THE GREEK TRAGEDY
IN NEW TRANSLATIONS

GENERAL EDITORS
Peter Burian and Alan Shapiro

SOPHOCLES: Antigone

SOPHOCLES

Antigone

Translated by
REGINALD GIBBONS
and
CHARLES SEGAL

OXFORD
UNIVERSITY PRESS

OXFORD
UNIVERSITY PRESS

Oxford University Press, Inc., publishes works that
further Oxford University's objective of excellence
in research, scholarship, and education.

Oxford   New York
Auckland   Cape Town   Dar es Salaam   Hong Kong   Karachi
Kuala Lumpur   Madrid   Melbourne   Mexico City   Nairobi
New Delhi   Shanghai   Taipei   Toronto

With offices in
Argentina   Austria   Brazil   Chile   Czech Republic   France   Greece
Guatemala   Hungary   Italy   Japan   Poland   Portugal   Singapore
South Korea   Switzerland   Thailand   Turkey   Ukraine   Vietnam

First published by Oxford University Press, Inc., 2003
198 Madison Avenue, New York, NY 10016
www.oup.com

First issued as an Oxford University Press paperback, 2007
ISBN 978-0-19-514310-2

Oxford is a registered trademark of Oxford University Press

The Library of Congress has catalogued the hardcover edition as follows:
Sophocles.
[Antigone. English]
Antigone / Sophocles ; translated by Reginald Gibbons and Charles
Segal.
p.   cm.
ISBN 978-0-19-514373-7
1. Antigone (Greek mythology)—Drama.   I. Gibbons, Reginald.
II. Segal, Charles, 1936–   III. Title.
PA4414.A7 G53   2003
882'.01—dc21   2002008966

The translations of the odes on Man, on the House
of Labdakos, and to Eros were first published in
Poetry magazine.

9 8 7 6 5 4 3 2
Printed in the United States of America

EDITORS' FOREWORD

"The Greek Tragedy in New Translations is based on the conviction that poets like Aeschylus, Sophocles, and Euripides can only be properly rendered by translators who are themselves poets. Scholars may, it is true, produce useful and perceptive versions. But our most urgent present need is for a *re-creation* of these plays—as though they had been written, freshly and greatly, by masters fully at home in the English of our own times."

With these words, the late William Arrowsmith announced the purpose of this series, and we intend to honor that purpose. As was true of most of the volumes that began to appear in the 1970s—first under Arrowsmith's editorship, later in association with Herbert Golder—those for which we bear editorial responsibility are products of close collaboration between poets and scholars. We believe (as Arrowsmith did) that the skills of both are required for the difficult and delicate task of transplanting these magnificent specimens of another culture into the soil of our own place and time, to do justice both to their deep differences from our patterns of thought and expression and to their palpable closeness to our most intimate concerns. Above all, we are eager to offer contemporary readers dramatic poems that convey as vividly and directly as possible the splendor of language, the complexity of image and idea, and the intensity of emotion and originals. This entails, among much else, the recognition that the tragedies were meant for performance—as scripts for actors—to be sung and danced as well as spoken. It demands writing of inventiveness, clarity, musicality, and dramatic power. By such standards we ask that these translations be judged.

This series is also distinguished by its recognition of the need of nonspecialist readers for a critical introduction informed by the best recent scholarship, but written clearly and without condescension.

Each play is followed by notes designed not only to elucidate obscure references but also to mediate the conventions of the Athenian stage as well as those features of the Greek text that might otherwise go unnoticed. The notes are supplemented by a glossary of mythical and geographical terms that should make it possible to read the play without turning elsewhere for basic information. Stage directions are sufficiently ample to aid readers in imagining the action as they read. Our fondest hope, of course, is that these versions will be staged not only in the minds of their readers but also in the theaters to which, after so many centuries, they still belong.

A NOTE ON THE SERIES FORMAT

A series such as this requires a consistent format. Different translators, with individual voices and approaches to the material in hand, cannot be expected to develop a single coherent style for each of the three tragedians, much less make clear to modern readers that, despite the differences among the tragedians themselves, the plays share many conventions and a generic, or period, style. But they can at least share a common format and provide similar forms of guidance to the reader.

1. Spelling of Greek names

Orthography is one area of difference among the translations that requires a brief explanation. Historically, it has been common practice to use Latinized forms of Greek names when bringing them into English. Thus, for example, Oedipus (not Oidipous) and Clytemnestra (not Klutaimestra) are customary in English. Recently, however, many translators have moved toward more precise transliteration, which has the advantage of presenting the names as both Greek and new, instead of Roman and neoclassical importations into English. In the case of so familiar a name as Oedipus, however, transliteration risks the appearance of pedantry or affectation. And in any case, perfect consistency cannot be expected in such matters. Reader will feel the same discomfort with "Athenai" as the chief city of Greece as they would with "Platon" as the author of the *Republic*.

The earlier volumes in this series adopted as a rule a "mixed" orthography in accordance with the considerations outlined above. The most familiar names retain their Latinate forms, the rest are transliterated; -os rather than Latin -us is adopted for the termination of masculine names, and Greek diphthongs (such as Iphigen*eia* for Latin Iphigenia) are retained. Some of the later volumes continue this practice, but where translators have preferred to use a more consistent practice of transliteration of Latinization, we have honored their wishes.

2. Stage directions

The ancient manuscripts of the Greek plays do not supply stage directions (though the ancient commentators often provide information relevant to staging, delivery, "blocking," etc.). Hence stage directions must be inferred from words and situations and our knowledge of Greek theatrical conventions. At best this is a ticklish and uncertain procedure. But it is surely preferable that good stage directions should be provided by the translator than that readers should be left to their own devices in visualizing action, gesture, and spectacle. Ancient tragedy was austere and "distanced" by means of masks, which means that the reader must not expect the detailed intimacy ("He shrugs and turns wearily away," "She speaks with deliberate slowness, as though to emphasize the point," etc.) that characterizes stage directions in modern naturalistic drama.

3. Numbering of lines

For the convenience of the reader who may wish to check the translation against the original, or vice versa, the lines have been numbered according to both the Greek and English texts. The lines of the translation have been numbered in multiples of ten, and those numbers have been set in the right-hand margin. The (inclusive) Greek numeration will be found bracketed at the top of the page. The Notes that follow the text have been keyed to both numerations, the line numbers of the translation in **bold**, followed by the Greek lines in regular type, and the same convention is used for all references to specific passages (of the translated plays only) in both the Notes and the Introduction.

Readers will doubtless note that in many plays the English lines outnumber the Greek, but they should not therefore conclude that the translator has been unduly prolix. In some cases the reason is simply that the translator has adopted the free-flowing norms of modern Anglo-American prosody, with its brief-breath-and emphasis-determined lines, and its habit of indicating cadence and caesuras by line length and setting rather than by conventional punctuation. Even where translators have preferred to cast dialogue in more regular five-beat or six-beat lines, the greater compactness of Greek diction is likely to result in a substantial disparity in Greek and English numerations.

Durham, N.C.
Chapel Hill, N.C.
2003

PETER BURIAN
ALAN SHAPIRO

PREFACE

The final stages of my work on the play overlapped with a Fellowship from the National Endowment for the Humanities, which was awarded for another project, but nevertheless contributed to the efficient completion of the book. I am deeply grateful to the Endowment for their support.

I completed work on this volume at a time when Antigone's lament about being between upper and lower worlds took on an intensely personal meaning as I faced a life-threatening illness. I cannot list all the friends, colleagues, and students, past and present, who offered their help, encouragement, and prayers, but they are all gratefully remembered. I would like particularly to thank my Harvard colleagues for their many kindnesses, especially Kathleen Coleman, Albert Henrichs, and Richard Thomas, chair of the department. I am deeply grateful to the medical professionals whose expertise and concern enabled me to finish my share in the volume and indeed to continue looking on the light of the sun: Drs. Christopher Colie, Keith Stuart, and David S. Rosenthal and Ms. Judith Podymatis, RN. My collaborator, Reg Gibbons, not only made several long trips so that we could work together in the best possible way, by face-to-face discussions, but remained a steadfast and involved friend on whom I could also count for support. I am grateful to George Steiner for taking the time to read the manuscript at a time when he was busy delivering the Norton Lectures at Harvard. To my wife, Nancy Jones, my gratitude for her ever-present love and devotion at a period of particular adversity goes beyond what words can express.

Cambridge, Massachusetts   CHARLES SEGAL
September 2001

CONTENTS

ANTIGONE

INTRODUCTION

For the nineteenth-century idealist German philosopher Hegel, *Antigone* is "one of the most sublime, and in every respect most consummate, work[s] of art human effort ever produced. Not a detail in this tragedy but is of consequence."[1] Hegel's dazzling accolade is typical of the high esteem for the play in the early nineteenth century.[2] For Hegel, *Antigone* plays a major role in the evolution of European consciousness, one of whose early stages is exemplified by *Antigone*'s conflict between State and individual, or more accurately between "the public law of the State and the instinctive family-love and duty towards a brother." This division in turn is an aspect of a larger conflict between Nature and Spirit and so a step toward the emergence of Spirit (*Geist*). The individual bearer of such consciousness is essentially tragic because he or she enters into the division between the divine law, embodied in the *polis* or state, and the human law, embodied in the family, and in entering into that division is destroyed. And yet "it is precisely this destruction," as George Steiner explains Hegel's view, "which constitutes man's eminent worth and which allows his progression towards the unification of consciousness and of Spirit on 'the other side of history.' "[3] In terms of Hegel's emphasis on action and his conception of fate in Greek tragedy, Antigone, rather than Kreon, is the full bearer of the tragic because she self-consciously decides to act and therefore chooses the path of her destiny.[4] The "classical" perfection of *Antigone* lies not only in the clarity and purity with which it develops this conflict but also in its representation of divinity, which

1. G. W. F. Hegel, *Philosophy of Fine Art*, quoted from the Osmaston translation (London 1920), in Anne and Henry Paolucci, eds., *Hegel on Tragedy* (Garden City, N.Y., 1962), 178.
2. See George Steiner, *Antigones* (Oxford, 1984), 1–19.
3. Ibid., 31.
4. Ibid., 36.

goes beyond the horrific chthonic gods of the old myths and the old religion to more impersonal gods, who do not appear on the stage as anthropomorphic beings and are more important for the principles they endorse than for any visual effects.

The weaknesses of Hegel's reading have long been clear.[5] It is as simplistic to identify Kreon with "the law of the State" as it is to identify Antigone with individualism *tout court*. Even Antigone's devotion to family love, or *philia*, is problematical, given the incestuous bonds within this family and her harsh treatment of her sister, Ismene. Antigone, to be sure, may be identified with the emergence of an individual ethical consciousness that resists the domination of certain laws that have been imposed by Thebes' present ruler, but the play calls into question whether these laws may be associated with an abstract, impersonal Law of the State. It is questionable to identify a small fifth-century city-state or *polis* with the modern abstract notion of State. The *polis* of *Antigone* is rather the total civic space in which the religious and the political, the private and the public are closely intertwined, and the fact that they are so intertwined creates the tragedy. Each protagonist sees only half of the whole, and each acts as if the two realms are independent of the other.

Nevertheless, Hegel's influence should not be taken lightly, and his articulation of his position in his earlier work offers a more nuanced and profound reading. In Hegel's dialectical thinking of this period, the position of human and divine changes places. The family, in its honoring of the dead, can also embody the divine law, while the city-state's law, as the creation of human beings and as the visible regulator of day-to-day affairs, can embody the human. In the fact that the two sides share in both human and divine law lies the irreconcilably tragic nature of the conflict. And this conflict is also gendered between the "feminine-ontological" and the "masculine-political," between the woman's domestic world of hearth and home and the man's public world of civic assemblies and legislative bodies.[6]

Political, historical, and social considerations add further nuances. Antigone is opposing not the city's Law (*nomos*) as a totality, but rather Kreon's specific "decree" forbidding the burial of her brother's body. She is primarily the champion not of the individual against the State but of the ties of blood and birth that rest on the solidarity of the family.

---

5. Among the earliest criticism is Goethe's, in J. W. von Goethe, *Conversations with Eckermann*, trans. John Oxenford (1850; reprint New York, 1998), 174–78 (March 28, 1827). For further discussion see, e.g., Steiner, *Antigones*, 49–51; T. C. W. Oudemans and A. P. M. H Lardinois, *Tragic Ambiguity* (Leiden, 1987), 110–17.

6. Steiner, 34–35.

More specifically, she opposes to Kreon's authority the traditional authority of the old aristocratic families to honor and bury their dead. The care for the dead was especially the prerogative of women, and it was increasingly restricted in Athens in the sixth and fifth centuries as the democracy sought to limit the power of the aristocratic clans, but it was nevertheless widely respected.[7] The Athenian institution of the public, city funeral for warriors who died in battle, established around the middle of the century, sharpened the conflict between the family's mourning and the public ceremony, and this conflict is doubtless in the play's background.[8] Against Kreon's laws (*nomoi*) Antigone sets the "unwritten laws" that pertain to the burial of the dead, which are also the "custom-laws" (another meaning of *nomoi* or *nomima*) that have a place within every city and rest on the sanctity, as she says, of "Justice, who resides in the same house with the gods below the earth" and on the authority of Zeus himself (translation 495–501 / Greek 450–55).[9] Thus, while she is so human and moving in the fragile strength of her defiance of the ruler, she has on her side the weight of religious tradition, the universal recognition of the rights of burial, and the performance of those offices for the dead that traditionally belong to women in the *polis* and in the family.

Viewed more broadly, *Antigone* brings down to earth and to purely human characters some of the conflicts of Aiskhylos' *Oresteia*. Antigone's position has some affinities with that of the Furies in Aiskhylos' conflict between Olympian and chthonic, upper and lower worlds, in the last play of the *Oresteia*, the *Eumenides*. Here the newer and younger Olympians, Apollo and Athena, who belong to the reign of Zeus, are identified with the male-dominated political institutions of the city, whereas the ancient gods, the Erinyes or Furies, daughters of primordial Night, defend the bonds of blood and birth and the rights of the mother and of Earth in their vengeful pursuit of the matricide, Orestes. To be sure, the issue of *Antigone* is burial, not vengeance; the cosmic order is in the background, not the foreground; and the focus is on the family as a whole and not on the rights of the father as against those of the mother. *Antigone* also presents the conflict in terms of the more impersonal "eternal laws of the gods" rather than through the

---

7. For the importance of female lament in the play see my *Sophocles' Tragic World: Divinity, Nature, and Society* (Cambridge, Mass., 1995), 119–20, 125–27, 135–36.

8. This aspect of the play is stressed by William Tyrrell and Larry Bennett, *Recapturing Sophocles' Antigone* (Lanham, Md., 1998), especially 5–14, 115–17.

9. Bernard Knox, *The Heroic Temper* (Berkeley and Los Angeles, 1964), 97, shows that the (literally) "unwritten and secure custom-laws (*nomima*) of the gods" of which Antigone speaks in 500–501 / 454–55 refer primarily to the sanctity surrounding burial rites. Yet her word *nomoi*, literally "laws," in 498 / 452, also indicates that broader issues are involved.

awe-inspiring mythical presences of the Furies. Nevertheless, the framing of this conflict between male and female and between civic order and primordial religious tradition bears comparison with the *Oresteia*. Antigone too looks for support from the divinities of the lower world (in the lines cited above; also in 593 / 542), and her vindication comes, finally from Hades and the Furies (1145–47 / 1074–75).

Comparison with the *Oresteia*, however, also reveals how poorly the Hegelian scheme of thesis-antithesis-synthesis fits the play. *Antigone* has none of the resolution that ends the *Eumenides*, where the Furies finally accept the Olympian persuasion of Athena and consequently are reconciled with the *polis* of Athens and transform themselves into the more benign and acceptable Eumenides, the "Kindly Ones." In *Antigone* the conflict between the blood ties within the family, to which the women are particularly devoted, and the realm of political action that belongs to men is played out almost entirely on the human level. The gods appear only as the remote agents of retributive justice; and the mortal representatives of family ties and civic duty respectively both suffer a terrible doom, Antigone by the despairing suicide of her death in her cave-prison, Kreon by the blows that leave him disoriented, isolated, and totally crushed at the end.

The Hegelian notion, however, that both sides have some degree of right on their side—or, as A. C. Bradley will later rephrase it, that there is a division in the ethical substance with a resultant "violent self-restitution of the divided spiritual unity"[10]—has the merit of getting us into the fundamental issues of the play. Conflict is the heart of this work, which is so structured that each protagonist can act only by attacking and destroying the central values of the other. The play offers conflicting definitions, explicit or implicit, of the basic terms of the human condition: friend and enemy, citizen and ruler, father and son, male and female, justice and injustice, reverence and irreverence, purity and pollution, honor and dishonor, and even (in the Ode on Man) conflicting judgments of what is *anthrôpos*, a human being—powerful or helpless, something "wonderful" or "terrible" (both of these, meanings of the same word, *deinon*). Not only are the definitions in conflict, but the terms themselves become ambiguous or (as in the case of Antigone's "holy wrongdoing") paradoxical.[11] Antigone and Kreon use the same words to mean different things, like *philos* and *ekhthros*, "dear

10. A. C. Bradley, "Hegel's Theory of Tragedy" (1909), in Paolucci (above, n. 1), 385.

11. On these conflicts and ambiguities in the larger context of the nature of Greek tragedy, see Jean-Pierre Vernant, "Tensions and Ambiguities in Greek Tragedy," in J.-P. Vernant and Pierre Vidal-Naquet, *Myth and Tragedy in Ancient Greece* (1972, 1986), trans. J. Lloyd (New York, 1990), 29–48, especially 41–43.

one" and "enemy," or *nomos*, law. Antigone's incestuous birth compli-
cates these ambiguities of language by confusing the basic terms of
kinship: in the family of Oidipous, son and husband, brother and son,
sister and daughter horribly coincide. What in fact sets the plot into
motion is the mutual slaughter of the incestuously begotten sons/broth-
ers, Polyneikes and Eteokles, who are simultaneously too close in their
claims on the inherited throne and too distant in their murderous struggle, simultaneously the nearest of "dear ones," *philoi*, and the most
bitter of "enemies," *ekhthroi*. The play's obsessive harping on words for
"self-," "common," "one another" is the verbal expression of this deadly
fusion of same and opposite that underlies the tragedy of the house of
Oidipous.

The ambiguities of *philia*, being near-and-dear, in this house are
enacted in the opening scene between the two sisters. The language
of intimate kinship in Antigone's opening address to Ismene is painfully
fractured by the end of that scene, and Antigone's virtual identification
with her sister in the opening line, with its untranslatable juxtaposition
of *koinon autadelphon*, literally, "shared/sharing self-sister," has turned
to scorn and near hatred by the time the two young women leave the
stage.

In this opening scene Antigone not only sets out the main issues but
also displays all the contradictions and dangers that define her character: her intensity of feeling, the single-mindedness of her devotion to
family, her unbending will, her readiness to defy the entire city in the
name of what she believes, her involvement with the dead, and her
willingness to face death if necessary. With sarcasm she shows her
independence and bitterness when she recounts that "the noble Kreon
has proclaimed" his order against the burial of Polyneikes (39–43 / 31–
34), while at the same time she personalizes the conflict and dramatizes
its immediacy and the consequent need to act decisively. She has a
visceral sense of Polyneikes' exposed corpse — she not only recounts that
"no one may hide it inside a grave, wail over it or weep for it," but
she also pictures it as horribly desecrated by vultures, "a sweet-tasting
treasure that birds will spy and feed on with their greedy joy" (34–38 /
27–30). That this image is distinctive, we see from comparing Kreon's
otherwise similar description of his decree later (229–35 / 203–6).[12]

The paradox of what Antigone calls her "holy crime" (90 / 74) shows
her understanding of her isolation but also signals the moral complexity

---

12. Kreon says "eaten by birds and dogs" and adds the epithet "shameful for anyone to see" (or
literally the detail of "disfigurement" or "outrage"), but he does not use Antigone's more vivid
expression.

of her forthcoming act.[13] When Ismene refuses to help, Antigone turns
abruptly from affection to hatred. She openly accepts the folly of her
own resolve, and she is determined to die the "noble death" of the
male warrior, on the model of the Homeric hero. Her claim to the
honor that she will win from her deed, her determination to "lie beside" her brother in death in her "holy wrongdoing," and her open
defiance of the city at a time of crisis, would almost certainly alarm
the audience of male Athenian citizens, accustomed to the view that
women do not challenge men (as Ismene states in 76–77 / 61–62),
especially in the all-male areas of politics and public life.

The ensuing ode, sung by the chorus of Theban elders, reveals the
one-sidedness of Antigone's position in the context of the city's fears
and so sets the stage for an initially sympathetic view of Kreon. The
chorus describes the battle of the preceding night in images of ani-
mality, blood, madness, and fire that show the horror of what the city
might have suffered had the fierce enemy warriors broken through the
walls. Entering directly after the ode, Kreon vehemently denounces
Polyneikes, the attacker who came to "burn their country and the temples with columns around them and the offerings inside" (328–29 /
285–87). On the other hand, the absolute refusal to bury a traitor's body,
though legally justified, could be perceived as harsh. A traitor's corpse
was often cast outside the city walls, where family members might bury
it and where the danger of pollution to the city would be avoided. This
is in fact the punishment specified for Polyneikes' corpse by Aiskhylos
in *Seven against Thebes* and by Euripides in *Phoinikian Women*.[14] Elsewhere too in Greek tragedy the refusal of burial is regarded as cruel
and impious, as in Sophokles' *Aias* and Euripides' *Suppliants*.[15] In the
latter play, Theseus, the civilizing hero and model king of Athens,
heeds his mother's plea to defy Kreon and the victorious Thebans, bury
the fallen Argive warriors, and thereby "stop them from overturning the

13. With 90 / 74 see the similar phrasing of 990–91 / 924 and 1011 / 943.
14. Aiskhylos, *Seven against Thebes*, 1013–25; Euripides, *Phoinikian Women*, 1629–30. See Patricia
E. Easterling, "Constructing the Heroic," in Christopher Pelling, ed., *Greek Tragedy and the
Historian* (Oxford, 1997), 26–28, who argues that Kreon's punitive treatment does not correspond
precisely to any known historical situation in the fifth century. The Aiskhylean version, however,
though specifying burial outside, does nevertheless include exposing the body to dogs (no birds,
however) and the prohibition against burial by the family (*Seven*, 1013–15). The date of the ending
of the *Seven*, however, remains controversial, and it may have been influenced by Sophokles: see
Appendix 2. For further discussion of the problem of the justification of Kreon's decree, see Steiner,
Antigones, 114–20, and Oudemans and Lardinois, *Tragic Ambiguity*, 101–2, 162–63.
15. For Euripides' *Suppliants* see the Note on 1153–58 / 1080–83. In *Antigone*, 1133–61 / 1064–86,
Teiresias is probably referring to the tradition that Theseus, King of Athens, intervened against
Kreon for the burial of the exposed corpses of the attacking Argive warriors: see Griffith's note on
Greek lines 1080–83.

custom laws (*nomima*) of all Greece" (*Suppliants* 311–12). The Kreon of *Antigone* even seems to relish his punitive authority as he dwells on the details of exposing Polyneikes' corpse and on his specific steps to ensure that body will remain unburied (230–35 / 203–6, 248 / 217, 451–58 / 408–14). He gives four lines (in the Greek) to the honors due to Eteokles, nine to the defiling of the traitor's body (217–35 / 194–206)—a touch of a cruelty that will be seen again later when he sends Antigone to her death.[16] The repeated first-person statements of his opening speech too, though innocuous enough in their context, also sound a note of authoritarian willfulness and self-important sententiousness that will emerge more ominously later (214–15 / 191, 223–24 / 198, 238–40 / 209–10).[17]

Both protagonists turn out to have a relation to the city-state (*polis*) different from what the opening scenes might suggest. Kreon's view of *nomos*, law, one of the crucial words in the play, proves to rest on too narrow a vision of the city. The word *nomos* also means "custom" and can refer to "practice" or "convention" so embedded in society that it has virtually the authority of the "laws" that derive from formal legislation. (The two meanings of *nomos* are particularly important in Sophokles' time, in democratic Athens of the fifth century, which is very much aware of the sovereign power of the assembled citizenry, the *dêmos*, to create new laws, abolish old, and replace or modify traditional "laws," and thereby codify as statute or written decree what had been more loosely defined as "custom-law.")

Both protagonists, however, assume that the gods defend their *nomos*. Kreon increasingly regards the law of the city as an extension of his own authority and assumes, erroneously, that the order of the gods is congruent with what he sees as the order of the *polis*. Antigone, in defying Kreon's laws on the grounds of the "unwritten laws" of the gods, opens up the definition of both law and the city in directions that Kreon does not understand. The city does, in fact, have obligations to the dead and to the chthonic divinities who protect them and watch over the rituals that separate the dead citizens from the living and move them to their appropriate realm in Hades. Later in the play the prophet Teiresias will announce the dire effect of violating these "unwritten laws" (1133–61 / 1064–86); and he will show that Kreon's attempt to absorb ritual practice and the politics of the gods into his own politics of the city rests on a one-sided vision of both the city and the gods.

16. See, e.g., 838–42 / 777–80 and 944–50 / 885–90, and the Notes on these passages.
17. On the reservations that the language of Kreon's opening speech may cause the spectator, see Felix Budelmann, *The Language of Sophocles* (Cambridge, Eng., 2000), 75–78.

If Antigone seems initially to disregard the legitimate claims and needs of the *polis*, the course of the action dissipates the sympathy for Kreon aroused by the first ode and by the civic sentiments of his opening speech. The turning point is the scene with Haimon, who, for the first time, allows other voices in the city to be heard (747–55 / 692–700). Antigone, defying Kreon to his face earlier, had said that the elders of the chorus shared her view but had their mouths sealed by fear of Kreon, whose rule she describes as *turannis*, "one-man rule" (556–58 / 506–7). The word does not yet carry the full associations of our word "tyranny," but it does connote autocratic power, the absolute rule of a single man, and it begins to undercut Kreon's claims to represent the city as a whole. Knowing his father, Haimon cannily begins with a declaration of loyalty and obedience but then endorses Antigone's position with increasing force. He might be thought a biased reporter of the citizens' sentiments when he echoes Antigone's words and defends her as one who merits "golden honor" (754 / 699). Teiresias' warnings, however, will validate this other voice and give it the authority of the gods.

In condemning Antigone to death, Kreon callously disregards her marriage with Haimon. "It's Hades who will stop this wedding for me," Kreon says to Ismene (626 / 575). But Hades in fact fulfills this marriage, later, in its way; as the messenger recounts, Haimon "in the end has had his wedding ceremony—but in the house of Hades" (1325–27 / 1240–41). "It's Hades who desires these laws" for the living and for the dead, Antigone says earlier, in defending herself before Kreon (570 / 519). Yet Kreon begins with confidence in his power to use Hades— that is, death—as an instrument of political control. However, Hades' laws operate more terribly on living and dead than even Antigone had imagined. "Only from Hades will he not procure some means of escape," the chorus had sung in their ode on the achievements of human civilization (403–5 / 361–62), and their pronouncement is spectacularly fulfilled in Kreon's doom.

Kreon carefully arranges Antigone's death to leave himself and his city free of pollution. But her suicide in the cave doubly undoes his schemes. She takes control of her own death and turns it into a polluting death after all.[18] She thereby initiates a cycle of pollutions in Kreon's house parallel to the pollutions that his nonburial of Polyneikes has brought to the city. At the end, when Kreon's wife's suicide leaves him totally bereft, he cries out, "Ah, Harbor of Hades never to be

---

18. On Antigone's polluted death, see Nicole Loraux, *Tragic Ways of Killing a Woman* (1985), trans. Anthony Forster (Cambridge, Mass., 1987), 31–32.

purified! Why, why do you destroy me?" (1371–72 / 1284–85). His house has now taken on the pollutions from Hades that he had tried to avoid for the city, and these will not be cleansed.

In his prophecy, Teiresias explains how Kreon has done violence to his own favored realm of the gods above, the Olympians, because he kept on earth what did not belong to them (1140–44 / 1070–73). As a result, the "late-punishing" avengers, the Furies of both Hades and the gods, lie in ambush for him (1145–47 / 1074–75). Like Antigone, he now suffers an immersion, while alive, in the realm of Hades, for he enters the tomb and sees her dead and his son mad with grief, and then also dead; and, like Antigone, Kreon suffers the deaths of his closest kin. This man of the city is left, like Oidipous, in a house emptied by the suicide of a wife and the bloody deaths of two sons. Kreon's wife, Eurydike, in her dying curse, calls him "killer of sons" and so makes him, like Oidipous, responsible for the death of his two sons (1391–92 / 1304–5).[19] In his first speech Kreon had referred to his intimate kinship with Oidipous as the basis for the legitimacy of his rule (194–95 / 173–74), but this close tie with Oidipous' house takes on a sinister meaning by the end of the play. In the tragic irony of his reversal, Kreon gains not just the city of Oidipous but the house of Oidipous as well.

Antigone, silenced by her being immured in the cave, is symbolically present at both stages of Kreon's doom, first in the recognition of the symmetries between upper and lower worlds in Teiresias' prophecy, which hark back to her defiant speech to Kreon on the Justice that dwells with the gods below (495–518 / 450–70), and later in the cries of lament that Eurydike utters over her last son, for these echo Antigone's cries over the body of her last brother.[20] Antigone's suicide too both anticipates Eurydike's suicide and motivates Haimon's. Yet the gods who have vindicated Antigone's chthonic Justice and her demand for the equal burial of both her brothers do not intervene for her as an individual. Their absence suggests Sophokles' deeply tragic world view, which includes the remoteness and inaccessibility of the divine

---

19. Although Oidipous' curse on his two sons is not explicitly mentioned in the play, it is a familiar feature of the myth from at least the sixth century BCE on and is dramatized by Sophokles in his *Oidipous at Kolonos*. It was also prominent in Aiskhylos' *Seven against Thebes*. In our play Antigone also alludes to the curse in her opening lines, and it is probably also in the background of the third ode (642–50 / 594–603). The "Fury in the mind" mentioned here (650 / 603) also suggests the curse, as parents' curses on children are regularly fulfilled by the Erinyes or Furies. Compare Teiresias' prediction later that the "Furies, who avenge Hades and the gods" (1146–47 / 107–76) will lie in wait for Kreon.

20. Compare 1389 / 1302 and 1402 / 1316 (of Eurydike) with 35–36 / 28 and 468–72 / 422–27 (of Antigone).

beings who permit the catastrophic waste and loss of the courageous and passionate young people who have championed their cause.

In retrospect, Antigone's unyielding commitment to her beliefs and the dignity and courage of her defiance of Kreon are perhaps the only things that illuminates the darkness of this tragic world. Hence to many, influenced by the highly politicized versions of Jean Anouilh and Bertolt Brecht in the 1940s, the history of the play is "the history of the European conscience."[21] And yet, in Sophokles' play, Antigone's very intensity of commitment has triggered the disaster. Given her devotion to her family and her passionate nature, the fact that she responds as she does bears the Sophoklean stamp of tragic inevitability. She resembles other Sophoklean tragic protagonists — Aias, Elektra, Philoktetes: admirable in her inner strength and integrity, but also dangerous to herself and to others in her one-sidedness, violent emotions, and unbending will.[22] Kreon, of course, is just as rigid as Antigone. Fresh in his authority, eager to display his full control of a crisis barely averted, and determined to assert his newly gained power, he cannot afford failure in this first challenge to his command. To be faced down by a woman, and in public, is particularly humiliating. He has, however, more options than Antigone, more space for yielding or finding areas for compromise. But in these heated circumstances and between these two personalities, no compromise is possible.

Interpreters of the play after Hegel have often idealized Antigone for her heroism and love of family. Jebb's remark, in the preface to his great commentary, is typical: "It is not without reason that moderns have recognized her as the noblest, and the most profoundly tender, embodiment of woman's heroism which ancient literature can show." Some half a century later, Cedric Whitman offered a brilliant reading of Antigone as the exemplar of an existential hero who holds bravely to her integrity and her grandeur of spirit in total isolation.[23] "In a world of hollow men, she is real." More recent critics, however, have increasingly questioned Jebb's alleged "tenderness" and stressed her darker side. With her "heart that's hot for what is chilling" (**105** / 88), she is more involved with her dead relatives than with her living sister

---

21. See Pierre Vidal-Naquet, *Le miroir brisé: Tragédie athénienne et politique* (Paris, 2001), 47–51; also Steiner, *Antigones*, 170–71, 193–94. See also Maria-Grazia Ciani, ed., *Sofocle, Anouilh, Brecht: Variazione sul mito* (Venice, 2001).

22. On these and related qualities in the Sophoklean hero, see Bernard Knox, *Heroic Temper*, 10–27, especially 16ff.

23. C. H. Whitman, *Sophocles: A Study in Heroic Humanism* (Cambridge, Mass., 1951), 88–91. The following quotation is from p. 90. In order to save Antigone's heroic perfection, however, Whitman has to delete lines 905–12 of the Greek text. See the Notes on **967–79** / 905–15. For views of Antigone similar to Whitman's, see Oudemans and Lardinois, 107–10.

or fiancé. In the grandeur of her unshakable certainty she towers above everyone else in the play, but as Bernard Knox has emphasized, she shares the harshness and intransigence of most Sophoklean protagonists, and precisely because of her nobility and integrity she brings terrible suffering to herself and those around her.[24]

One can agree with the later Hegel that Kreon (initially, at least) may have some "right" on his side, but the tragic situation consists in the intertwined, interactive responsibility of both protagonists. The play, like most of Sophokles' extant plays, as we now increasingly acknowledge, has not one but two foci of tragic concern.[25] In the uncompromising sharpness of her personality, and the brazenness and stiffness of her defiance, Antigone undercuts whatever hope of compromise there might have been and calls forth from Kreon a complementary intransigence that destroys them both. The passions of the young— Antigone's all-absorbing family loyalty in this moment of loss and Haimon's love and despair—meet the stubbornness and inflexibility of their elders at a crisis when the city's safety has only just been secured. Interpreters who view Kreon as a champion of civic values and communal solidarity stumble against his increasingly autocratic behavior and the final judgment of the gods. Their intervention, as expounded by Teiresias, retrospectively clarifies and supports Antigone's instinctive knowledge of what she had to do and why.

As always in Sophokles, the interaction of human circumstances and human character are sufficient to account for the tragedy. Sufficient, perhaps, but not final—for in Sophokles' tragic view, human life is always part of a larger continuum, which includes the natural world and the divinities whose power, immanent in the world, makes it what it is. Antigone follows and reveres her values with an intensity for which she is ready to pay with her life. Yet she lives in a world defined by the needs of a city that she rejects. Both antagonists have limited horizons, but Kreon ultimately proves to be more disastrously limited, and he must finally yield to Teiresias' larger prophetic vision. His power buckles, but too late for Antigone to be saved.

DRAMATIC STRUCTURE

In the prologue Ismene sets out the weakness of Antigone's position. Should she persevere in her plan to bury Polyneikes, she, a mere

---

24. Knox, *Heroic Temper*, chapter 1, especially 19–23, and also 62–67; R. P. Winnington-Ingram, *Sophocles* (Cambridge, 1980), 128–29, 135.

25. This important point is established by Albert Machin, *Cohérence et continuité dans le théâtre de Sophocle* (Hauteville, Québec, Canada, 1981), especially 366–76. See my review in *American Journal of Philology* 107:3 (1986), 594–99.

woman, with a woman's weakness, will be defying men and the male authority of the city (75–79 / 61–64). We should keep in mind that for fifth-century Athens political life is an area of male autonomy, freedom, and control. Women are excluded from direct political activity, may not control or administer property (including their own property), cannot enter into contracts, or represent themselves in a court of law, and remain subject to the authority of their male relatives (which of course does not mean that they were without respect, rights, and influence of other kinds).[26] Except for religious festivals, they are expected to remain inconspicuously in the house (*oikos*), which is their domain.[27] The *polis* is a male work of art, an artificial system of rules, limitations, and eligibilities of man's own making, a creation of intellect and conventions, located within its natural setting, to be sure, but also separate from it in the special kind of secondary order that the city imposes on its world by its walls, temples, monuments, and of course its institutions. Yet the city also depends on the order of nature for its fruitful and harmonious relation with the land, and it depends on its women for the procreation of new citizens.[28] With procreation come sexual desire, maternity, and the strong ties of family. All these have an important role in *Antigone* and shape its tragic form.

Kreon's *polis* proves to be not so autonomous after all, and his role as father and husband throws him back into the network of the unpredictable, biological bonds that his construction of his world and of himself would exclude. Although he harshly rejects the ties of blood and marriage that connect him to his niece, Antigone, and views her "crime" solely in terms of the law she has violated, he cannot escape the power of those bonds of blood. As his wife's last words show (as reported by the Messenger at 1387–92 / 1301–5), Kreon has lost his elder son, Megareus, who, presumably, sacrificed himself, or was sacrificed, to save the city.[29] Kreon never speaks of this loss, but the silenced grief returns in the sorrow of the mother, first in an oblique hint (1265–66 / 1191) and then in

---

26. This is not to say that women were completely without rights or various forms of personal power and influence. For a good survey of women in fifth-century Athens see Elaine Fantham, Helene Foley, Natalie Kampen, Sarah Pomeroy, and Alan Shapiro, eds., *Women in the Classical World* (Oxford, 1994), chapter 3, especially 74–75, 79–83; Roger Just, *Women in Athenian Law and Life* (London, 1989), especially chapters 2 and 3.

27. It remains controversial whether women were allowed to attend the dramatic performances at the City Dionysia, the festival in honor of Dionysos. See the discussion and references in my *Oedipus Tyrannus: Tragic Heroism and the Limits of Knowledge*, second edition (New York, 2001), 21–22, with n. 8, p. 23.

28. The "interconnectedness" of man and nature, with the latter's uncontrollable ambiguities, in contrast to their rationalistic separation, is a main theme of Oudemans and Lardinois, e.g., chapters 3–4.

29. See the Note on 1387–92 / 1301–5.

the outburst of emotional and physical violence with which she ends her life. And everywhere in the background is the house of Oidipous, destroyed by just those bonds of blood that Kreon dismisses. The power of the tragic reversal, as we have observed, consists in part in the fact that Kreon's house comes increasingly to resemble that of Oidipous.

Like many tragedies of divine retribution, the action has an hourglass shape (though not completely symmetrical) as the power flows from Kreon to Antigone. He is tested by a series of challenges until he is completely destroyed in the last scene. The encounter with Haimon brings the challenge closer to home as his own son questions his authority over both city and house. In sending Antigone to her death in the cave, Kreon reasserts his power, but the entrance of Teiresias shifts the balance back to Antigone. The reversal (peripeteia) reaffirms the two areas that Kreon has tried to subordinate to his civic authority, the underworld and family ties. He enters the dark cave where he has ordered Antigone immured and where both she and Haimon kill themselves. He thereby makes a symbolical journey to the underworld, parallel to Antigone's, and this subterranean space now wreaks its vengeance on him and fulfills Antigone's parting curse (992–96 / 925–28).

The crushing blow comes from the house and particularly from female mourning and sorrow within the house. His wife, Eurydike, whom he never actually confronts alive within the play, comes on stage from the house just long enough to hear the news of Haimon's death.[30] Her subsequent suicide inside the house demonstrates the power of everything that Kreon had disvalued in his single-minded exaltation of civic values: women's emotions and their intense involvement in the bonds of family and in pollution, lament, and death itself. The last third of the play centers on Kreon; yet his collapse is implicitly measured against the absent Antigone's strength and integrity.

Kreon's entrance immediately after the first ode consolidates the weight of authority that now rests on him as commander-in-chief of a city that has survived a deadly attack. His presence intimidates the elders of the chorus, and he obviously savors his new role as leader of the city and spokesman for the civic ethos, on which he moralizes expansively in his platitudinous opening speech. The Guard who arrives soon after with the bad news of the "burial" of Polyneikes—in fact, a ritual sprinkling of dust—is also terrified of Kreon's power but not entirely cowed. When the Guard returns with Antigone as his pris-

---

30. Eurydike is presumably played by the same actor who played Antigone. For her role at the end, see my *Tragedy and Civilization* (Norman, Okla., 1999), 194–95, and my *Sophocles' Tragic World*, 133–36.

oner after the first stasimon (the second ode), he is relieved to escape any further expression of Kreon's wrath, although he also has a small word of sympathy for Antigone (481–84 / 436–39).

Antigone's defiance of Kreon in the following scene contrasts with the submissiveness of both the chorus and the Guard. Her rejection of Ismene's attempt to claim a share in the crime increases her isolation. If, with the manuscripts, we assign to Ismene line 619 / 568, in which she asks if Kreon will "kill [his] own son's bride-to-be," then the implication of this line is that Antigone is so completely absorbed in her determination to bury her brother, despite the threatened punishment by death, that she herself seems to have no thoughts of Haimon. At this crisis of her spiritual life, Haimon lies below the horizon of her moral vision. We admire Ismene's courage too, for Kreon, in response to her expressed solidarity with her sister, quickly arrests her as a co-conspirator and will not release her for some two hundred lines (830–31 / 770–71). But Ismene's gesture does nothing to help Antigone and in fact separates her even further from her one remaining blood relative.

Haimon's entrance after the second stasimon brings the first open defense of Antigone's position, and for the first time stymies Kreon in his attempt to suppress opposition. His encounter with Haimon formally resembles his encounter with Antigone. In both scenes, initial statements of principle are followed by sharp antithetical debates in the line-by-line exchange known as stichomythia. In the previous scene, that statement of principle was Antigone's powerful assertion of her reverence for the gods below, which Kreon answered by asserting the authority of the city's and his laws (495–518 / 450–70 and 521–47 / 473–96, respectively). Haimon's challenge strikes more deeply at Kreon's basic conception of himself. Kreon is pleased and relieved at his son's opening expression of loyalty, which encourages him to make a characteristically expansive speech on his favorite virtues, after the manner of his first speech in the play: Kreon's view of the proper order in the family exactly matches his view of the proper order in the city, for both rest on hierarchy and absolute obedience (686–95 / 639–47, 709–34 / 659–80). The young and impetuous Haimon, however, is very different from the timid chorus of elders. He sketches an image of the city that infuriates his authoritarian father—a city that holds and utters voices and opinions antithetical to Kreon's.

The angry exchange pushes Kreon to his revealing statement, "Isn't the city held to be his who rules?" to which Haimon replies, "You'd do well as the single ruler of some deserted place." Kreon rebuts him with "It seems this man is fighting on the woman's side!" (798–800 / 738–40), extending his authoritarian principles to another area of hierarchy, the subordination of female to male with which he had ended his previous tirade on obedience (731–34 / 677–80).

Haimon's open challenge to Kreon's rule in fact exposes the latter as very close to the *turannos*, the man who seizes sole power in the city and concentrates it entirely in his own hands. Kreon is not actually a "tyrant," for he has gained his authority legitimately, through inheritance, not through force or trickery. Yet his behavior emerges increasingly as that of a *turannos* in his identification of the *polis* with himself and his obsession with obedience, conspiracy, and money.[31] (Some interpreters have suggested that Sophokles has thus expressed an underlying criticism of Perikles' control over Athens, which technically was shared with the other elected officials, but in fact approached autocratic power.[32] In a famous passage of his *History of the Peloponnesian War* Thukydides describes Athens under Perikles as "in word a democracy but in deed rule by the first man" [2.65.10].) Kreon makes no attempt to engage in a serious discussion of Haimon's arguments. Instead he unleashes a series of *ad hominem* insults, culminating in the threat that Haimon will never marry Antigone while she lives (810 / 750), an ironic foreshadowing of the marriage-in-death that will in fact occur.

The scene begins and ends with fatal misunderstandings.[33] Although Haimon explicitly begins by putting his father ahead of his fiancée (684–85 / 637–38; cf. 801 / 741) and never appeals to the marriage as an argument for saving Antigone, Kreon, finally, can see his son only as Antigone's betrothed. Kreon's response escalates the violence to a new level. Taking an oath by Olympos, he orders his guards to lead Antigone out and kill her at once, "beside her bridegroom" (821 / 761). This cruel order, although not carried out, both provokes and foreshadows the couple's subsequent marriage-in-death.

Haimon begins with praise of his father's counsel and ends by accusing him of madness (824–25 / 765). It adds to the irony that he urges Kreon to yield in terms that are not wholly dissimilar from Kreon's own statements to Antigone about a stubborn will being broken (cf. 521–28 / 473–79 and 768–75 / 710–14). Haimon's nautical metaphors also hark back to Kreon's sententious posturing in his opening speech (cf. 775–

---

31. On Kreon's concern with money as characteristic of the *turannos*, see Richard Seaford, "Tragic Money," *Journal of Hellenic Studies* 118 (1998), 132–34. For Kreon as *turannos*, see Winnington-Ingram, *Sophocles*, 126–27.

32. For this view and other aspects of Kreon's possible connections with Perikles, see Victor Ehrenberg, *Sophocles and Pericles* (Oxford, 1954), 95–98, 145–49.

33. For good comments on the misunderstandings in this scene, see David Seale, *Vision and Stagecraft in Sophocles* (Chicago, 1982), 97–98.

77 / 715–17 and 212–13 / 189–90). But passion, not reason, now dominates, and no voice of calm and clarity will be heard again — until it is too late.

A scene that opened with broad generalizations about obedience and submission ends with wild threats whose meaning will be revealed only later. Sensitive to any questioning of his authority, Kreon misconstrues as a threat to his own person Haimon's promise that Antigone's death will kill someone else.[34] When Haimon exits, the chorus comments, "The man has gone off quickly in his anger! The mind, at his age, can become weighed down by grief" (826–27 / 766–67), unknowingly foreshadowing Haimon's probable meaning, suicide, for elsewhere in Sophokles the verb translated here as "he has gone," *bebêke*, often refers to death; and the mind "weighed down," or "heavy" or "resentful," foreshadows the ominous silent exit of Eurydike (1342 / 1256).[35] Kreon, however, remains impervious to criticism. Although he agrees to release Ismene, he continues with his intended execution of Antigone, and he ends with a cruel remark that "she'll learn at last what pointless waste of effort it is to worship what is down below with Hades" (840–42 / 779–80).

Eros is the subject of the immediately following ode. Eros is not "love" in our sense but the dangerous, irresistible, elemental force of passion. The ode stands at the midpoint of the play and sets the tone for the rest. The irrational forces of the previous ode, on the sufferings in the house of Oidipous, now become dominant. Begun as an ode sung by the chorus, the Eros ode leads directly into a lengthy lyrical exchange (known as a *kommos*) between the chorus and Antigone. This song echoes the play's opening exchange between Ismene and Antigone and, to lesser extent, the debate between Kreon and Antigone, but it takes those previous exchanges to a new register of emotional intensity. Antigone now expresses the pathos of what it means to become "Hades' bride." She will leave this world unlamented by any friends or family (935–41 / 876–82) — exactly the fate that she has tried to prevent for Polyneikes at the cost of her life.

Still intimidated by Kreon, the chorus offers only grudging and fleeting sympathy.[36] They cannot hold back their tears at the sight of the

34. Haimon's threat at 811 / 751 is in fact left somewhat ambiguous, for at the end he does attack Kreon with his sword, presumably to kill him (1316–17 / 1232–34).

35. Cf. the similar ominous exit of Iokasta in *Oidipous Turannos*, 1073–75, and the similar phrasing in the account of Deianeira's death in *Trakhinian Women*, 813–14 and 874–75.

36. Some scholars have thought that Kreon is present on stage during this ode, but it seems to us unlikely that he is there during Antigone's lament, which follows directly upon the ode: see the Note on 838–42 / 777–80.

girl about to be led off to the cave to die, but they continue to identify themselves with the collective political consciousness of the city. In the one place where they acknowledge her "reverence," they contrast it with the "power" of the ruler, which must not be transgressed (931–34 / 872–75). Kreon, who probably reenters just as Antigone is finishing her lament, hardheartedly dismisses her mournful song as an attempt to delay the inevitable, and his brusque response deepens the pathos of her isolation (942–43 / 883–84). He sends her to her death satisfied that he is ritually "pure," that is, unpolluted by shedding the blood of kin; but the ending will show his failure to escape so easily from pollution.

Antigone's last speech, once more in the dialogue meter of iambic trimeter, is addressed to the cave/tomb/bridal chamber that she is about to enter. Cut off from the human world, she turns to her dead family members in Hades. She addresses Polyneikes three times, once by name (964 / 902) and twice by the untranslatable periphrasis, literally "head of my brother" (960–61 / 899, 978 / 915), a phrase that echoes her address to Ismene in her opening line and so serves as another measure of her present isolation from the living. She already looks back at her mortal existence from the perspective of death. Forgetting Ismene, she sees herself as the last of her family whom Persephone, queen of the dead, has received in the underworld (954–56 / 894–96).

In the context of her absorption into the world below, Antigone makes the famous assertion that she would not have sacrificed her life to bury a husband or a child but only a brother, for with her parents dead she can have no other siblings. This is the *nomos*, the "law" or "custom," she says, by which she dared to become a criminal in Kreon's eyes (976–79 / 913–15). This "law" seems very different from those eternal, god-given, unwritten laws on which she based her earlier defiance of Kreon (495–518 / 450–70). The apparent contradiction between the two statements has troubled interpreters, some of whom, following Goethe's romantic reading, would excise the lines as a later interpolation based on a similar line of argument in Herodotos.[37] But

37. Herodotos, *Histories*, 3.119. Goethe objected that the passage was unworthy of Antigone's "noble motives . . . and the elevated purity of her soul" and that it "disturbs the tragic tone and appears to me very far-fetched—to savor too much of dialectical calculation." He also says, "I would give a great deal for an apt philologist to prove that it is interpolated and spurious": *Conversations with Eckermann* (above, n. 5), 178 (March 28, 1827). Goethe has found many champions, and these lines have often been regarded as a later interpolation based on Herodotos. But, as Herodotos was working on his *History* in the late 440s, there is no serious chronology problem with his priority. See the Note on lines 967–79 / 905–15. The authenticity of the lines is also supported by the citation of part of the passage in Aristotle, *Rhetoric*, 3.1417a29–33. For a cogent defense of the

Antigone's two accounts of her motives are complementary, not contradictory. Now she reveals that more personal, emotionally vulnerable side that she had already expressed in the preceding lyrical exchanges with the chorus.[38]

That more intimate tone is also appropriate to her present situation. Not only is she on the verge of death, but she is addressing her dead kin, particularly her mother and brothers, whom she expects to join imminently in the underworld. In the poignancy of these last, reflective moments, she finally expresses her bitterness and sorrow at her loss of marriage and children. The speech obviously wins sympathy for her as the young victim of cruelty and injustice. In this loneliness and despair, she even questions the gods, who have thus let her die, when her "reverence has earned [her] charges of irreverence" (990–91 / 924), but she does not forget her anger as she asks the gods to make her enemies suffer no more, and no less, than they have made her suffer (992–96 / 925–28).

In this final moment when we see her alive, Antigone reveals again her capacity for hatred and steely determination alongside her softer side of devotion to the intimate bond of *philia* or family love. We recall the curses of other Sophoklean good haters in their last moments, notably Aias as he commits suicide.[39] Her curse, though uttered at her lowest ebb of despair, also looks ahead to the shift in the balance of power that will take place when the gods, through Teiresias, do in effect answer her plea for vengeance and justice. But evidently they will not act on behalf of the girl who has served them. Antigone leaves the stage, and the mortal world, with a final, hopeless appeal to the city and citizens of Thebes, once more singing in lyric meter to the chorus (1005–11 / 937–43). Her isolation is total as she regards herself, again as if Ismene did not exist, as the only survivor of "the royal house" of Thebes (1008–9 / 941). At the end of her previous speech, in the dialogue meter of iambic trimeter, she looked to the gods for justice (992–96 / 925–28). Now she looks for sympathy to the human world that has punished her for her "pious impiety," her third use of such an expression and her last utterance in the play. Yet in all of her long lament she expresses sorrow but no regret and no weakening of resolve.

The following ode, the fourth stasimon, is one of the most complex

authenticity of the lines see Knox, *Heroic Temper*, 104–7. Some authoritative contemporary scholars still regard them as spurious, e.g., Winnington-Ingram, *Sophocles*, 145, with n. 80.

38. On Antigone's more vulnerable and so sympathetic side in this scene and the preceding lament, see Winnington-Ingram, *Sophocles*, 138–46.

39. Sophokles, *Aias*, 835–44. Cf. also Oidipous' curse on his sons in *Oidipous at Kolonus*, 1370–96, and Polyphemus' curse on Odysseus, *Odyssey*, 9.528–35.

and controversial in Sophokles. The chorus continue to distance themselves from Antigone, but their mythical exempla have a potential multiplicity of meanings that is appropriate at this critical moment in the action. All three of the myths they allude to illustrate imprisonment and so can easily point to Antigone. Yet all three also have implications that extend to Kreon as well.

The enclosure of Danae in her tower of bronze seems clearly enough to refer to Antigone. Yet the moral drawn from it, the inevitable power of the gods, will also come to refer to Kreon, particularly as Danae's myth includes the destruction of the powerful older king, Akrisios, who imprisoned her.[40] The chorus's next example, the Thracian king Lykourgos who persecutes Dionysos and is punished with a madness in which he kills his own son, has even stronger relevance to Kreon, whose anger and folly cause the death of his son. The third myth, a less familiar tale of jealousy between a wife and an ex-wife that results in the bloody blinding of two sons, evokes the sufferings of the house of Oidipous, but it also has implications for the doom that is about to overtake the house of Kreon, in which an angry, vengeful wife will wreak self-destruction with a bloody instrument. The chorus, of course, does not know what is going to happen and does not understand the full implications of their mythical exempla. As often in Sophokles, and in the Greek tragedy generally, the chorus members say more than they know; and the full meaning of their words appears only later, in retrospect.

The ode's closing reference to "the Fates, that live long ages" sets the tone for the entrance of the old blind prophet of Thebes, Teiresias, led on stage by a young boy or slave. After previous scenes with the Guard, Antigone, and Haimon, Kreon now meets a fourth challenge to his authority, but this time from an older rather than a younger man, and from the gods rather than from mortals. The prophet's opening address, "Lords of Thebes" (1050 / 988), like Antigone's last address to the leaders of Thebes (1008 / 940), in itself implies a less autocratic view of the city's government than Kreon had assumed, as he has been addressed earlier as the single "lord" of the land (e.g., 254 / 223, 319 / 278).[41] Kreon responds to Teiresias, as before to the previous challenges,

40. For the death of Akrisios at the hands of Danae's son by Zeus, Perseus, see Apollodoros, *Library of Mythology*, 2.4.4.

41. Kreon himself addresses the elders of the chorus merely as "men," *andres*, whereas Antigone calls them "citizens of my native land" (866 / 806), "men of the city, with all your possessions" (902–3 / 843–44), and "you rulers of Thebes" (1008 / 940). It may be that she does not want to address Kreon, from whom she can expect no sympathy, and wants to empower those whom she still has some hope of moving; but she also seems to envisage a government more broadly shared among the Thebans than Kreon's autocratic or tyrannical model.

with angry and defensive accusations of bribery and conspiracy (cf. 321–59 / 280–314). Teiresias, however, is not Kreon's subordinate, but truly an authoritative spokesman for the divine order, and he replies to Kreon's insults with a prophet's foreknowledge, which takes even Kreon aback (1133–72 / 1064–97). For the first time Kreon acknowledges weakness ("my mind is confused," 1170 / 1095), asks for advice, and submits to another's advice: "What must I do? Tell me! I will obey" (1174 / 1099).

Even in yielding to the divine message, however, Kreon still gets his priorities wrong. The chorus's advice is clear: first release Antigone, then bury the body (1175–76 / 1100–1101). With a misplaced concern for the political rather than the personal and for the soldier rather than the girl, he attends to the corpse first. By the time he reaches Antigone, it is too late.[42]

Kreon exits with the promise to release Antigone: "I am afraid it's best to observe the established laws through all one's life, to the end" (1189–90 / 1113–14). These "established laws" look back to the religious laws (or customs) pertaining to burial that Antigone had cited in her great speech of defiance (495–501 / 450–55), and in Kreon's mouth the word "laws" now tacitly acknowledges her victory. Yet the phrase "to the end" is ominous and foreshadows the horror that is approaching. (In contrast to Antigone, who remains steadfast, Kreon is afraid and "gives way." True heroism, of the unbending Sophoklean type, rests with her, not with him.[43] Her last words are about piety, his about fear.)

The fifth stasimon, the sixth and last regular ode in the play, is a prayer to Dionysos for help and purification at this time of crisis for Thebes. Dionysos is a major divinity of Thebes, his birthplace; but the ode also invokes the god's broader association with Italy and Eleusis, associations that point to mystery cults that promise initiates happiness in the afterlife. The allusion to Dionysos' maenads, his frenzied female worshipers (1201–5 / 1126–30), also reminds us of the female emotions that Kreon has tried to suppress by violence and imprisonment. It is as if these Dionysiac figures, like the murderous wife of the previous ode, become nightmarish projections of the female "madness" that Kreon

42. Kreon's reply inverts the order of events but nevertheless suggests that he might in fact go first to Antigone while his attendants go to bury Polyneikes (1183–90 / 1108–14). As we learn later, however, he accompanies his attendants first to Polyneikes' corpse and then goes to Antigone's cave (1271–83 / 1196–1205). F.J.H. Letters, *The Life and Work of Sophocles* (London, 1953), 157–59, attempts to defend Kreon's choice on the grounds that Teiresias' prophecy has emphasized the importance of burying Polyneikes for the welfare of the city. But this view does not take account of the advice of the elders, who are equally concerned with the city, nor that part of Teiresias' prophecy that includes the burial alive of Antigone as part of the disruption of the relation between upper and lower worlds (1133–44 / 1064–73).

43. See, in general, Knox, *Heroic Temper*, 62–75, 109–10.

attributes to Antigone and Ismene (see 542–43 / 491–92; 612–13 / 561–65). In the myths about these maenads, such as that of Pentheus dramatized in Euripides' *Bakkhai*, the god's female followers eventually triumph over resistance from a king. The chorus ends with a characteristically Dionysiac prayer for the god's epiphany, calling to him: "O You that lead the dance of the stars that breathe out fire, You that watch over the voices sounding in the night" (1218–20 / 1146–48). They thus point toward the powers of nature, the gods, and the world-order beyond human control.

In the play's first ode the chorus invoked Dionysos primarily as the local god of Thebes, to be honored in the all-night choruses of the citizens' victory celebrations (171–73 / 152–54). But the Dionysos of the last ode reaches far beyond the city of Thebes. His all-night choruses consist not of Theban citizens but of the fiery stars in the heavens. The fire-bearing enemy Kapaneus, trying to scale Thebes' walls in the first ode, was compared to a bakkhant in the madness of his wild rush against the city (152–55 / 134–37); but the fiery bakkhantic madness of this last ode belongs to the god and will not be driven away from the city. The bright ray of the sun that heralded Thebes' salvation in that first ode is now answered by nocturnal dancers outside the city; and the whole city, far from enjoying victory (167 / 148) or salvation, is in the grip of a "sickness" that may cause its doom (1214–15 / 1140–41).[44]

Once Kreon acknowledges his mistake, events move rapidly. The answer to the chorus's prayer for release from pollution is the Messenger's entrance with the news of a polluting death within Kreon's own house. Kreon is now in a state of living death (1238–40 / 1166–67), a fitting punishment for one who confused the relation between the living and his dead (cf. 1137–44 / 1068–73). At first the Messenger gives only the barest account of Haimon's suicide, until Eurydike, Kreon's wife, enters from the palace. Sophokles has carefully contrived this scene so that the Messenger makes his full report not to the chorus but to Eurydike. He thus makes us witness the bloody violence in Antigone's cave through the eyes of the mother and wife who will soon become the instrument of completing Kreon's tragedy.

The Messenger's narrative is one of the most powerful in Greek tragedy, and it vividly brings before us the ruin of Kreon's house. Having buried Polyneikes first, Kreon and his attendants approach Antigone's cave. He enters and finds her dead and Haimon in a frenzy. Now

---

44. The contrast between the first and last odes is also suggested by the earlier joyful invocation to "Nike, the goddess of victory, with great name and glory" (167 / 148), in a mood very different from the desperate invocation to Dionysos here as the "god of many names" (1191 / 1115).

in the role of supplicant (**1313** / 1230), not an all-commanding father, Kreon begs his son to leave the cave; but the boy, looking "wildly at him with fierce eyes," spits in his face, lunges at him with drawn sword, and, after he misses, stabs himself. He then falls in a dying embrace on Antigone's lifeless body, matching, as bridegroom, her role as a bride of death itself (**1317–23** / 1234–39).

Antigone's defiance of Kreon is now fulfilled in Haimon's, and it is a defiance that utterly undoes Kreon's authority over his son, over Antigone, and over his city. Kreon prided himself on his patriarchal authority, his good sense, his rational approach to life, and his superiority to women. Haimon overturns all these principles. He rejects the father for the promised bride, surrenders to the wild passions surrounding love and death, and chooses the cave's Hades-like prison of a condemned woman over the *polis*-world where he should succeed his father in ruling the city. The two houses, Kreon's and Antigone's, are joined together by a fearful marriage-in-death; and it is as if with that union Antigone, the heiress, transfers to the house of Kreon all the pollutions in the house of Oidipous: the suicide of the mother, the death of two sons, and the fulfillment of a terrible prophecy.[45]

The Messenger concludes with a generalization about the dangers of foolish behavior, but Eurydike makes no reply. She slips away in silence, like Iokaste in *Oidipous Turannos*, and it is a silence that strikes both the Messenger and the chorus as ominous. But before they can absorb its meaning, Kreon enters with the body of Haimon, either actually in his arms, as the chorus says (**1344** / 1258), or on a bier or wagon that Kreon accompanies with his arms around his dead son. It is a mournful tableau, and the contrast with Kreon's first entrance is shocking. Instead of making authoritative civic pronouncements in the proud bearing of a victorious ruler, he utters cries of lament and misery. Instead of generalizations about statecraft he sings a funeral dirge, the traditional task of women, punctuated by sharp cries of grief, indicated in the Greek text by *aiai aiai*, *oimoi*, or *pheu pheu* (**1354** / 1267, **1358** / 1271, **1362** / 1276). This is also the first time in the play that he sings extensive lyrical passages, accompanied by the *aulos*, the double wind instrument (probably with a reed, like a clarinet or oboe) that was felt by the Greeks of Sophokles' era to be particularly emotional.[46] This change of musical and emotional registers marks his shift from absolute

---

45. On hearing the cry from the cave Kreon had exclaimed, "Am I a seer?" (**1291** / 1212; cf. **1252** / 1178).

46. Prior to this passage, Kreon has only two short anapestic exchanges with the chorus about sending Antigone into the cave (**999–1000** / 931–32, **1003–4** / 935–36); otherwise, he speaks only in iambic trimeters.

power to total helplessness, and he continues to sing in lyrics to the end of the play.

More suffering lies in store. The messenger returns from the royal house to announce the death of Eurydike. The manner of her end intensifies Kreon's pain, for she has killed herself in a particularly horrible way, stabbing herself at the household altar in the courtyard, cursing her husband as the killer of both his sons—Haimon and an elder son who died earlier, here called Megareus, who is left obscure but is possibly to be identified with the Menoikeus of Euripides' *Phoinikian Women*, who leaps from the walls of Thebes to fulfill a prophecy that only the voluntary death of a descendant of Thebes' autochthonous inhabitants could save the city.[47]

Eurydike's curse turns the two generative roles in the house, maternity and paternity, toward death, the appropriate punishment of one who has interfered with the basic ties of family in Antigone's house. The messenger calls her *pammêtôr nekrou*, literally "the all-mother" of the corpse, the mother in the fullest sense of the word ("mother absolute," at 1368 / 1282).

Also, Eurydike's final, suicidal lament recalls the cries of Antigone over the body of Polyneikes at the moment when she was caught, and in fact Sophokles uses the same verb of both women's cries (468 / 423, 1389 / 1302). Again like Antigone, Eurydike combines lament with curse (473 / 427 and 1391–92 / 1304–5). The close verbal parallels bring Kreon's suffering into direct causal connection with his actions in a way that is expressive of the retributive justice that the Greeks call *dikê*. Taking full responsibility for the deaths that he has caused, Kreon now sees himself as "no more than nothing" (1408 / 1325). The man who spoke in metaphors of keeping things straight and upright now finds his whole world awry: he says, "everything is twisted in my hands" (1425–26 / 1342).

MYTHS AND ODES

The six odes of the play are among the most poetically elaborate of those in the extant Sophokles and provide a commentary parallel to the main action on the ambiguities of Kreon's controlling power and the atmosphere of doom surrounding Antigone.[48] The parodos, as we have noted, celebrates the city's victory over its enemies and so sets the

47. See Griffith's note on 1302–3 and our Note on 1387–92 / 1301–5. Eurydike's accusatory epithet for Kreon, "killer of sons," may refer only to the death of Haimon, but the passage can also be read as implying that Eurydike holds Kreon responsible for the deaths of both sons.
48. For the place of the odes in the rhythm of the action, see my *Tragedy and Civilization*, 197–206.

stage for Kreon's entrance. Yet its Dionysiac language and the all-night civic choruses return with very different meanings in the last ode, when something of the emotional violence and frenzy that also belong to Dionysos make their appearance.

The first stasimon, sometimes called the Ode on Man, is one of the most famous passages of all Greek literature (377–416 / 332–75).[49] Its triumphant list of the achievements of human civilization is often read as a hymn to the confidence, humanism, and rationalism of the Periklean Age, which saw so many advances in the arts and sciences. Yet the opening words, "At many things—wonders, terrors—we feel awe, but at nothing more than at man," are deeply ambiguous, as the translation of the word *deinon* implies, for *deinon* means "wonderful" but also "fearful," "strange," "terrible," "uncanny." Antigone uses it, for example, of the "terrible" suffering that she is ready to undergo for defying Kreon (114 / 96) and the Guard of the "terrible" things he fears from Kreon (278 / 243). The ode's opening, furthermore, echoes the beginning of a famous ode of Aiskhylos' *Libation Bearers* on the destructive passions and crimes of evil women (*Libation Bearers* 585ff.).

It is tempting to associate with Kreon the Ode on Man's attitude of proud, rationalistic domination of the world. Yet both he and Antigone, in different ways, embody the quality of the "wonderful/terrible" with which the ode begins; and both protagonists ambiguously shift between being "high in his city" and "outside any city" (412–13 / 370). Many of the items listed as the proud achievements of humanity return later with their meaning reversed. The human conquest of earth, sea, and the birds of the skies returns later as a human failure to control. The conquest of disease, for example, comes back ominously in the disease of pollution with which Kreon's acts afflict the city (1079 / 1015; cf. 1215 / 1141 and 467 / 421). The juxtaposition of "inventive" (literally "all-devising") and "without invention" or "device" 401–2 / 360 points to the paradoxical collocation of the human strength and weakness enacted by both protagonists. The qualification of human power in the next line, "Only from Hades will he not procure some means of escape" (403–5 / 361–62), looms large in a play so much concerned with the underworld and the ways in which the dead destroy the lives of the living. Kreon's tragedy in particular follows a trajectory from his confident assertion of authority over love and marriage ("It's Hades who will stop this wedding for me," 626 / 575) to his miserable cry that his house is a "harbor of Hades" whose pollution he cannot cleanse (1371 / 1284). The ode's insistence on human cleverness and intellect con-

---

49. For further discussion and references, see my *Tragedy and Civilization*, 152–54.

trasts, of course, with the bad judgment of the ensuing action. In their closing lyrics, the members of the chorus blame the absence of "good sense" for the tragic outcome (1427 / 1348, 1431 / 1353).

The taming of "Gaia, the Earth, forever undestroyed and unwearying, highest of all the gods" (382–83 / 337–39) by agriculture comes early in the ode, paired with the conquest of the sea. However, it is not Earth as highest but as it is associated with both the realm of the dead below and with the dust of burial that determines the course of the tragedy. When Antigone is apprehended performing burial rites for Polyneikes' body, a mysterious whirlwind, as the Guard describes it, lifts the dust from the earth as a "storm of trouble high as heaven," which "filled up the whole huge sky," so that those watching the body suffer a "supernatural plague" (462–67 / 415–21), as if some divine power were inverting upper and lower realms. The next ode describes the murderous curse in the house of Oidipous in the bold metaphor of the "blood-red dust of the gods under the earth" (if we can trust the manuscript text) reaching up to "reap" "the last rootstock of the House of Oidipous" (647–50 / 599–602). This second stasimon begins by associating the dark sand stirred from the depths by violent storms at sea with the doom of the house of Oidipous (633–44 / 582–95) and then contrasts that submarine turbulence with the immutable radiance of Zeus high above on Olympus (651–57 / 604–10). At the peripeteia or reversal, Teiresias traces the spread of pollution to Kreon's inversion of what belongs above and below the earth (1133–48 / 1064–76).[50]

In fact, the mood of this second stasimon is virtually the reverse of that of the first stasimon. The Ode on Man begins with the conquest of the sea; but the second stasimon, as we have noted, uses the sea as a metaphor for exactly the opposite meaning, associating the dark, stormy Thracian sea with the irrational sufferings that have afflicted Antigone's family. Taking the afflictions of the ancient house of Oidipous as its paradigm, this ode dwells on the irrational aspects of mortal life. Its tone proves justified, for the chorus immediately introduces Haimon (673–77 / 626–30), who is now the bearer of the uncontrollable passions in Kreon's own house.

From this point on, the odes run parallel to the increasing emotional and physical violence of the action. The third stasimon (fourth ode), on the invincible power of Eros, forms the transition between the fatal quarrel of Haimon and Kreon and Antigone's final lament with the chorus. It thus joins the two destructive forces operating in the background, Eros and Hades, love and death. The complex fourth stasimon

50. For the upper/lower axis in the play, see my *Tragedy and Civilization*, 170–73, 178–79.

(fifth ode), as we have already noted, narrates myths of passion and violence that are applicable, in different degrees, to both protagonists. Finally, the Dionysiac themes of the last ode, suggesting a possible fusion between the city and the natural world, are different from the views of both the parodos (the first ode, on Thebes' victory) and the Ode on Man. Dionysos' maddened female worshipers here (1222–24 / 1150–52) also anticipate the release of dangerous female passion in the play's closing movement, the suicides of both Antigone and Eurydike.

If Kreon implies that he sees the sisters as something like maenads, maddened or running wild (see 542–43 / 491–92 and 630 / 579), Antigone on the contrary sees herself as a bride of Hades, that is, as Kore, the Maiden, who is also called Persephone, carried off to the underworld.[51] Young women who die before marriage are conventionally regarded as "marrying" Hades. For Antigone, however, the motif of wedding Hades is part of a dense network of associations. She will not just wed Hades figuratively, for by the manner of her death she will actually go underground, entering Hades while alive. And there in fact a marriage of sorts will be enacted in Haimon's bloody embrace of her corpse as he dies from his self-inflicted wound. Her death as a bride of Hades makes horribly literal what is only a convention of speaking. She is being sent to her Hades-like cave, moreover, because she has valued the dead and their gods above her life on earth; and, as we have observed, she is vindicated by Teiresias' accusation of Kreon's interference with the relation between upper and lower worlds.

As a bride of Hades, Antigone is a Persephone carried off violently by the god of the lower world. Yet she is a Persephone who will remain unmarried and will never return to the upper world in the seasonal alternations of winter and spring that are essential to the Demeter–Persephone myth, as told in the *Homeric Hymn to Demeter*. "Go send the girl (*korê*) up from her deep-dug house," the chorus advises Kreon when he finally gives in to Teiresias (1175–76 / 1100–1101). Their word, "send up," evokes the motif of Persephone's ascent when Hades must return her to Demeter with the return of the earth's fertility in the spring.[52] Yet the Kore/Persephone that Antigone envisages is a goddess

---

51. For the role of Persephone and Demeter in the mythical background of the play, see my *Tragedy and Civilization*, 179–81. For the fusion of marriage and death in tragedy, see Richard Seaford, "The Tragic Wedding," *Journal of Hellenic Studies* 107 (1987), 106–30; Gail Holst-Wahrhaft, *Dangerous Voices: Women's Laments and Greek Literature* (London and New York, 1992), 41–42; Rush Rehm, *Marriage to Death* (Princeton, 1994), especially 59–71.

52. In the Homeric *Hymn to Demeter* the verb "send up" describes Demeter's allowing the grain to grow on earth (lines 307, 332, 471).

of death, not of renewed life, she who "has received [Antigone's] dead among the shades" (954–55 / 893–94).

Antigone's role as an unrisen Persephone parallels that of Haimon as the young man who dies "out of season," *aôros*, a term that is used of youths who will not make the transition between the bloom of adolescence and adulthood but will die before their time. In this respect the two suicides are symmetrical in their perversion of the normal pattern of life-generating marriage. Antigone remains too close to her house of origin. Instead of going to the house of the bridegroom — the usual pattern of patrilocal marriage in classical Athens — she goes to the Hades that holds her parents and brother. She thereby reenacts the introverted kin ties characteristic of the house of Oidipous.[53] Marrying Hades, staying in her house of origin, and being the child of an incestuous marriage are all in a way equivalent aspects of Antigone's tragic situation, her sacrifice of the normal progression to womanhood to the bonds of family and to devotion to the dead. The incest of her parents is the inverse of her nonmarriage, but it belongs to a similar failure of "normal" family life. The excessive closeness of incest (same staying with same) short-circuits the union of same and other in normal marriage and so parallels Antigone's refusal to separate herself from her natal family in a union with a bridegroom of another house. Haimon, analogously, undoes all the expectations of the groom. He not only goes to his bride's "house" (instead of bringing her to his) but also attacks his father (recalling Oidipous' patricide) and then consummates the marriage in an act of reverse penetration that leads to the spilling of his blood, like the maiden's, instead of seed.

In Antigone's long lyrical lament as she prepares to enter the cave, she looks to another female model from the realm of myth, Niobe, the grieving mother who weeps incessantly for her lost children and is turned into a rock from which streams of water flow perpetually (883–93 / 823–33). The chorus objects that Niobe is a god and Antigone a mere mortal, and in response Antigone feels pain at what she takes to be mockery (899ff. / 839ff.). There is irony too in the fact that Niobe is the mother of many children, Antigone of none. Yet Antigone can identify with the eternity of lament into which this *mater dolorosa* is frozen forever. Both the eternity and the stony end speak to her condition. The image of Niobe is also a negation of the fruitful aspect of

---

53. For the way in which the house of Oidipous is characteristic of a Theban pattern of introverted family ties, see Froma I. Zeitlin, "Thebes: Theater of Self and Society in Athenian Drama," in J. J. Winkler and F. I. Zeitlin, eds., *Nothing to Do with Dionysus?* (Princeton, 1990), 130–67, especially 150–52.

the mother figure in the Demeter–Persephone myth. It evokes Demeter's role as a mother of sorrows, lamenting her lost daughter, Persephone, as she wanders over the earth in her desperate search for the abducted girl. This is also the aspect of Demeter that applies to the other mother figure in the play, Kreon's wife, Eurydike, whose name, literally "of broad justice," or "wide-ruling," is also an epithet for the queen of the dead. As the "all-mother" of the dead Haimon, as we have noted, she is associated with grieving maternity. Antigone, doomed to die childless, is also drawn into the model of the grieving mother when she laments over the body of Polyneikes like a mother-bird that finds her nest emptied of fledglings (469–71 / 423–25). The simile of grieving motherhood once more points to the unfulfilled life of this bride of Hades. She is a Persephone who will not ascend and a sorrowing Demeter/Niobe who will always lament.

The images of the mother in this play, in fact, are all of the mourning, dying, or murderous mother, not the fertile mother. This is true even of the fourth stasimon's myth of Danae, imprisoned like Antigone and "made to exchange the light of the sky for a dark room bolted with bronze" (1012–14 / 944–47). She will, of course, be impregnated by Zeus' golden shower and bear his son, Perseus (1017–18 / 950), but the ode dwells rather on her imprisonment and on the ineluctable doom given her by the Fates or Moirai (1018–20 / 951–53). The final strophe of the ode tells the story of another imprisoned mother and centers on the blinding of her two sons by the jealous stepmother. And in the background is Iokaste, who "violently disfigured her own life" by suicide (67–68 / 53–54) but by whom Antigone feels loved and whom she hopes to see soon in the underworld (960 / 898).

Of the six formal odes, only the first stasimon, the Ode on Man, seems to have no immediate connection with the events enacted on stage. Yet on further reflection it has profound implications for the meaning of the play as an interpretation of the human condition.[54] The ode's celebration of the confident domination of nature by human intelligence and technology is undercut by the themes of the subse-

---

54. For further discussion, see my "Sophocles' Praise of Man and the Conflicts of *Antigone*," in my *Interpreting Greek Tragedy* (Ithaca, N.Y., 1986), 137–61. Noteworthy is Martin Heidegger's celebrated existentialist interpretation of the ode as a reflection on the mysterious and "uncanny" nature of our humanness, which makes us both violent and creative, both citiless outcasts and all-powerful conquerors of a world that, nevertheless, eludes and defeats us as we are "tossed back and forth between structure and the structureless," between order and the ultimate nothingness of death: Martin Heidegger, *An Introduction to Metaphysics*, trans. Ralph Manheim (New Haven, 1959), 146–65, conveniently accessible in Thomas Woodard, ed., *Sophocles: A Collection of Critical Essays* (Englewood Cliffs, N.J., 1966), 86–100. The quotation is on 97. See also Steiner, *Antigones*, 174–77.

quent odes and by the subsequent actions. Sophokles' contemporaries might well read this contrast as a critique of the human-centered rationalism of Athens' Periklean Age. The achievements of this extraordinary period include the high classical art and architecture that extol the human form (especially the male body) as the standard of beauty and a rationalistic view of religion, law, medicine, history, language, and the founding of cities, and so on, as creations of human intelligence and progress, not gifts of the gods. Influential here are the theories of the Sophists, such as Protagoras or Hippias, and of scientists and philosophers, such as Anaxagoras, Parmenides, or the atomist Leukippos, and of medical writers such as Hippokrates.

While it would be simplistic to identify this spirit of scientific inquiry with Kreon, the play does insist on his materialism and shallow rationalism. In the face of events that might have a supernatural cause, like the initial burial of Polyneikes, where there are no signs of human or animal presence (284–94 / 249–58), or Teiresias' announcement of widespread pollution, Kreon's first response is an accusation of bribery and conspiracy. Men, he assumes, always act for "profit," one of his favorite words. But in Antigone, as later in Haimon and Teiresias, he encounters motives that cannot be reduced to material gain or to his mode of reasoning. Antigone dismisses all calculation of personal advantage, including life itself. "If I die before my time," she says in her speech of defiance to Kreon, "I count that as my profit" (508–10 / 461–62). Until he finally backs down in the face of Teiresias' prophecy, Kreon assumes that he understands the ways of the gods and that their values coincide with his. Hence his anger and scorn at the chorus's suggestion that the gods might have buried Polyneikes (319–20 / 278–79), a possibility that the play in fact leaves open.[55] Such too is his

---

55. On the much discussed question of the so-called double burial, see H. D. F. Kitto, *Form and Meaning in Drama* (London, 1956), 138–44, 152–54, and my *Tragedy and Civilization*, 159, with the references cited in n. 25, 442–43. In favor of possible divine intervention are the absence of any marks of human agency, the fact that the first watch of the day (288 / 253) finds the body while Ismene and Antigone are still speaking in "this very night" (21 / 16), and Antigone's return to bury the body on the occasion when she is caught, even though the first "burial" would suffice for the funerary ritual (290–93 / 255–56). On the other hand, interpreters have argued that Antigone's response when she sees the body uncovered and her curses on those who have uncovered it (468–73 / 423–28) imply her having performed the initial burial: see Winnington-Ingram, *Sophocles*, 125, with n. 31. Yet Sophokles' language even here is vague enough to leave open other possibilities. In any case, the gods seem to be working through Antigone, even if they do not intervene directly, and the play offers a double perspective on the events in the contrast between the mysterious details in the background and Kreon's insistence on what is visible and tangible: so Seale, *Vision and Stagecraft*, 87–91. Kitto, 154, suggests that the gods and Antigone "are working on parallel paths." Analogously, Ruth Scodel, *Sophocles* (Boston, 1984), 55–56, suggests that the gods may not directly intervene in either burial but help Antigone's success in performing the rites on both occasions. In any case, the chorus's explicit suggestion of divine intervention

confidence in the narrow legalism of putting Antigone to death in a manner that avoids pollution to the city (in contrast to his original threat of punishment by public stoning, 46–47 / 36), his bold assertions of what can and cannot bring pollution, and his use of death or Hades as an instrument of political control.

All these views turn on him with terrible consequences. The Ode on Man warns that death is the one thing that humankind's technological progress cannot overcome. The marriage that Kreon thinks Hades will stop (626 / 575) takes place in the Hades-like cave, from which comes the final wave of death and pollution that submerges Kreon's life. The association of Eurydike's name with the underworld, noted earlier, further suggests that death and Hades, far from being something that Kreon can inflict on others, are already deep within his own house. The Ode on Man suggestively links Kreon's attitude of domination and control with a larger worldview in which nature is an inert resource to be exploited by human technology. The ode's description of yoking the horse, for example, echoes Kreon's metaphor of the yoke for power over the Thebans (336 / 291–92). His first response to Antigone's speech of defiance is also a metaphor of tempering iron by fire and taming horses with the bit (521–28 / 473–79). When Haimon offers alternative images of trees by a flooding river that bend with the current or ships that slacken sails in high winds instead of fighting the winds (768–77 / 710–17), Kreon responds with anger at being chastised by a younger man (786–87 / 726–27).

The sharpest opposition comes, of course, from Antigone, who values the invisible world of the dead over the surface, material world that Kreon would dominate as the plow of the Ode on Man wears down the surface of the inexhaustible earth and renders it serviceable for humankind. Kreon translates his political and legal conflict with her into a conflict of genders, male versus female. He may be reflecting some of the anxieties of Greek males about strong women's assertion of power; but he also reflects a deeper polarization of worldviews.[56]

(319–20 / 278–79) is particularly important, for it strongly signals the possibility of divine interaction. It suffices for the play that the possibility is raised and has some plausibility, even if the play offers no definitive answer.

56. On the male-female conflicts in the play, see my *Tragedy and Civilization*, 183–86. Helene P. Foley, "Antigone as Moral Agent," in Michael S. Silk, ed., *Tragedy and the Tragic* (Oxford, 1996), 49–73, drawing in part on the work of Carol Gilligan, suggests that the two protagonists represent contrasting notions of moral responsibility; she contends that Antigone thinks in terms of specific and personal contexts, involving "care and responsibility," whereas Kreon operates with more abstract and impartial notions of rights and justice (64). See, however, the critique by Michael Trapp, ibid., 74–84, and Mark Griffith, "Antigone and her Sister(s): Embodying Women in Greek Tragedy," in André Lardinois and Laura McClure, eds., *Making Silence Speak: Women's Voices in Greek Literature and Society* (Princeton, 2001), 117–36, especially 126–35, on the range and

Where Kreon stresses differentiation by political allegiance, Antigone stresses the unifying bonds of kinship, notably in her famous exchange of 562–76 / 511–25. Where he insists on the political labels of "friend" or "enemy" as the defining terms, Antigone insists that both her brothers have an equal right to burial under "Hades' laws," and asserts, "My nature's not to join in hate but to join in love" (574 / 523).[57]

In comparing herself to Niobe, as we have seen, Antigone conveys her image of eternal devotion to family, lament for dead kin, and funerary ritual. But her comparison also suggests a dissolution of the barrier between the human form and the natural world. Niobe is a grieving mother whose body has now become an ivy-covered mountain from which the waters flow as tears would flow down a human face. In Antigone's insistence on the sanctity of death, she also affirms, indirectly, the sanctity of life and the value of those bonds within the family that derive from generation and blood kinship, not political and legal institutions.[58] Yet if Kreon forgets that the civic institutions also rest on smaller, more intimate units like the family, Antigone equally forgets that the family is also part of the city. That the ties within her own family are so fraught with the double pollutions of incest and fratricidal self-slaughter is one of the play's deep tragic ironies. Her convoluted family ties, as the second stasimon, on the house of Oidipous, indicates, belong to what is dark, mysterious, and irrational in human life. The chorus's first two odes celebrate, respectively, the victory of the city over wild, bakkhantic aggression and of human intelligence over the physical and animal world. But the play ends with the darker vision of catastrophe unleashed by the uncontrollable passions of grief and love, bad judgment, and irreverence.

The final lines on good sense, piety, cautious speech, and learning wisdom by great suffering in old age offer little comfort. Kreon's old age is the bleakest possible; but the tragedy has also afflicted the young, the new generation of the two houses, who come together only for violent death, whether at the gates of Thebes, as do Polyneikes and Eteokles, or in the Hades-like cave of perverted union, as do Haimon and Antigone. Ismene, of course, is still alive, but she has not been mentioned for some six hundred lines (since (830–31 / 770–71), and her survival hardly counts.

---

fluidity of the female voice in tragedy and the problems of constructing a model of "female" behavior or language.

57. See the Note on 574 / 523.

58. Steiner, *Antigones*, 287, remarks of the play, "No poet or thinker, I believe, has found a greater, a more comprehensive statement of the 'crime against life.'"

The chorus's closing advice, far from offering consolation, implies a world hedged about by dangers and limits, a world that is far removed from the triumphant domination of nature in the Ode on Man. The Hades that seemed only a secondary qualification or an afterthought in the Ode on Man is now frighteningly near, and the "gleaming marble heights" of Olympos, where Zeus rules in his timeless power, hopelessly remote (**651–57** / 604–10).[59]

To return to Hegel, the play does not show any synthesis of two antithetical positions, but it does reveal the terrible wholeness of a reality of which Kreon and Antigone separately perceive only a part. Each ignores the modicum of truth that the other's worldview might hold. And yet Antigone has a reverence for the hidden powers of the divine world that Kreon increasingly flouts, carried away as he is by the arrogance of his human power, until his open defiance of the spokesman of the divine order provokes the curse that seals his punishment. Indeed, Antigone speaks of the gods more than does any other character in the play.[60] Unshaken in her convictions, she is cast in the mold of the true Sophoklean hero. Kreon, when we see him last, is a broken man. The emptiness that surrounds him at the end contrasts with the spiritual fullness of Antigone's death, lonely and despairing as it is.[61] It is interesting to compare his cries of utter misery at the end with those of Oidipous in the *Oidipous Turannos*, written a decade or so later. Oidipous gives voice to similar utterances of despair and misery at the moment of tragic reversal, but these are not his final words. His play, unlike Kreon's, continues for another 300 verses, in which he discovers a new kind of strength and a new kind of heroism. No such discovery awaits Kreon.[62]

The ending justifies Antigone, but too late to save her life; it brings learning to Kreon but too late to protect him from the polluted "Harbor of Hades" into which he has fallen. "Good sense is the first principle of happiness," the chorus moralizes as it moves toward closure (**1427–28** / 1347–48). But whatever "good sense" Kreon has learned "in old

59. The "weariless passing of the months" (**653–54** / 607), or more literally, "the untiring months" (*akamatoi mênes*) associated with these remote, eternal gods, may evoke Earth the "unwearying" (*akamatan*) of the Ode on Man (**383** / 339). The succession of the months is beyond human control and thus a sign of the ultimate human frailty rather than human power. See also the similar description of the Olympian realm in the second stasimon of *Oidipous Turannos* (863–72).

60. See Budelmann, *Language of Sophocles*, 175–79.

61. See Karl Reinhardt, *Sophocles* (1947), trans. H. and D. Harvey (Oxford, 1979), 93.

62. Compare especially **1403–26** / 1317–46 with *Oidipous Turannos* 1307–68. For further discussion, see my *Oedipus Tyrannus: Tragic Heroism and the Limits of Knowledge*, 132–33.

age," in the play's final lines, contains no trace of happiness, only the dazed, barren, and lonely old age into which we see him frozen as his attendants lead him offstage.

CHARLES SEGAL

ON THE TRANSLATION

Some nuances of the text of *Antigone*, as of every Greek tragedy, must have been thrown into view by performance, especially since this was so stylized—the language markedly different from speech, many passages chanted or sung to accompanying music and dance, the dialogue exchanges punctuated by commentary within the play itself in the form of the choral odes. And the actors' masks would have shifted all facial expressiveness to the voice and body. The very artificiality of ancient performance could not help calling attention to the language itself rather than to action or the apparent personalities of the characters (something in which we take more interest than did the ancient Greek poets, for whom the play was an exploration not so much of character as of ultimate questions of human fate and freedom). We do not know how ancient audiences reacted to the theatrical convention of actors changing roles, yet surely the stagecraft would have had some effect on the audience's sense of the language they were hearing. For example, how could one not listen very keenly to such remarkably staged moments as the beginning?—when, as George Steiner concisely describes it, "the masked male actor who impersonates Antigone addresses the masked male actor who impersonates Ismene" (206). Then it is very probably the actor who plays Antigone who also returns as her betrothed, Haimon—and then as Teiresias, and then as Haimon's mother, Eurydike! This *actor*'s changing of roles *enacts* a striking idea: that each *character* who in vain challenges Kreon brings back on stage the futile challenges of the others. This theatrical practice is scarcely ever repeated today, nor, on the page, is there any way to "translate" the effect of that actor appearing in different roles, or of the actor playing Ismene returning as the Guard and the Messenger. Or to "translate" the strange stubbornness of role of the one actor who plays only the stubborn Kreon: he remains on stage for most of the play, while the other figures appear and disappear around him. (The Greek text includes no stage directions, but in this translation we provide them to give the reader our conjectures about what is likely to be happening on stage.)

LANGUAGE AS AN ELEMENT OF STRUCTURE

Antigone opens after the slaughter and fright of war have come to the very gates of Thebes but have been kept outside. The heroine's two brothers have already killed each other, one heroically defending their native Thebes, the other cruelly attacking it. These life-and-death bodily conflicts are an emblem of the intense conflicts of words and beliefs with which the play begins and continues—which is only to say that *Antigone* (like all Greek tragedy) includes much argument, and that the argument arises from, and leads to more of, an inordinate amount of dying and death and suicide. Warfare has left rotting bodies outside the city walls, and then come the suicides of three of the six main characters of the play—Antigone, Haimon, and Haimon's mother Eurydike. (Still alive but offstage at the conclusion are Ismene, of whom we see nothing in nearly the last two-thirds of the play, and Teiresias, the seer; on stage at the end is Kreon, whose self-satisfaction in his rule and whose emotional investments in life have been utterly destroyed.)

Returning again and again to dire confrontations and conflict, and to descriptions of appalling acts, the play repeatedly returns also to certain ideas and words. Some of the individual words themselves are sites of struggle between the new ruler Kreon and his series of antagonists, as he and they fight from opposite points of view to control the meaning of the language they use. For instance, Kreon and Antigone argue over who can properly be called "friend" and who "enemy," over what is just and honorable and reverent, and what is unjust and dishonorable and irreverent. Sometimes the characters launch competing words at each other, so that, for example (in the words of Mark Griffith):

> [W]e can trace an implicit struggle for validation between the calculating "intelligence," "counsel," and "thought" . . . recommended by Kreon and other (male) characters, as against Antigone's intuitive "knowledge" and "certainty" . . . and among the male characters, we may contrast Kreon's emphasis on "calculation" and rigid "straightness" with Haimon's and Teiresias' recommending of "learning" and "bending." (42)

(I have translated the Greek word here represented by "bending" as "yielding" and also "giving way.")

The play is not a long text, and its diction is repetitive, so as Sophokles draws out the complexity of meaning in attitudes, beliefs, and words, many of the associations and connotations around each key Greek word are eventually brought to light, sometimes with grim and sorrowful tragic irony. The structural effect of such language is of a highly deliberate wovenness (a favorite ancient metaphor for poetry) that is both intellectually beautiful and artistically effective; to achieve an analogous effect in translation, the translator can try to repeat an English word to match the repetitions of a particular Greek word. For example: "You'd do well as the single ruler of some deserted place," Haimon bitterly tells his father (799 / 739), using the same word (*erê-mos*) that Sophokles will just afterward give to Kreon, both when he plans to "lead [Antigone] out to some deserted place" (833 / 773) and when he specifically orders her to die "alone, deserted" (946 / 887); finally Sophokles gives the word to Antigone herself, who laments that she has been "deserted by those close" to her (984 / 919).

However, working against the translator is the dispiriting historical fact that any particular word in contemporary English has its own associations and connotations that have nothing whatever to do with the Greek ones, but instead are the traces of centuries of use in other times and cultures, and of our own particular, present-day linguistic environment. The word that is repeated several times in Greek, turned by Sophokles this way and that to reveal the nuances and implications of its use in different phrases and circumstances, is necessarily represented by a word in English without those nuances and implications and with a number of new implications that are irrelevant. However, there is no other way but repetition—when this is possible without forcing English to be unidiomatic—to signal Sophokles' method of bringing words back in new contexts to show which underlying ideas are relevant to a moment of struggle between characters. Fundamentally, the repeated words structure the play both in that weaving way I mentioned earlier and also in setting out the binary oppositions between which Sophokles dramatizes a conflict of belief, feeling, and real power. (For example, when Kreon utters with contempt the word "woman," an ideological axis of the play comes immediately into view.)

Standing on the shoulders of Charles Segal and the scholarly editions of *Antigone*, I offer below just a few key words with some of their connotations and associations in Greek—on which I myself am far from being an authority.

(1) It turns out to be impossible to echo consistently in English the repetitions of the several words derived from or related to Greek *philos*. "Loved," "beloved," "those close to us," and so on, are among the

different articulations of this idea in English that I have used for the same word in Greek, because no one word in English is adequate. As Griffith notes, "Given the wide semantic field occupied by *philos*— covering 'family member,' 'loved one,' 'friend,' 'ally,' even 'one's own' (limbs, etc.), and extending even further with the usage of [related words]—contradictions constantly arise, as members of the same family or political group (= *philoi*, by definition) become 'hateful/hostile' to one another as a result of their behavior" (40–41). Kreon even uses a derivative of *philos*, translated as "money-loving," when accusing Teiresias of greed (see point 5, below). And to Kreon—whose character Sophokles convincingly portrayed, even if character as such was not foremost among the poet's interests—a form of *philos* can quickly suggest its opposite: hatred and the enemy.

(2) The famously untranslatable first line of the play uses three of the often repeated key words of the play: *koinos*, meaning what is shared in common; *autadelphon*, a word for sister or brother that includes as prefix the root word *autos*, meaning "self"; and *kara*, a noun meaning "head," but used idiomatically as an elevated periphrasis expressing endearment and emotional involvement. Every use of the word "self" in the translation—such as "self-killing," "self-will," "he himself," and so on—echoes Sophokles' use of some form of *autos* in the Greek, as I tried to represent Sophokles' restless inquiry into how much of suffering is brought on oneself by one's own decisions, as opposed to how much is ordained by the gods. In this translation, *koinos* is represented by the words "shared" and "common" singly or together (and these English words are not used to represent any other Greek word); and the noun *kara* by the adjectives "dear" or "true," as when Antigone calls the dead Polyneikes her "own dear brother" (978 / 915).

(3) The polar opposites that I have rendered as "reverence" and "irreverence," and related forms, appear often, but if my goal had been to achieve variety in the diction of the translation, the Greek words could have been translated at least some of the time as the opposites "pious" and "impious." Kreon believes it is impious or irreverent with respect to the gods of the city—presumably Dionysos and Zeus, among others—to give funeral rites to Polyneikes, because the latter made himself an enemy of the city, while Antigone believes it is irreverent or impious to the gods of the underworld, Hades their chief, *not* to give proper ritual burial to the dead. However, the action of the play finally implies that Kreon has been blasphemous; since Kreon is destroyed, we do not doubt that some of the gods, at least, are punishing him.

(4) I have used the words "right" and "straight" and related words to

represent the Greek word *orthos* and its derivations (and have not used "right" otherwise). *Orthos* is one of Kreon's favorite words. In following his "straight" course, Kreon manifests his rigid and stubbornly mistaken thinking. He claims he stands for what is "right" and he tries to establish the authority of his concept.

(5) Kreon is convinced that the reason people do what they do is for *kerdos*, "profit," material gain. His reiterations of this word, sometimes even when it does not appear to be relevant, make it seem that Sophokles wished to show how, as we might say in our day, Kreon keeps attributing to others a motive of his own that he keeps secret, even from himself; perhaps he is excited that he may profit from his having come into the position of ruler of Thebes. We cannot know; the play is not psychological in this way. Antigone counters that her profit, by contrast, is *not* material but instead is a noble or honorable death (508–12 / 462–64). Perhaps the idea of profit is on the mind of the culture itself, so to speak. After all, even though Teiresias was not present earlier to learn of Kreon's rage at the guards' presumed willingness to be bribed, the seer happens to conclude his opening speech by urging Kreon to accept a metaphorical "profit" from good advice. Kreon, though, takes the word literally and he bitterly accuses everyone, including Teiresias himself, of profiting somehow by betting on his decisions. With a devastating turn, the word *kerdos* is used last by the chorus, who in effect say to Kreon (1409 / 1326): you were obsessed with profit; well, your own has finally come, but only in the form of your agonized and belated understanding.

(6) A Greek word for the worst of fates is *atê*. Griffith glosses it this way: "*Atê* is a rich and evocative term, especially in tragedy, suggesting both *outcome* ('delusion,' 'ruin,' 'misery'), and *cause* (often a mixture of human folly and supernatural sabotage)" (121). Later, Griffith adds that *atê* is an "inescapable complex of delusion, error, crime and ruin" (219). Since the idea of the *cause* of ruin effectively implicates human decisions, whether these seemed bad or even good when made, *atê* also suggests the emotional state, the mistaken impulse, the ill-advisedness or foolishness, that leads someone to ruin. Yet the ancient Greeks often regard this bad impulse as having been sent, for sometimes unknowable reasons, by the gods. I have used "ruin" to represent *atê*, throughout.

(7) The idea of human folly leads me to two other structures of polar opposites informing the play that deserve brief comment. In *Antigone*, events seems to turn on whether decisions by a man—or a woman—are sensible or foolish. A large family of words denoting these ideas is based on the Greek root *boul-* but cannot be translated so as to echo

a single root word in English. The repeated echoing of *boul-* in various forms in Greek, I have had unfortunately to disperse in the translation into disparate English words, but I hope that the polarity of concept— well-advised versus ill-advised, good counsel versus bad, and so on— remains visible. In fact, in the repetition of the large number of Greek words for mind, thought, judgment, ascertainment, and so on, we seem to see a cultural preoccupation different from our own.

Another structure of opposites has to do with freedom versus slavery. For example, Kreon relegates women to the status of slaves when he speaks contemptuously of how Antigone's ambition to violate his order is not only wrong but also inconceivable, since she is not a man (526– 28 / 478–79). Again, Antigone argues passionately that the brother who died and still lies unburied outside the city walls "was no slave" (568 / 517). But although the same Greek word for enslaved war captives may be used also for the servants and attendants of Kreon and his wife Eurydike, I have translated many instances as "servant" or simply "man" in the sense of "Kreon's man" (or "men"), because while slavery was a notable part of the social and political fabric of Sophokles' Athens, the complex differences between Athenian and American slavery make it unwise to imply in the American linguistic, historical, and political context an easy identification of these two "peculiar institutions."

RHYTHMS

One great problem of translating ancient Greek poetry is that, for un- avoidable historical and cultural reasons, the language we ourselves speak and write no longer makes any use of a poetic lexicon—a special register of word-choice that is generally felt to be "poetic." So a trans- lator can create scarcely any effects at all that are *analogous* to those that the ancient poets created for their audiences (and conversely, some of the effects created by the translation would be unrecognizable to ancient audiences). Also, we live in a world of print and media images that can override our sense of the rich complexity of linguistic expres- sion; compared to the consciousness of the ancient Greeks, our con- sciousness is saturated proportionally less by the rhythms of language spoken *between* living human beings and more by language aimed by media *at* passive listeners. Furthermore, for the translator, the difficul- ties of representing the intensity and liveliness of the language of the ancient Greek stage, and of particular words or kinds of words, are really only first problems; next comes the problem of the different man- ner of speaking of each of the characters in the ancient play, and then the problem of differences between sorts of stage language in general— dialogue, chanted lines, and sung lines. Sung lines appear both in odes and in certain scenes, when it's as if the sheer intensity of feeling—in Antigone, as she is about to be sealed up alive in a tomb, and then in Kreon, after the deaths of Haimon and Eurydike—pushes them from agitated speech into anguished singing.

In this play, especially, *agôn*, contest, is nearly everything—a debate, after war, for new life-and-death stakes. When the characters are speaking to each other in one-line utterances (the stichomythia), I would have liked to produce iambic lines all of the same length, but this was impossible because of the extraordinary compression of ancient Greek in general and especially of Sophokles' language. For the sake of faithfulness to the pace of the play in Greek, I have kept all these utterances to one line in English too, but the length of that line varies from five to six or occasionally seven metrical feet. And the stichomythia is not the only contest of words in the play—the characters, each using a particular tone and diction, dispute each other in longer speeches also. In these, Sophokles sometimes creates structural symmetries—two lines from one character are answered by two from another, or forty-two spoken by Kreon answered by forty-two spoken by Haimon, and so on. To preserve the symmetries of the number of lines in the briefer exchanges, I have sometimes lengthened lines to fit everything in, but in longer speeches I considered instead that the consistent rhythm of blank verse was more important than the precise length of the speech.

The ancient dynamic of argument points to a larger difference between Greek tragedy and the modern theater (although psychologically, *Antigone* does seem among the most "modern" of all the surviving tragedies), which is the way the Greek writers saw the play as both an action on stage and also as word-work, the performance of language. Andrew Brown notes that Sophokles and Euripides almost always include a messenger speech in their (surviving) plays, and says that these, "with their opportunities for vivid and exciting narrative, were deliberately cultivated by the tragedians, and not regarded as regrettable necessity imposed by the limitations of the Greek stage" (217). These narrative passages require a rhythm at least distantly related to epic poetry, but the odes sung by the chorus, and the sung portions of the play's final moments, require a markedly different rhythm, and they too are composed and structured rhythmically, thematically, and by diction and symmetries of length. I have put the rich and densely figurative lines of sung passages into free verse, using hemistichs, or half-lines, to produce more opportunities in English for word-emphasis and more vigorous rhythmic movement. I have also reproduced symmetries of stanza-size and a few other symmetries in the pairs of matching ode-stanzas called *strophe* and *antistrophe*.

LANGUAGE LITERAL AND SENSUOUS

Of the odes, Griffith writes, "If it is characteristic of lyric poetry in general to be dense and ambiguous, these odes must be counted among the most opaque—as well as the most adventurous—in all of Greek tragedy" (18). Sophokles is known for the compression of his effects, both of metaphor and syntax. (Rather than calling some of his most difficult metaphors "mixed"—which is what we could call them, given our contemporary expectations of poetic practice—classicists call them "bold," since they belong to a somewhat different, ancient, aesthetic. And yet the wonder is how much of Sophokles' practice as a poet— apart from meter—is immediately comprehensible, in technical terms, to us, 2,500 years after he composed the play.) What has struck me most about Sophokles' language is its density of metaphor and image— its cognitive boldness, to be sure, but also at other moments its literalism of effect—especially when words (either abstract or concrete) are brought back to achieve also that effect of wovenness. Perhaps when classicists themselves do not always translate very literally, it is because they believe some of the metaphors in the Greek to have been already dead in Sophokles' time or because they are intent on conveying to readers of their translations the general sense of an utterance rather than its texture. (An example is that word *kerdos*, profit, mentioned earlier. In rendering the moment at the end of the play when the chorus turn this word against Kreon as a metaphor, two of the classicists on whose great scholarship I have depended resort to paraphrases that entirely lose the effect of this devastating reiteration.) Even more complicated is Sophokles' use of metaphor in the odes.

My goal in translating metaphors was not to smooth out the language of the play but to get as close to the Greek as I could, in an English that can reproduce at least some of the poetic qualities of this magnificent long poem-for-performance. An example: at the beginning, after Antigone has slipped out of the city in the dark and Ismene has reentered the royal house, the chorus of Theban elders see Kreon approaching and they wonder why he has assembled them. At Greek line 158, literally they say, "What plan [or counsel or thought] does he stir-as-with-an-oar?" Sophokles frequently makes use of metaphors that are this vivid if taken literally, but yet are ordinary in his linguistic context; these are difficult to catch hold of in our contemporary American English, which has almost completely lost touch with the immediacy of the pre-technological physical world that was the basis of ancient Greek figures of speech. For this line, Sir Richard Jebb gives us (in his marvelous 1900 edition of the play: "What counsel is he pondering?" Mary Whitlock Blundell, in her excellent scholarly translation, writes, "What plan is he plying?" To provide more information, she annotates the line—an option that literary translators must avoid if they want to produce a text that is playable. Like Blundell, two other classicists preserve the oar's movement, but not with the implication of an oar, specifically: Andrew Brown offers, in the literal version accompanying his edition of the Greek, "What plan is he putting in motion?" (and he annotates the line) and Elzabeth Wyckoff (in David Grene's well-known edition of 1954) translates, "What plan . . . beats about his mind?" So what is the translator to do with that stirring-as-with-an-oar? Is it worth trying to keep hold of?

The problem with the stirring or rowing lies not only in its vital immediacy in ancient Greece, where the sea was the path of the Athenians' trade and military conquests, but also in its lack of immediacy in our lives. Merchant ships and naval triremes had both oars and sails, but in our epoch sails belong to pleasure boats and oars are mostly thrown underneath beached, overturned aluminum rowboats awaiting an energetic vacationer. To put the word "rowing" or "oar" into the translation of the Greek line is to try to catch hold of something both vigorous and solemn, something *telling*, in Sophokles, and simultaneously to throw that meaning away because of the bathos of *our* oar. The translator is always translating both *out of* and *into*, and the lack of a fit can be found on either end of the transaction, or on both at once.

I say solemn, because after the chorus has thought of the stirring of water when the oarsman propels his boat or turns it, Kreon immediately launches (182 / 162) his own principle metaphor—his ship of state—for the seriousness of what faces Thebes in the aftermath of the failed attack by the traitorous Polyneikes. (Note also that following this scene—in which Kreon hears from the newly arrived guard that Polyneikes' body has been given a funeral ritual, although not a full burial, against Kreon's orders and under penalty of death—the stasimon that follows [the Ode to Man], one of the great poems in all of ancient Greek, says of man that among his wondrous accomplishments is that in his ships he courageously "sails the gray- / White sea running before / Winter storm-winds, he / Scuds beneath high / Waves surging over him / On each side.") And in Kreon's ship of state, everyone must pull at the oars together and in the same direction, especially through dangerous waters. But Antigone refuses to do so, or even to use this kind of language.

Later, Sophokles writes for Ismene, in the scene when Antigone, Ismene, and Kreon are all on stage, a line of pained fellow-feeling for her sister that brings that ship and that rowing back into our minds;

Ismene uses another nautical verb (592 / 541) when she says, "But amidst your troubles I am not ashamed / To sail beside you through your suffering." (The verb is in an untranslatable number, neither singular nor plural but dual—meaning that only she and Antigone have done this, against all others.) So we would not want to have missed, in English, the sense that the earlier "stirring-as-with-an-oar" evokes seafaring, for out of echoes like this Sophokles builds the language of his play. My own solution (178–79 / 158), as much to avoid "oar" and "rowing" as to capture the idea of a boat, is merely like Blundell's: "What course does he plan to steer?"—all I have done is point the metaphorical sense of the line toward the ocean, so that Kreon can then imagine his metaphorical ship of state sailing across dangerous seas, and thus initiate in English, too, Sophokles' *sequence* of nautical metaphors. This sequence will lead eventually to Haimon's metaphor of a sailing ship that has capsized and must be captained upside down (775–77 / 715–17). In fact, once Kreon's house has been turned upside down by death, he is incapable of serving as captain any longer. In an outburst of anguished metaphor that concludes Sophokles' nautical sequence, Kreon sees Hades as a harbor clogged with the bodies of the dead (1371 / 1284).

There is an important contrasting metaphor that is all too easy to leave buried. (And in a play about burial, a translator should think twice about what should be buried and what most certainly should not—Antigone should not be buried at all, much less alive, nor should the living vividness of Sophokles' language. A translator is tempted to say that Antigone the character is, among other things, a figure for the very livingness in language, which is an irrepressible gesture of resistance—in this case, Antigone's resistance to Kreon's attempt to control not only her life but also her language and thought.) Hugh Lloyd-Jones translates the chorus's line about thinking as a kind of rowing (the same Greek line I have just discussed) as "What plan is he turning over?" But if "turning over" suggests anything in the physical world, it is not the oars reaching out from the sides of a Greek ship, feathered as the oarsmen turn them before attacking the water on the next stroke, but rather the plow that turns over the soil. Yet for what the chorus says, an implicitly landlocked image about Kreon could not be more wrong, for the soil is associated by Sophokles with Antigone and her fierce allegiance to the gods of the earth—as, for example, when she is described as having poured handfuls of dust on the dead body of her brother Polyneikes, or when she thinks of the reiteration of the doom of her father as (literally) "thrice-plowed" (of which, more later), or even when she is associated in Kreon's mind with the passivity of cultivated soil; he uses a brutal metaphor, when, with Ismene and Antigone standing before him, he says—echoing language of the ancient patriarchal Athenian marriage-contract, according to Griffith (216)—that Haimon can find another bride: "There are other furrows he can plant" (620 / 569). Antigone's *tripolistos* (919–20 / 859), "thrice-plowed," is often rendered in English translations as "repeatedly." Even if this metaphor is already dead in Sophokles' time, he revives it: the word "thrice" numbers the generations of Antigone's family who have borne an apparent curse of the gods; and the word "plowed" suggests the gods of the earth, of dirt and dust, to whom Antigone gives reverence. To me it would seem a mistake to erase this repeated plowing with the generality "repeatedly." After all—to refer once more to the Ode to Man—the play says that one of the characteristics of this strange creature, man, who is so ingenious at both good and evil, is that the most ancient of the gods, Gaia (who deserves greatest reverence from men because without her there is no world at all), is also for man merely dirt to be plowed again and again, as if he sought to wear Her out (382–86 / 337–41).

I describe these few word-motifs to emphasize that a poetic translation usually cannot afford to go right through a metaphor as if it were transparent and arrive at some general sense behind it. It is bad enough that the intricate patterns of the play of sounds in ancient Greek are far beyond any possible translating. To lose also most of the metaphorical compression and synthesizing of ideas, themes, motifs, and so on would be to drain the lifeblood out of the poem. It seems to me that when translating, metaphor above all is what has to be lifted safely past a tempting explanatory, general language, for it to be grasped in its vividness and multiple signifying. It is a common practice of scholarship and criticism, in general, to read poetry for the ideas, themes, even information, that it contains, but readers turn to poetry for pleasures—of being engaged with language that signifies richly through its diction, its rhythms and sound, and the ways it is structured—pleasures of language that heighten our somber reflection on even the most tragic of subjects. This play, above all—which for 2,500 years, for all sorts of readers, has resisted giving away a definitive sense of how to resolve the conflict between Antigone and Kreon—would be travestied if one cared only about decoding the positions that Sophokles gives to his characters, or guessing what he himself, behind them, believes. The complexity of the characters' stances is in the very density and beauty of the language, which is not just an aspect of the play but is itself the meaning of the play—the difficulty of the language continually enacts at the level of word and syntax and rhythm the uncertainty and acutely competing forces represented by the play as a drama.

I could unfortunately give many more examples of metaphors of literal and sensuous immediacy in Greek that I could not quite unbury in English, any more than Haimon—or even Kreon, once his mind was able to think right again—could rescue Antigone.

METHOD AND SOURCES

Working with Charles Segal, first on Euripides' *Bakkhai* and then on Sophokles' *Antigone*, has led me in a new way to the deep pleasures of artistic problems. Our method was for me to produce successive drafts of the translation, to each of which Charlie brought suggestions, corrections, nuances, and clarities of interpretation, while also pointing out verbal reiterations in the Greek that were too subtle or distant from each other for me to have noticed on my own. Together we wished to produce a translation as "fine-woven" (1303 / 1222) as Antigone's fatal veil. There were some problems we could not solve—one was the frequently repeated interjections (*ômoi, pheu, iô,* and so on) for which almost nothing in contemporary English will do, since the choices are between the outdated "alas!" and many contemporary expressions lacking gravity. Another unsolved problem is the reliance of the language of tragedy on relatively few words, often repeated, for people who have been ruined, are miserable, wretched, ill-fated, and so on. Scarcely any of the available words in English for a bad fate have the ring of deeply felt, ultimate misfortune—partly because our sense of "unhappy" no longer includes anything of fate in it, but instead refers to feeling. Another problem is avoiding the chance occurrence in English of words sounding too much alike—which is why, since the translation must often use the word "profit," I did not use "prophet" but "seer," and why I tried to minimize the use of the word "counsel," an idea which is so necessary to the play, because it sounds like "council."

As in translating Euripides' *Bakkhai*, I have preferred to use transliterations of Greek for proper names except for the most familiar Latinized names and the occasional word, like "chorus." For help with the Greek text I relied above all on Charles Segal, but I also drew on sources to which he sent me: Griffith, Jebb, and Brown, cited at the head of the Notes, and Hugh Lloyd-Jones's edition and translation (*Sophocles II*, Cambridge, Mass., 1998), and Mary Whitlock Blundell's translation of *Sophocles' Antigone* (Newburyport, 1998). I have also consulted Charles Segal's masterful *Sophocles' Tragic World* (Cambridge, Mass., 1995), his *Tragedy and Civilization* (1981; reprinted Norman,

Okla., 1999), and separate essays. Also important to my understanding of the play, and of what might be made of it today, was George Steiner's remarkable *Antigones* (Oxford, 1984). Although Charles Segal provided me with characteristically wise and kind counsel regarding every aspect of meaning and interpretation, and of course made all necessary decisions regarding textual problems and variants, whatever flaws of sense and sound that may remain in the translation should be ascribed solely to me.

I end this brief essay with thanks—to good fortune, to Oxford University Press, and to series editors Alan Shapiro and Peter Burian for the opportunity to translate the play with a scholar of such great learning and wisdom. Much too soon after finishing his introduction and notes to this *Antigone*, and after he and I had completed our work together on the translation, Charles Segal died on January 1, 2002. I have known no one else who achieved a longer, more Sophoklean view of human life and death, or who gave more thoughtful attention to those around him; Charlie believed that the value of scholarship and poetry was deep and that at their best these have added wise counsel, humane ideals, and intellectual beauty to our entire civilization, and will continue to do so. In a way, this book is a most fitting memorial to Charlie, for it represents by his example the good of seeking to understand and revivify elements of the human past that belong to us all. This is a good in which Charlie believed wholeheartedly. Our *Antigone* also exemplifies Charlie's supreme learning and intelligence and his gift for bringing Sophokles to light for others.

REGINALD GIBBONS

ANTIGONE

CHARACTERS

ANTIGONE a young woman of about sixteen to eighteen years of age, daughter of Oidipous

ISMENE her sister, probably younger

CHORUS OF ELDERLY THEBAN MEN citizens who counsel Kreon, sometimes speaking singly, sometimes together

KREON ruler of Thebes, maternal uncle of Antigone and Ismene

GUARD a low-ranking soldier

HAIMON the young son of Kreon, betrothed to his cousin Antigone

TEIRESIAS an aged, blind seer

MESSENGER one of Kreon's men

EURYDIKE the wife of Kreon and mother of Haimon

VARIOUS MALE ATTENDANTS servants; slaves

ETEOKLES *and* POLYNEIKES, *sons of self-blinded* OIDIPOUS, *have been at war,*
ETEOKLES *having refused to alternate the rule of Thebes with his brother, as he*
had promised, and POLYNEIKES *having led an army of military allies from Argos*
against the city. OIDIPOUS *had put a curse on his two sons that they would kill*
each other, and in fact, on the day before the play opens, amidst battles surround-
ing the city, these two older brothers of ANTIGONE *and* ISMENE—ETEOKLES, *de-*
fending one of the seven gates of Thebes, and POLYNEIKES, *leading the attack*
against him—have fought and killed each other. Now, well before dawn in
Thebes, the sisters ANTIGONE *and* ISMENE *are standing—surprisingly—outside the*
great main doors of the house where they were born and where, under the guard-
ianship of their uncle, KREON *(their dead mother's brother), they have again been*
living since the death of OIDIPOUS. POLYNEIKES' *Argive alliance has now retreated*
during the night and abandoned the war and its dead warriors, whose bodies lie
on the plains outside the walls of Thebes.

ANTIGONE   Ismene, my own true sister, Oh dear one,   1
           Sharing our common bond of birth, do you know
           One evil left to us by Oidipous,
           Our father, that has not been brought down on
           The two of us by Zeus, while we still live?
           Among our woes, both yours and mine, there's
                 nothing
           Painful to us, nothing that's not weighed down
           By ruin, no shame and no dishonor, that I
           Have not already seen. And now, what is
           This proclamation they say the general   10
           Has issued for all the citizens—the men?
           Have you heard anything? Or have you not
           Noticed that evils of our enemies
           Are marching now against our friends and dear ones?

ISMENE   No talk of friends we love has come to me,
         Antigone—neither welcome nor painful,

Since that moment when we two sisters were
Dispossessed of our own two brothers—killed
On one day by twin blows of each other's hands.
And since the Argive army went away   20
This very night, I know no more, nor whether
I'm closer to good fortune or to ruin.

ANTIGONE   I thought so! That's why I called you outside
The courtyard gates, alone, to listen to me.

ISMENE   What is it? It's certain your words will be as dark
as dye.

ANTIGONE   But hasn't Kreon honored only one
Of our two brothers with a tomb and dis-
Honored the other? They say he has covered
Eteokles with earth, as justice and law
Require, so down below among the dead   30
He will be honored. But the body of poor
Polyneikes, who died so miserably—
They say a proclamation has been cried
To all the citizens that no one may
Hide it inside a grave, wail over it
Or weep for it, it must be left unmourned,
Unburied, a sweet-tasting treasure that birds
Will spy and feed on with their greedy joy.
And this is the very order that they say
The noble Kreon has proclaimed to you   40
And me—to me, to me he says it!—and then
To make it clear to those who don't yet know,
He's coming here, and he does not treat this
As some small matter: anyone who does
What he has now forbidden will be put
Before the people and by public stoning
Murdered.
                There you have how things stand, and soon
You will show whether you are noble, or—
Despite high birth—are low and cowardly.

ISMENE Oh my poor sister!—but if things are knotted up   50
        This way, then how could I unravel them?

ANTIGONE Think about joining in my action and my burden!

ISMENE What sort of dangerous act? What have you decided?

ANTIGONE Will you join with this hand of mine to lift the body?

ISMENE What? You're thinking you will bury him,
        When this has been forbidden to the city?

ANTIGONE My brother, yes—and yours—if you don't want to!
          I will not be caught betraying him.

ISMENE Hard, headstrong girl!—even though Kreon bans it?

ANTIGONE It's not for him to keep me from my own.   60

ISMENE Oh! But sister, you must understand—
        Our father, after beating out his eyes
        Himself, with his own self-striking hand, then died
        Infamous and detested, because of crimes
        That he himself discovered he'd committed!
        Then his mother and wife—the woman had
        Two titles—with a twisted loop of rope
        Violently disfigured her own life.
        Third, our two brothers on a single day,
        A wretched pair, with hands aimed at each other,   70
        Killing themselves have shared a doom in common.
        And now we two, the last ones left—consider
        How much worse death will be for us if we
        Defy the law and flout the rulers' vote
        And power—we must keep in mind that first,
        We're born as women, we're not brought into being
        To war with men; and second, that we are ruled
        By those whose strength is greater, and we must yield
        To this—and to much that's worse than this. So I

Will plead with those under the earth to feel   80
For us and pardon us, because I'm forced
To act as I do, and I'll obey the rulers,
For it makes no sense to do things that are futile.

ANTIGONE I won't insist. And even if you wished
To do this, now, it wouldn't make me happy.
So be as you decide to be—but I
Will bury him. For me it's noble to do
This thing, then die. With loving ties to him,
I'll lie with him who is tied by love to me,
I will commit a holy crime, for I   90
Must please those down below for a longer time
Than those up here, since there I'll lie forever.
But you, if that is what you decide, then leave
Dishonored that to which the gods give honor!

ISMENE I don't dishonor them! But to defy
The citizens is beyond what I can do.

ANTIGONE Offer that excuse. But I will go heap earth
In a grave-mound for my beloved brother.

ANTIGONE *begins to leave.*

ISMENE Oh poor Antigone—I'm frightened for you.

ANTIGONE Don't fear for me! It's your life you should put right.   100

ISMENE At least don't tell a soul what you will do,
But keep it secret, and with you, I'll do the same!

ANTIGONE Oh—denounce me! I'll hate you even more if you
Keep quiet and don't proclaim all this to
everyone.

ISMENE You have a heart that's hot for what is chilling.

ANTIGONE But I know I'm pleasing those I must please most.

ISMENE If you succeed! But you're in love with what's
        impossible.

ANTIGONE Then when I'm out of strength—but only then—I will
        be stopped.

ISMENE But it's wrong to go hunting for what's impossible.

ANTIGONE If you say that, you will be hated by me.   110
        And justly to the dead man you'll remain
        A hated enemy. So let me and
        This ill-considered plan of mine endure
        This terrible thing—for I will suffer nothing
        So bad as to deny me a death with honor.

        ANTIGONE *leaves, on the side leading out beyond*
                     the city walls.

ISMENE If you think so, then go. But know you're foolish
        To go, yet rightly dear to your dear ones.

        ISMENE *goes into the royal house. The* CHORUS *of fif-*
     teen elderly Theban men, Kreon's counselors, enter from
        the side that leads in from the city, while performing
                    their choreographed song.

CHORUS Flashing ray of   *Parados*
            Sun, most beautiful   *strophe a*
    Light ever to
            Appear at seven-
    Gated Thebes, at
            Last you, the   120
    Eye of golden
            Day, appeared—
    You came
            Slanting over
    The River Dirkê,
            You made that
    Argive warrior

With silver-
White shield run
Headlong in
Frightened flight,
His armor heavy
And a sharp bit
Stabbing him!

Chanting.

Urged on by
Furious two-sided
Quarrels of divisive
Polyneikes,
He had risen and
Flown to our land, he had   130
Come against us
Shrieking like
An eagle that
Spreads out its snow-
White wings, its
Weapons, over
Us, and with all his
Horse-tailed helmets.

Singing.

Over our rooftops he   *antistrophe a*
Loomed, with blood-
Thirsty gaping he
Surrounded us, his
Murderous spear-
Talons at our seven
Gates, but then he was
Gone before he could
Glut his jaws with
Our streaming blood and
Before pine-fed flames
Of the fire-god could   140

Seize our city's crown
                    Of towers. The loud
Clashing of war was
                    Stretched taut at
His back, for this wrestling
                    Was too hard
For one who matched himself
                    Against the Theban serpent!

                                        Chanting.

For Zeus utterly
                    Hates the noise
Of an arrogant bragging
                    Tongue, and as He
Watched those men
                    Come like a flood at us
In their brazenness of
                    Clanging gold, He
Struck with His
                    Hurled fire one
Man who already had
                    Raced to his goal   150
Atop our walls to
                    Shout of victory.

                                        Singing.

This man was tumbled   *strophe b*
                    Crashing to the hard ground—
He who panting with
                    Bakkhic fury had leapt
At us bearing torch-
                    Fire and blew his breath
Of hatred on us like
                    Hot winds. But finally
These things went
                    Otherwise: Instead,
Ares the great war god,

Strong as a charioteer's
Lead horse, struck men
            Hard and gave to some
Men one fate and
            To others, another.

                                        Chanting.

Seven captains attacking
            Seven gates abandoned   160
Their bronze weapons
            That now become
A tribute to battle-turning
            Zeus, the god of trophies —
Except for those two
            Doomed, cursed men who
Though born from one father
            And one mother thrust
Their two mutually
            Victorious spears into
Each other and shared one death in common.

                                        Singing.

But — since Nike, the goddess of victory,   *antistrophe b*
            With great name and glory
Has come, and her
            Joy answers the
Joy of Thebes,
            City of many
Chariots, let us
            Forget this war   170
That is over and
            Let us go
To the temples of all
            The gods to celebrate
In whirling dance
            All night and may

Dionysos, Earth-shaker
      Of Thebes, lead us!

The CHORUS *notice the unannounced approach of*
KREON, *with attendants, from the side that leads*
                                        in from the city.

                                                    Chanting.

But now comes the
                  King of the land,
The son of Menoikeus,
                  Kreon,
Newly crowned in these
                  New circumstances
That the gods have given us.
                  What course
Does he plan to steer, that
                  He would convene
This special conclave
                  Of elders,   180
Having sent us all a summons in common?

            FIRST EPISODE / SCENE II

KREON Men, the gods have tossed our ship of state
       On rolling seas and set it upright again.
       I sent my messengers to summon you,
       Away from everyone else, because I know
       That you always honored the power of the throne
       Of Laios, and also that you did the same
       When Oidipous set this city right, and also
       That when he died, you held his children steadfast
       In your own thoughts. And since both of his sons,   190
       Doubly destined, have died on the same day,
       With their own hands both striking and struck down
       In their own polluting murder of one another,
       Now I hold all the power and the throne,

Because of my close kinship to the dead.
　　It is impossible to know completely
The soul, the mind, the judgment of a man
Until we see his mettle tested against
His duties and his way with the laws. In my view,
A helmsman of the city as a whole   200
Who fails to lay his hand on the best advice
Yet is afraid of speaking and locks up
His tongue seems now and always the worst of men.
And any man who feels that someone close
To him is more important than his own
Fatherland—him I count as belonging nowhere.
May great all-seeing Zeus now be my witness:
If I saw doom instead of deliverance
Marching against my fellow citizens,
I would not be silent, nor would I love   210
An enemy of my land as a close friend—
Knowing that this ship keeps us safe, and only
When it sails upright can we choose friends for
　　ourselves.
　　These are the laws with which I make our city
Grow strong. And like a brother to these is the one
I have proclaimed to the citizens concerning
The sons of Oidipous: that Eteokles,
Greatest in glory with his spear, who died
In battle for this city, we will bury,
We will perform all pure and proper rites   220
And we will make the offerings to be sent
Down to the noblest of the dead, below;
But his brother by blood—I'm speaking now
Of Polyneikes—an exile who came back,
Who wanted to set fire to his fatherland
And to the gods of his own people and burn
Everything down from high to low, who wanted
To devour the blood he shared with his own kin,
And to enslave the others—this man!: for him
It has been proclaimed throughout the city   230
That no one is permitted to honor him
With burial or funeral gifts, or to wail

For him with grief, that he must lie unburied,
A corpse eaten by birds and dogs and torn
To pieces, shameful for anyone to see.
That's my intention. Never from my hand
Will come a greater honor for the evil
Than that which goes to the just. But him who bears
Good will toward this city—I honor him
Equally whether he is dead or living.   240

CHORUS   Son of Menoikeus, it pleases you
To do as you wish to him who bears ill will
Toward the city and him who's friendly. No doubt
You have the power to use any law
In dealing with the dead or us the living.

KREON   Make certain, then—watch over what I ordered!

CHORUS   Appoint some younger man to take this task.

KREON   Guards are on watch already near the corpse.

CHORUS   Then what else are you commanding us to do?

KREON   Not to join with those who disobey this.   250

CHORUS   No one's such a fool as to be in love with dying.

KREON   And that will be the price! But often, hope
For profit has destroyed men utterly.

> *Approaching hesitantly from the side that leads in*
> *from beyond the city walls, a* GUARD *speaks as*
> *he nears* KREON.

GUARD   My Lord, I cannot say that I'm arriving
Quite out of breath from running rapidly
And with light feet—I have had numerous
Worries along the way that made me halt,
And revolve myself, to go back whence I came.

My spirit spoke to me, quite often, saying
"Pathetic creature, why are you on the way   260
To where you'll have to pay the penalty?
And once more you cease your locomotion, fool?
And yet—if Kreon comes to know of this
From someone else, won't you be subject
     to pain?"
And as I cogitated this in my thoughts
I quickly kept on going, slowly, and so
I turned a short path into a long road.
What won at last was coming here to you.
If what I say is nothing—still, I'll say it,
Because I'm holding to the hope that what   270
I'll suffer can't be more than what's my due.

KREON Why then do you show such a lack of heart?

GUARD First, I'd like to tell you about myself:
I didn't do this thing, or see who did,
Nor would it be just if I were harmed.

KREON You take aim at me. Yet you fence the thing
Around. Yet clearly you have news you could reveal.

GUARD What is terrible makes one hesitate.

KREON Out with it! Then take yourself away.

GUARD I'm telling you! That corpse—just now some person   280
Has buried it and gone, and he sprinkled it
With thirsty dust and performed the proper rites.

KREON What are you saying? What man dares do this?

GUARD I do not know! There's no mark of a pickax,
No dirt dug up with a mattock. No—the ground
Is hard and dry, unbroken, without wheel tracks.
Whoever did this left no sign at all.
And when the first man of the day-watch showed us,

We all were much alarmed and amazed. The corpse
Had disappeared—not covered with a mound   290
But with a little dust thrown over him,
As if by someone trying to avoid
Pollution. There was not a sign of beast
Or dog that might have dragged and torn the body.
    Then came an uproar of evil words among us,
With guard accusing guard; and we might have come
To blows, in the end, without someone to stop us—
It was as if each one of us had done it,
Yet none of us was clearly the one. But each
Of us pleaded that he knew nothing of it.   300
All of us were ready to pick up
A lump of red-hot iron in our own hands,
Ready to walk through fire, ready to swear
By all the gods we hadn't done this thing,
We didn't know who had conspired in it
Nor did we know who was the one who did it.
But after all our searching turned up nothing,
One of us said something that made us hang
Our heads toward the ground in fear. We had
No answer, and no matter what we did,   310
We saw no way to come out well, for what
He said was that we must report to you
What had been done, not hide it. And this gained
The day, and I, the unluckiest—I won
The grand prize when we shook lots from a helmet.
So here I am—most unwelcome, I know.
Against my own will, too, since no one loves
A messenger who brings with him bad news.

CHORUS LEADER   My Lord, my own thoughts have advised me anxiously
For a while that this was all directed by the gods.   320

KREON   *To* CHORUS LEADER.

Stop!—before your words give me my fill
Of anger, or you'll all be taken for fools
As well as elders. What you say is not

To be tolerated, when you say the gods
Care about this corpse. So was it they
Who covered it, because they honored him
For his good deeds toward them?—he who came here
To burn their country and the temples with columns
Around them and the offerings inside,
He who came to shatter laws and customs?   330
Or in your eyes, do the gods give honor
To persons who are evil? That cannot be!

   Yet for a long time in this city, men
Who barely can put up with me have raised
A secret uproar, they've been tossing their heads,
They haven't kept their necks under the yoke—
As justly they should have done—and been content
With me. I know what this is all about.
Those are the ones who bribed the guards to do it.
For nothing current grows among us worse   340
For men than silver: money ravages
The cities, it forces men to leave their homes,
It teaches mortals with good thinking to turn
To shameful deeds, it shows men how to commit
All crimes, and know all kinds of irreverence.
But those who hired themselves out to do this thing
Have now made sure they'll pay the penalty.

To GUARD.

   If Zeus gets any reverence from me,
Know this—I swear it on my oath!: if you guards
Don't find out who with his own hand has done   350
This burying, and bring him into my sight,
Then Hades won't be punishment enough,
And before you're dead you'll hang alive until
You throw some light on this outrage. And that
Will teach you in the future where to get
Your profit from when you steal, and teach you not
To love this profiting from anything
And everything. One sees more people ruined
Than rescued by such shameful earnings as yours.

GUARD Will you allow me to say a word, or should I turn
    and go?   360

KREON Do you still not know how much your words annoy
    me?

GUARD Would it be your ears or your spirit that they sting?

KREON Why are you trying to diagnose where I feel pain?

GUARD He who did it hurts your mind; I hurt your ears.

KREON Ugh! It's plain that you were born to talk and talk!

GUARD That may be so. But I never did this thing.

KREON Yes, you did! What's more, you sold your spirit for
    some silver.

GUARD Ah!
    It's terrible for him who believes to believe what's
    false.

KREON Be clever with the word "believe"—but if
    You don't reveal who did this, you'll confess   370
    That dirty profits make for suffering!

            KREON *goes into the royal house with his men.*

GUARD   *Speaking to the departing* KREON, *who does*
                             not hear him.

May he definitely be caught! But whether
He is or is not found—which chance will decide—
You won't see me come here again! Beyond
My hopes and calculation, I've been saved!
And now I owe the gods great gratitude!

He leaves on the same side from which he entered,
heading out beyond the city walls again.

The CHORUS *perform their choreographed song.*

Second ode / first stasimon

CHORUS At many things—wonders,   *strophe a*
                    Terrors—we feel awe,
         But at nothing more
                    Than at man. This
         Being sails the gray-
                    White sea running before
         Winter storm-winds, he
                    Scuds beneath high   380
         Waves surging over him
                    On each side;
         And Gaia, the Earth,
                    Forever undestroyed and
         Unwearying, highest of
                    All the gods, he
         Wears away, year
                    After year as his plows
         Cross ceaselessly
                    Back and forth, turning
         Her soil with the
                    Offspring of horses.

         The clans of the birds,   *antistrophe a*
                    With minds light as air,
         And tribes of beasts of
                    The wilderness, and water-
         Dwelling sea creatures—
                    All these he
         Catches, in the close-
                    Woven nets he   390
         Throws around them,
                    And he carries them
         Off, this man, most

68

            Cunning of all.
With devices he
            Masters the beast that   ⸍
Beds in the wild and
            Roams mountains—he harnesses
The horse with shaggy
            Mane, he yokes
The never-wearied
            Mountain bull.

He has taught himself   *strophe b*
            Speech and thoughts
Swift as the wind;
            And a temperament for
The laws of towns;
            And how to escape
Frost-hardened bedding
            Under the open   400
Sky and the arrows
            Of harsh rain—inventive
In everything, this
            Man. Without invention he
Meets nothing that
            Might come. Only from
Hades will he not
            Procure some means of
Escape. Yet he has
            Cunningly escaped from
Sicknesses that had
            Seemed beyond his devices.

Full of skills and   *antistrophe b*
            Devising, even beyond
Hope, is the intelligent
            Art that leads him
Both to evil and
            To good. Honoring the
Laws of the earth
            And the justice of   410
The gods, to which

69

> Men swear, he stands
> High in his city.
> > But outside any
> City is he who dares
> > To consort with
> What is wrong: let
> > Him who might do
> Such things not
> > Be the companion
> At my hearth nor have
> > The same thoughts as I!

SECOND EPISODE / SCENE III

> *The* CHORUS *notice the* GUARD *returning on the side
> that leads in from beyond the city walls, as he
> brings* ANTIGONE *with him as his prisoner.*

CHORUS LEADER   *Chanting.*

> What monstrous thing is this,
> > Sent by the gods? —
> My mind is divided — how can I
> > Say this girl is not
> Antigone, when I recognize
> > That she is?
> Oh unfortunate child of your
> > Unfortunate father,   420
> Oidipous, what does this mean?
> > Can it be you
> They are bringing here,
> > For having dis-
> Obeyed the laws of
> > The king — You,
> Seized at the height of your folly?

GUARD Here's who did the deed! We caught this girl
In the act of burying. But where is Kreon?

CHORUS   *As they speak,* KREON *comes out of the royal house
with attendants.*

Just when we need him, here he comes from the
    house.

KREON What is it? What has chanced to make my coming
    timely?

GUARD My Lord, mortals should not swear anything's
    Impossible!—since later thoughts can prove   430
    One's judgment quite mistaken: after your threats
    Came coldly storming at me, I resolved
    That I would be reluctant to return,
    But due to the fact that the happiness for which
    One prays, beyond one's very hopes, exceeds
    All other pleasures, here I am again—
    Although I solemnly swore I never would be.
        I bring this girl! We caught her at the grave
    Performing funeral rites. This time we cast
    No lots—this piece of luck belongs to me   440
    And no one else. So now, My Lord, you take her
    Yourself, question and convict her. By rights,
    I should be free to be let off this trouble.

KREON This woman whom you bring, how did you catch her?
    Where?

GUARD She was burying the man herself. Now you know
    everything.

KREON Do you grasp—are you saying right—the things you
    speak?

GUARD Yes! I saw her burying the corpse against
    Your orders. Now is what I'm saying clear and plain?

KREON How was she spotted and then seized while doing it?

GUARD Well, what happened was, when we went back there—   450
    After those awful threats you made—we brushed
    Off all the dust that was on the corpse, we did

A good job of uncovering the body,
Which was slimy; and then upwind, on top
Of a hill, we sat, to keep ourselves away
From the stink, so that it wouldn't hit us. Each man
Helped by keeping another awake and warning
Him loudly if he seemed to shirk the task.
This lasted till the time when the blazing circle
Of the sun had put itself at the midpoint   460
Of the sky and we were melting in the heat.
Then suddenly a whirlwind raised a pillar
Of dust from the ground, a storm of trouble high
As heaven, it spread across the lowland, it tore
Away the leaves of the trees and it filled up
The whole huge sky. We shut our eyes and endured
This supernatural plague.

                          After a long while
The thing died down and this wailing child is seen . . .
The way a bird will give sharp cries when she finds
That her nest and bed are empty and her young   470
Are gone — it was like that when this girl sees
The corpse all bare, she moaned with wailing grief,
She cursed those who had done this, and at once
She carries in her hands the thirsty dust
And holds up high a fine bronze pitcher and then
She pours libations three times round the corpse.
When we see this, we rush to hunt her down
But she was not afraid, and we accused her
Of what she'd done, before, and what she now
Was doing. She did not at all deny it —   480
Which to me brought both satisfaction and pain,
Because to flee bad things yourself feels good,
But it is painful to lead one of your own
To something bad.

                          Of course, all of these things
Are less to me than safety for myself.

KREON   *To* ANTIGONE.

You! You turning your head away, to the ground —
Do you admit or deny that you did this?

ANTIGONE I admit I did it; I do not deny it.

KREON   *To* GUARD.

> You can take yourself wherever you want
> To go—you're freed from serious charges, now.   490

> *As the* GUARD *leaves,* KREON *turns to* ANTIGONE.

> You—answer briefly, not at length—did you know
> It was proclaimed that no one should do this?

ANTIGONE I did. How could I not? It was very clear.

KREON And yet you dared to overstep the law?

ANTIGONE It was not Zeus who made that proclamation
To me; nor was it Justice, who resides
In the same house with the gods below the earth,
Who put in place for men such laws as yours.
Nor did I think your proclamation so strong
That you, a mortal, could overrule the laws   500
Of the gods, that are unwritten and unfailing.
For these laws live not now or yesterday
But always, and no one knows how long ago
They appeared. And therefore I did not intend
To pay the penalty among the gods
For being frightened of the will of a man.
I knew that I will die—how can I not?—
Even without your proclamation. But if
I die before my time, I count that as
My profit. For does not someone who, like me,   510
Lives on among so many evils, profit
By dying? So for me to happen on
This fate is in no way painful. But if
I let the son of my own mother lie
Dead and unburied, that would give me pain.
This gives me none. And now if you think my actions
Happen to be foolish, that's close enough
To being charged as foolish by a fool.

CHORUS LEADER   *To* KREON.

It's clear this fierce child is the offspring of her fierce
Father! She does not know to bend amidst her
            troubles.   520

        KREON   *To* CHORUS LEADER.

Understand that rigid wills are those
Most apt to fall, and that the hardest iron,
Forged in fire for greatest strength, you'll see
Is often broken, shattered. And with only
A small sharp bit, I've noticed, spirited
Horses are disciplined. For grand ideas
Are not allowed in someone who's the slave
Of others . . .
            First, this girl knew very well
How to be insolent and break the laws
That have been set. And then her second outrage   530
Was that she gloried in what she did and then
She laughed at having done it. I must be
No man at all, in fact, and she must be
The man, if power like this can rest in her
And go unpunished. But no matter if
She is my sister's child, or closer blood
Relation to me than my whole family
Along with our household shrine to Zeus himself,
She and her sister by blood will not escape
The worst of fates—yes, I accuse her sister   540
Of conspiring in this burial, as much
As she.

                                                To his men.

        Go get her!

                        Some of KREON's *men go into the royal house*
                                to find ISMENE.

To CHORUS LEADER.

Earlier I saw her
Inside, raving, out of her wits. The mind
Of those who plan in the dark what is not right
Will often find itself caught as a thief.
But I hate even more those who when captured
In evil acts then want to make them noble.

ANTIGONE Now you've caught me, do you want something more
than my death?

KREON I don't. If I have that, then I have everything.

ANTIGONE Then why delay? To me, your words are nothing   550
Pleasing, and may they never please me; likewise,
My nature displeases you. And yet, for glory,
What greater glory could I have gained than by
Properly burying my own true brother?
These men would say it pleases them—if fear
Did not lock up their tongues. But one-man rule
Brings with it many blessings—especially
That it can do and say whatever it wants.

KREON You alone among the Thebans see it this way.

ANTIGONE These men see it, but shut their craven mouths
for you.   560

KREON You feel no shame that you don't think as they do?

ANTIGONE No—no shame for revering those from the same
womb.

KREON Wasn't he who died against him of the same blood?

ANTIGONE Of the same blood—the mother and the father, the
same.

KREON Why do you grace with irreverent honor that other
        one?

ANTIGONE Eteokles' dead body won't testify to that.

KREON It will, if you honor him the same as the irreverent
        one.

ANTIGONE It was no slave—it was my brother who died!

KREON Attacking this land!—the other stood against him, in
        defense.

ANTIGONE And yet it's Hades who desires these laws.   570

KREON But the good should not get equal honor with the
        evil.

ANTIGONE Who knows if down there that is not considered holy?

KREON An enemy, even when he's dead, is not a friend.

ANTIGONE My nature's not to join in hate but to join in love.

KREON Then go down there and love those friends, if you
        must love them!
        But while I am alive, a woman will not rule!

The doors of the royal house open, and ISMENE *is led
on stage by the men who had gone in search of her
inside the house.*

CHORUS   *Chanting.*

And here, outside the
                  Courtyard gates,
Ismene has come,
                  With tears of sister-

Love falling from her.
                              A storm-cloud over
Her brow mars
                              Her flushed face   580
And wets her lovely cheeks.

KREON   *To* ISMENE.

And you—hiding unnoticed in the house
Like a snake that drank my blood! I didn't know
I raised a double ruin to bring down
The throne! Come, tell me, do you admit your part
In this burial, or swear that you know nothing?

ISMENE I did this deed—if she will allow me that—
         And I too take the blame for my part in it.

ANTIGONE But Justice won't let you, because you did not wish
           To act with me, nor did I share this with you.   590

ISMENE But amidst your troubles I am not ashamed
         To sail beside you through your suffering.

ANTIGONE Hades and those below know whose the deed is.
           I don't like a loved one who only loves with words.

ISMENE Sister, no! Do not dishonor me by not
         Letting me die with you and purify our dead!

ANTIGONE Do not share my death, do not take as your own
           That which you did not touch! My death will be
              enough!

ISMENE How can I want to live if I am left without you?

ANTIGONE Ask Kreon! He's the one whose side you take!   600

ISMENE Why do you grieve me so, when it doesn't help you?

ANTIGONE Yes, mocking you hurts me instead, if I *am* mocking.

ISMENE   Then how can I still try to help you now?

ANTIGONE   Save yourself! I won't resent your escaping.

ISMENE   Must I, in my misery, fall short of your fate?

ANTIGONE   Yes—because you chose to live, and I to die.

ISMENE   But I did not leave these words of mine unsaid!

ANTIGONE   To one side you seemed right; to the other, I did.

ISMENE   Yet we are both blamed equally for doing wrong!

ANTIGONE   Be brave! You are alive—but my life has died   610
Already, for the sake of helping the dead.

KREON   I'd say one of these girls now stands revealed as out
Of her senses, and the other one was born that way.

ISMENE   Yes, My Lord, good sense that is innate
In people deserts them in the midst of troubles.

KREON   Yours did, when you chose to do evil with evildoers.

ISMENE   How can I live my life alone without her?

KREON   Don't speak of her—for she does not exist.

ISMENE   But will you kill your own son's bride-to-be?

KREON   There are other furrows he can plant.   620

ISMENE   Not the way he and she were fitting for each other.

KREON   Evil wives for my son are something I detest!

ISMENE   Dearest Haimon, how your father dishonors you!

KREON You irritate me too much!—you and your marriage-
           bed.

ISMENE And will you really rob your son of her?

KREON It's Hades who will stop this wedding for me.

ISMENE It seems decided then, that she will die—

KREON By you and by me! No more delays! You men!—
           Take them inside. From now on they must be
           Women—not to be let run loose, for even   630
           Bold men will try to make their escape when they
           See Death begin to come too near their lives.

           Some of KREON's *men take* ISMENE *and* ANTIGONE *into*
           the royal house. KREON *remains on stage with the rest*
                                        of his attendants.

                  The CHORUS *perform their choreographed song.*

                              Third ode / second stasimon

CHORUS Fortunate are they whose   *strophe a*
                  Lives do not
           Taste of woe; but among
                  Those whose house the gods
           Shake, no ruin is absent
                  As it creeps over a
           Multitude of generations like
                  A storm tide of the salt
           Sea driven by northern
                  Gales from Thrace—waves
           That speed over the ocean
                  Depths dark as the under-
           World and churn
                  Up black sand from the sea-

79

Bed and with harsh
                    Winds hurl it beating   640
Against headlands
                    That groan and roar.

From ancient times come   *antistrophe a*
                    These afflictions of the
House of the Labdakids
                    That I see falling one
After another on yet
                    Earlier afflictions of the dead;
Nor does one generation
                    Release another, but some
God batters them instead; nor
                    Do they have any
Way to be set free.
                    The last rootstock of the
House of Oidipous,
                    In light that was spreading,
Is reaped by blood-
                    Red dust of the gods
Under the earth, for foolishness
                    Of speech and a Fury in the mind.   650

Zeus, what transgression   *strophe b*
                    Of men could overcome
Your power? Neither
                    Sleep that catches
Everyone in its nets
                    Nor the weariless passing
Of the months named
                    For gods can
Overcome it—You,
                    The Generalissimo immune
To time, hold
                    The gleaming marble heights
Of Mount Olympos.
                    For what is now and
What comes after and
                    What came

Before, only one
        Law can account,
Which is that into the life
        Of mortal beings comes   660
Nothing great that lies
        Beyond the reach of ruin.

It is wide-wandering   *antistrophe b*
        Hope that brings
Benefit to many
        Men, but it deceives
Many others with desires
        Light as air. When
It comes upon
        A man, he cannot
See clearly until already
        He has burnt his
Foot on live coals.
        Wisely someone has
Kept before us the
        Famous saying that
A moment will come
        When what is bad
Seems good to the
        Man whom some   670
God is driving toward
        Ruin. Only a short
Time does he stay
        Beyond the reach of ruin.

HAIMON *enters from the side leading in from the city.*

CHORUS LEADER   *Chanting.*

Here is Haimon, your
        Last and youngest offspring.
Does he come here
        Grieving over the fate
Of Antigone, whom he
        Would wed, and to rage

At the great pain of
                    Being cheated of his
Royal marriage to the
                    Girl he had betrothed?

THIRD EPISODE / SCENE IV

KREON Soon we'll know, better than the seers. My son,
Do you come to rage at your father, having heard
My final vote on your bride-to-be? Or are we   680
Still loved as your own, whatever we may do?

HAIMON Father, I'm yours. And as your judgments are
Both good and upright, then I'll follow them.
No marriage could be a greater prize for me
To win than being guided well by you.

KREON Yes, what's best is for you to hold that, son,
In your heart and stand behind your father's will
In everything. For this is why men pray
To bring up dutiful offspring and to keep them
At home: so they'll pay back a hated foe   690
With trouble, and giving honor, love the friends
Of their father as he does. Of him who breeds
Useless children, what else can you say but that
He only begets more burdens for himself,
And more mockery among his enemies?
So do not, son, throw out your own good sense
For the sake of pleasure in a woman—you
Should know an evil wife in bed with you
At home is something that soon enough grows cold
Wrapped in your arms. What could fester deeper   700
Than someone closely tied to you who's evil?
So spit this girl out as an enemy!
And let her marry someone else—in Hades.
Now that I've caught her as the only one
In all the city who openly defied me,
I won't be seen as false to my own word
By all the city—I'll kill her.

                              In the face
          Of that, let her sing her hymns in praise of Zeus
          The god of bonds of blood! If those I've raised
          And kept become rebellious, then those outside   710
          The family will become so, even more.
          He who is a good man in his own house
          Will also be seen to be just in public life.
          A man like that—I'm confident he would
          Rule well and wish to be well ruled; he'd stand
          His ground where ordered, even in a storm
          Of spears—a just and worthy fellow soldier.
          But any criminal who violates
          The laws or thinks he can give orders to those
          Who rule, will not get any praise from me.   720
          Whoever is put into power by
          The city must be obeyed in everything—
          In small things, and what's just, and the opposite.
          There is no greater evil than lack of rule.
          This is what brings cities to ruin, it's this
          That tears the household from its roots, it's this
          That routs the broken ranks of allied spears!
          No—what does save the skins of most of those
          Who act right is obedience! Therefore—
          We must safeguard the orders of the rulers,   730
          And we must never be defeated by
          A woman—better to be overthrown,
          If we must be, by a man; then we will not
          Be said to have been beaten by the women.

CHORUS   If age has not misled us, you seem to speak
          Sensibly about the things you speak of.

HAIMON   Father, the gods endow men with good sense—
          Highest of all the things that we possess.
          And I could not say in what way your words
          Are wrong—and may I never be capable   740
          Of knowing how to say that. But someone else
          Might have a good thought, also. My natural role

Is to watch out for you—for the things that people
Might say or do, or what they might blame you for.
And to the common citizen, when you
Dislike some word he says, your eye becomes
A terror. But I hear what's in the shadows—
How the city mourns for this girl, and how
She of all women least deserves the worst
Of deaths for the most glorious of deeds—   750
Since she did not allow her own true brother,
Fallen in slaughter, still unburied, to be
Destroyed by flesh-eating dogs and birds of prey.
Isn't golden honor what she merits?
Such talk is spreading secretly in the dark.

    To me, Father, there's no possession more
To be sought than your well-being—for in what
Could children feel a greater pride than in
A father with a flourishing reputation?
Or what is greater for the father than   760
The sons of whom he's proud? So don't invest
Your being in one single way to feel—
That what you say, but nothing else, is right.
Whoever thinks that only he himself
Owns all good sense, that he and no one else
Has such a tongue and mind—when men like that
Show what's inside them, then we see they're empty.
    Even a man who's clever should feel no shame
In learning things—however many they are—
And in not keeping himself so tightly strung.   770
You see how all along a river swollen
By winter rain, the trees that bend with the current
Save themselves and even their twigs, but those
That stand straight are annihilated, root
And branch. And a man who pulls his rigging tight
And will not slacken it capsizes and then . . .
He simply has to sail on—upside down.
Let go of your anger, allow yourself to change.
    Now, if there's judgment in the young, like me,
Then I would say it's best by far if a man   780
Is completely filled with knowledge by his nature.

But since things aren't inclined to be that way,
It's also good to learn from what's well said.

CHORUS My Lord's it's only fair, if he speaks to the point, that
              you learn
          From him—and Haimon, you likewise. Both sides
              speak well.

KREON Should men of my age be taught what to think
          By someone who has only reached as yet his age?

HAIMON In nothing that's not just. If I am young,
          Do not look at my age, but at what I do.

KREON Oh—is what you do revering rebels?   790

HAIMON I'd never tell you to revere an evildoer.

KREON Isn't that the sickness that infects this girl?

HAIMON That's not what people of Thebes, who share
              this city, say.

KREON Should this city tell me what commands to give?

HAIMON See how you say that like a young new lord?

KREON Must I rule this land for someone else, not myself?

HAIMON There is no city that belongs to one man only.

KREON Isn't the city held to be his who rules?

HAIMON You'd do well as the single ruler of some
              deserted place.

KREON It seems this man is fighting on the woman's side!   800

HAIMON If you're the woman—for it's you I'm looking after.

KREON By unjust accusations of your father, you worst
of men?

HAIMON Because I see you doing wrong to justice.

KREON So I'm doing wrong to show some reverence for
my rule?

HAIMON You show no reverence trampling on the honors the
gods deserve!

KREON A filthy way to think—submitting to a woman!

HAIMON At least you won't find me brought down by something shameful.

KREON What you say is all on her behalf, though.

HAIMON And yours! And mine! And that of the gods down
below!

KREON You will never marry this girl while she's alive.   810

HAIMON Then she will die. And dying, she'll destroy—
someone else.

KREON Are you so insolent as to attack me with threats?

HAIMON What threat is it to speak against such empty thinking?

KREON You'll regret lecturing when your own thoughts
were empty.

HAIMON If you were not my father, I'd say that you can't think.

KREON You slave of a woman—don't you prate at me!

HAIMON You want to speak, but never hear the one you
speak to?

KREON What!? By high Olympos you won't keep on
　　　Abusing me so freely!

To his men.

　　　　　　　Lead in the girl—
　　　The hateful thing—so she may die at once!　　　820
　　　Here, beside her bridegroom, in his sight!

Some of KREON's *men go into the royal house in search
of* ANTIGONE.

HAIMON　　　　　*As he leaves to the side leading out beyond
　　　　　　　　　　　the city walls.*

　　　No! Don't even think she'll die beside me!
　　　And you will never see my face again
　　　With your own eyes—so go rave on among
　　　Whoever would still want to be your friend!

CHORUS My Lord, the man has gone off quickly in his anger!
　　　The mind, at his age, can become weighed down
　　　　　by grief.

KREON Let him do it! Let him go and have grand thoughts
　　　Too big for a man. He won't save those girls from
　　　　their fate!

CHORUS Is it your thought, then, to kill both of them?　　　830

KREON Not the girl who did not touch the deed—well said!

CHORUS And with what sort of death do you plan to kill her?

KREON I'll lead her out to some deserted place
　　　Where mortals do not go, and seal her up,
　　　Still living, in a tomb dug into rock,
　　　With just enough to eat—for our expiation,
　　　So that the city as a whole avoids

Pollution. There, where she can pray to Hades,
The only god whom she reveres, perhaps
She will be spared from dying—or else she'll learn   840
At last what pointless waste of effort it is
To worship what is down below with Hades.

> KREON *goes into the royal house with the rest of his*
> *men; the* CHORUS *perform their choreographed song.*

Fourth ode / third stasimon

CHORUS Eros, unconquered in   *strophe a*
                    Combat! Eros, that
        Leaps down upon
                    The herds! You
        That pass the night-
                    Watch on a girl's
        Soft cheeks, You
                    That cross the
        Open sea and
                    Roam from hut to
        Hut in the far
                    High fields—neither
        The immortals nor
                    Man, who lives only a day, can escape
        From you, and he
                    Who has you   850
        Inside himself
                    Goes mad.

        You that pull   *antistrophe a*
                    The reins of just
        Minds toward in-
                    Justice, disfiguring
        Men's lives; You
                    That stir up this
        Strife between two
                    Men of the same
        Blood, while victory

                         Goes to the force
             Of love in the gaze: the
                         Desiring eyes of
             The bride shine with
                         Wedding joy—this Power on its throne
                         rules
             Equally with the great
                         Laws, for the goddess
             Aphrodite at her play
                         Cannot be conquered.   860

                    ANTIGONE *is brought out of the royal house
                         by* KREON's *men.*

CHORUS   *Chanting.*

             But I myself, at the sight
                         Of this, swing wide off
             The track, beyond the
                         Limits of what the Laws allow.
             Now I can no longer hold
                         Back the streams of
             My tears when I see Antigone
                         Fulfilling this final journey—
             To that bridal chamber where all must sleep, at last.

                    FOURTH EPISODE / SCENE V

ANTIGONE   *Singing.*

             Look at me,   *strophe b*
                         Citizens of my native land!—I
             Am walking
                         The last road,
             I am seeing for
                         The last time
             The radiance
                         Of the sun and
             Never again!
                         While I am   870

89

Still alive, Hades,
                    Who makes us all
Sleep, at last,
                    Is leading me to
The banks of the River
                    Akheron. I have
No share of marriage
                    Rites, nor did
Any hymn of marriage
                    Sing me to
My wedding.
                    Instead my marriage will be to Akheron.

CHORUS   *Chanting.*

Do you not go with glory and
                    Praise when you disappear
Into that place where the
                    Bodies of the dead are
Hidden? Not struck down by
                    Diseases that waste one
Away, not having earned
                    The deadly wages of   880
The sword, but answering only
                    To the law of yourself, you
Are the only mortal who
                    Will go down alive into Hades.

ANTIGONE   *Singing.*

I have heard it   *antistrophe b*
                    Told that the pitiable Phrygian stranger,
Daughter of Tantalus,
                    Died at the
Peak of Mount
                    Sipylos — rock
That grew like
                    Ivy wound
Around her
                    Tightly till it

Stilled her, and
                    Men say that
She, melting in
                    Rain and snow
That never cease,
                    Dissolves into   890
Tears running
                    Down the mountain
Ridges beneath
                    Her brow: divine
Power takes
                    Me, who am most like her, to bed.

CHORUS   *Chanting.*

But you know she is a goddess and
                              Was born of gods, and we
Are mortals born of mortals.
                              Yet for a woman who
Has died it is a great thing
                              Even to be spoken of as having
The same fate as those
                              Who are like gods,
Both when alive and
                              Then afterward, when dead.

ANTIGONE   *Singing.*

Ah, I am laughed at!   *strophe c*
                    Why, by the gods of my fathers, do you
Insult me not
                    After I have gone   900
But when you see
                    Me still before you?
Oh city, Oh men
                    Of the city, with
Your many possessions!
                    Ah, springs of Dirkê
And sacred ground

91

Of Thebes of the
Beautiful chariots—at least
You will be
Witnesses to how I go, un-
Lamented by any
Friends—and because of what
Kinds of laws?—to the high-
Heaped prison of my
Tomb, my strange and
Dreadful grave. Ah,
Unfortunate that I am—
Neither living among those
Who are alive, nor   910
Dwelling as a corpse
Among corpses, having
No home with either
The living or the dead.

CHORUS   *Singing.*

Stepping ahead to the very
Limits of audacity,
You have struck your foot
Against the throne
Of Justice and fallen,
Oh child! And for
Some torment of your
Father's, you are paying, still!

ANTIGONE   *Singing.*

Of all my cares, you   *antistrophe c*
Have touched the one most painful
to me:
My father's doom—recurring
Like the plowing
Of a field three
Times—and the ruin
Of us all—the famed
Family of the Labdakids!   920

Ah, my mother's disaster
          Of a marriage bed,
And the self-incestuous
          Coupling of my father
With my ill-fated
          Mother! From such
As they, I—
          Who have been made
Miserable in my mind—
          Was begotten! Under a
Curse, unmarried, I
          Go back to them, having
No other home but
          Theirs. Ah, my brother!—
You who aimed at
          And won a marriage
That brought doom,
          You have died
And then killed
          Me, who am still alive!   930

CHORUS   *Singing.*

To show reverence
          Is indeed some reverence.
But power, in him
          Who holds power,
Is absolutely
          Not to be opposed—
Your self-willed temper
          Has destroyed you.

          As ANTIGONE *sings these last verses of her lament,*
               KREON *comes out of the royal house with*
                         more of his men.

ANTIGONE   *Singing.*

Without anyone's   *epode*
          Weeping, without friends,

Without a marriage-
          Song, I in my
Misery am
          Led to the road
Prepared for me,
          No longer am
I allowed to
          See this fiery
Eye of heaven. For
          My fate, there are   940
No tears or cries from any
          Beloved friend.

KREON Don't you know that no one would stop their singing
       And moaning before death if they didn't have to?

                                              To his men.

       Take her off! Quickly! Let the close-walled tomb
       Wrap arms around her, as I've ordered, leave
       Her there alone, deserted, where she can choose
       Either to die, or in that sort of house
       To go on living, in the tomb—as for us,
       We're pure as far as that girl is concerned.
       But she'll be deprived of any house up here!   950

ANTIGONE Oh tomb! Oh bridal bedchamber! Oh deep
          Cave of a dwelling-place, under guard forever,
          Where I must go to be with my own dear ones,
          Most of whom Persephone has received
          Dead among the shades! And I, the last
          Of them, will go in the worst way of all
          Down there before my portion of this life
          Comes to me.
                    But as I go I hold strong hopes
          That I will arrive as one loved by my father,
          Loved by you, mother, loved by you, my own   960

Dear brother—for when you died I washed and
    laid out
Your bodies properly with my own hands
And poured libations at your graves.

                          And now!—
Polyneikes—for tending to your body,
This is my recompense! Yet those who have
Clear thoughts think I did well to honor them.
   For I would never have assumed this burden,
Defying the citizens, if it had been
My children or my husband who had died
And had been left to rot away out there.   970
In deference to what law do I say this?—
Were my husband dead, there could be another,
And by that man, another child, if one
Were lost. But since my mother and my father
Are hidden now in Hades, no more brothers
Could ever be born—

                This was the law by which
I honored you above all others, Oh
My own dear brother, but Kreon thought that I
Did wrong, that things I dared were terrible.
And now by force of hands he's leading me   980
Away, without a nuptial bed, without
A wedding ceremony, and receiving
No share of marriage nor of rearing children.
Deserted by those close to me, and destined
For ill, I come while still alive to the cave
Of the dead dug deep underground.

                       And what
Justice of the gods have I transgressed? And why
Should I, in my misfortune, keep looking to
The gods for help? To whom should I call out
To fight as my ally, when my reverence   990
Has earned me charges of irreverence?
If all this does seem good to the gods, then I
Through suffering would know within myself
That I did wrong; but if these men do wrong,
May the evils that they suffer be no more
Than what they are unjustly doing to me!

CHORUS   *Chanting.*

> The same storms of
>   Her spirit, hurling
> The same blasts,
>   Still possess this girl.

KREON   *Chanting,* KREON's *men having been reluctant to lead*
                                              ANTIGONE *out.*

> And these men
>   Leading her will
> Soon begin to wail,
>   Because of their slowness!   1000

ANTIGONE   *Chanting.*

> Oh! That pronouncement
>   Comes very near
> To death!

KREON   *Chanting.*

> I cannot encourage
>   Anyone to be so bold as
> To think that these
>   Orders are not final.

                        KREON *goes into the royal house.*

ANTIGONE   *Chanting.*

> Oh city of Thebes, of
>   My fathers and my land!
> Oh gods of my ancestors!
>   I'm not going
> To be led away—I'm
>   Led away now!

KREON's men begin to take ANTIGONE *toward the side
leading out beyond the city walls.*

Look!—you rulers of Thebes—
                    On the last, solitary
Member of the royal
                    House! What things,
From what men,
                    I must suffer   1010
For having been
                    Reverent toward reverence!

The men and ANTIGONE *leave. The chorus perform their
choreographed song, addressing* ANTIGONE *even though
she is absent.*

Fifth ode / fourth stasimon

CHORUS Even Danae's lovely   *strophe a*
                    Form was made to
Exchange the light of
                    The sky for a dark
Room bolted with
                    Bronze. Yoked by
Force, she suffered—Oh
                    Child, child!—imprisonment
As in a chamber like
                    A tomb, although
She was of much-
                    Honored descent and entrusted with the
                        raining gold
Of the seed of
                    Zeus. But the power
Of fate—whatever that is—
                    Fills us with terror and
Awe. Neither wealth nor
                    Weapons nor high walls   1020
Nor dark sea-battered
                    Ships can escape it.

97

Likewise tamed under   *antistrophe a*
            A yoke was
The king of the
            Edonians, the angry
Son of Dryas, for
            Mocking with quick temper
The god Dionysos, who
            Confined him in a
Prison of rock. What he
            Had done, the terrible
Blooming of his madness,
            Drained out of him there. Then he
            recognized the god
Whom he had madly
            Assaulted with his
Mocking words. He had
            Tried to suppress the women
Quickened by the god,
            And their fire of Dionysos;   1030
That god's Muses, who
            Love the flute, he enraged.

Where indigo waters   *strophe b*
            Of two seas beat against shores of the
                        Bosporus
Is the Thracian
            Place called Salmydessos, and there,
From his neighboring
            Land, Ares saw
An accursèd
            Blinding wound
Fall on the
            Two sons of
Phineus, their wide
            Eyes—that would
Demand reprisals—
            Beaten blind by
His savage wife
            With her sharp

Shuttlepoints in her
        Blood-stained hands.   1040

Wasting away in   *antistrophe b*
        Sadness, they lamented their sad fate,
                these sons
Of a mother cast
        Out of her marriage. And yet she
And her seed
        Reached back to
The ancient family of
        The Erekhtheids and in
Faraway caverns she had
        Been raised among the
Storms and gales of Boreas,
        Her father—she was a
Child of gods, flying as
        Fast as horses over peaks
Too steep to be crossed
        On foot. But on her, too,
The Fates, that live long ages,
        Pressed hard, Oh child!

FIFTH EPISODE / SCENE VI

As the blind seer TEIRESIAS, *an old man led by a boy,
enters from the city, he calls out to the* CHORUS
of elders.

TEIRESIAS Lords of Thebes!—we come here sharing the road,   1050
Two persons seeing through the eyes of one. Thus go
The blind, with someone else to show the way.

                KREON *enters abruptly from the royal house,
                        with attendants.*

KREON What news do you have, old Teiresias?

TEIRESIAS I will explain—and you will obey the seer!

KREON I never shunned your thinking, in the past.

TEIRESIAS That is why you captained this ship of a city rightly.

KREON I am a witness, from experience, to your services.

TEIRESIAS Know that your fortunes stand once more on the
                razor's edge!

KREON What is it? What you say gives me a shudder!

TEIRESIAS You'll understand if you attend to the signs   1060
                Of my craft. For as I sat at the ancient site
                Of my bird-divining, where all sorts of hawks
                Gather, I heard an unknown noise as they
                Screeched their barbaric maddened gibber-jabber!
                I knew that with their talons they were tearing
                Murderously at each other—for the flurry
                Of wings was not without significance.
                At once, frightened, I tried to sacrifice
                On an altar blazing properly. However,
                Fire-god Hephaistos did not flare brightly up   1070
                From the offerings—instead, the fatty thighbones
                Oozed slime onto the embers, that smoked and
                        sputtered;
                And gall exploded, spewing high in the air,
                The thighbones dripped with grease and lay exposed,
                Without the fat that had covered them.
                                                These things—
                Failed signs from rites that did not signify—
                I learned from this boy who's leading me, as I
                Lead others. And it's from your thinking that
                The city is sick. Our altars and our hearths
                Are filled with food brought by the birds and dogs   1080
                From the dead ill-fated son of Oidipous!
                And this is why the gods still won't accept
                Our prayers at holy sacrifice or the flames
                That burn on thighbones, nor are the clamorous
                        shrieks
                That birds cry out good omens, for they have eaten
                The blood-streaked fat of a slaughtered man!
                                                Know this,
                My son: making bad choices is something shared

100

By all men, but when a man goes wrong, he's not
Still ill-advised and not ill-situated
If he tries to rectify the evil he   1090
Has fallen into and stops insisting that
He will not move. Stubbornness will earn
The charge of botching things! Give way to the dead.
Don't keep stabbing at him who is destroyed.
What prowess can there be in killing the dead
Yet again?
             I do regard you well, so I
Speak well to you. It's sweetest to learn from one
Who speaks well, if his speaking assures your profit.

KREON Old man—you all, like archers, shoot your arrows
At me as if I were some target! You work   1100
Against me even with your divinations.
By people like you I have been bought and sold
And shipped like merchandise. So take your profit!
Go trade in silver alloys and in gold
From India, if that is what you wish.
But you will not put that man in a grave.
And even if the eagles of Zeus want
To seize him and to carry him as food
Up to the throne of their god!—not even then,
From fear of pollution will I let this man   1110
Be given burial! For I know well
That no man has the power to stain the gods.
And even mortal men of striking, awe-
Some skill take shameful falls, Teiresias,
You old man, when they make a lovely speech
Of shameful language for the sake of profit.

TEIRESIAS Ah!
Does no man know, does no man understand—

KREON What is this great shared truth that you're
          expounding?

TEIRESIAS —to what extent the best of all we own is prudence?

KREON Yes—to the same degree wrong thinking is the worst.   1120

TEIRESIAS But that's the very sickness that fills you!

KREON I do not wish to return the seer's insult.

TEIRESIAS But you do, when you say my oracles are false!

KREON Since the whole breed of seers is money-loving.

TEIRESIAS And that of tyrants loves its shameful profiting.

KREON Do you not know that your words blame your
          sovereign?

TEIRESIAS I know. It was through me that you have saved this
          city.

KREON You are a skillful seer—but you love what's unjust.

TEIRESIAS You'll make me say what should stay deep within my
          mind.

KREON Do it!—so long as you don't speak for the sake of
          profit.   1130

TEIRESIAS Is that what you think I have done, so far?

KREON Know that you will never buy and sell my judgment!

TEIRESIAS Then know this well: that you will not complete
          Many swift courses of the racing sun
          Before you yourself, from your own gut, will give
          One corpse for other corpses, in exchange,
          Because you thrust down there someone from here
          Above, dishonorably compelling her,
          A human spirit, to live inside a tomb,
          While here you're keeping someone who belongs   1140
          Below—a body with no share of the gods,

102

No share of a tomb, no holiness—and this
Has nothing to do with you or the gods above,
And yet by you, violence is done to them!
And that is why the devastating late-
Destroying ones, the Furies, who avenge
Hades and the gods, now lie in wait for you,
So you will be caught up in these same horrors.
Ponder whether I would tell you this
Because I was given silver! Time will test   1150
My mettle and will soon reveal much wailing
For the men and women of your own household.
And all the cities are rioting with hatred
Because only dogs, beasts, and wingèd birds
Of prey have purified in burial
The torn and mangled bodies of their dead,
Carrying back to the city and its hearths
A stench of unholiness.
                        With anger, now,
And like an archer, I have let these arrows
Fly at your heart, since you torment me so—   1160
And you will not outrun their hot pain.
                        Boy!
Lead me home, so that this man may let fly
His anger at some younger men and learn
To keep his tongue more quiet and his mind
Much better at thinking than it is right now.

> TEIRESIAS *and the boy leave, on the side leading*
> *out of the city.*

CHORUS My Lord, he's gone—with terrible predictions.
And for as long as this hair—now white, once
        black—
Has covered my head, I know that never yet
Has he pronounced a thing untrue to this city.

KREON I myself know this; and my mind is confused: 1170
It's terrible to give way. But to resist
And strike my soul with ruin—is terrible.

CHORUS Son of Menoikeus, be well-advised!

KREON What must I do? Tell me! I will obey.

CHORUS Go send the girl up from her deep-dug house!
Build a tomb for the one who lies there, dead!

KREON Do you approve of this? You think I should give way?

CHORUS As fast as possible, My Lord! The gods' swift-footed
Bringers-of-Harm cut down the evil-minded.

KREON Oh! This is hard—but I change my heart. I'll do it!   1180
One cannot fight against necessity.

CHORUS Then go and do these things! Do not leave them
to others!

KREON I'm going now, immediately! You men!
All of you here and all the others, too!
Go! Go! Take tools and hurry to the place
You see out there! And I, since my decision
Has taken this turn—I who have put her there
In prison will be there to set her free
Myself. I am afraid it's best to observe
The established laws through all one's life, to the end.   1190

KREON *and his men rush out of the city.*

The CHORUS *perform their choreographed song.*

Sixth ode / fifth stasimon

CHORUS God of many names!—   *strophe a*
Glory of the young wife from the clan
Of Kadmos, child
Of thundering Zeus,
Guardian of magnificent
Italy, ruling where
The folds of the
Hills pleat the lap

Of Eleusinian Demeter,
          Shared by all,
You, Oh Bakkhos,
          That live in
Thebes, mother-city
          Of the Bakkhai,
By the flowing
          Waters of Ismenos
And on the very
          Ground where the
Savage serpent's teeth
          Were planted;   1200

You, whom the sputtering   *antistrophe a*
          Smoking flames of pine torches
                    have seen,
Up beyond the
          Double peak of
Rock, where the
          Korykian nymphs
Walk with Bakkhic
          Step and Kastalia
Flows down;
          You that the ivy
Slopes of Nysaian
          Hills send forth
To lead them in
          Procession, and the
Green coast rich with
          Grapes, while immortal
Followers cry out
          The Bakkhic chant as
You watch over
          The Sacred Ways of Thebes —   1210

This place that   *strophe b*
          You and Your
Mother, she who
          Was struck by
Lightning, honor

As highest of all
Cities: now, when
The force of
Disease holds the
City fast and all
Its people, come
Cleanse us! Stride over
The slopes of Parnassos or
Cross the moaning narrows to us,

Oh You that   *antistrophe b*
Lead the dance
Of the stars that breathe
Out fire, You that
Watch over the voices
Sounding in the night,   1220
Child of Zeus, His
Son, show us Your
Presence as a god, Oh
Lord, with Your
Bakkhantic Nymphs who
Whirl around You in worship
And celebrate You in frenzied dance
All the long night, Iakkhos! Generous
giver!

SIXTH EPISODE / SCENE VII

*Arriving from the side leading in from beyond the city
walls, a* MESSENGER *addresses the* CHORUS.

MESSENGER All you who live near the houses of both Kadmos
And Amphion—there is no person's life
That I would praise or blame, no matter what
The circumstances of it now, because
Fortune puts right and fortune topples down,
Always, the fortunate and unfortunate.   1230
Of things that stand established for us mortals,
No seer can predict what is to come.
Once, in my view, Kreon was enviable—
Because he saved this land of Kadmos from

Its enemies, and took sole, absolute
Command of this domain and governed it,
Having sown the seeds of noble children.
All that has flown. For when a man's enjoyment
Betrays him, I don't think of him as living
But as a dead man who can still draw breath.   1240
Pile up your wealth at home, if you so wish,
And live in the style of a king—but if enjoyment
Of things like these is absent, I wouldn't pay
The shadow of thin smoke to anyone
For what's left afterward, compared to joy.

CHORUS   But what new grief of the royal house do you bring
        with you?

MESSENGER   They're dead. And for their dying, the living are
        to blame.

CHORUS   Who is the murderer? And who lies dead? Tell us!

MESSENGER   Haimon is killed—bloodied by a hand close to him.

CHORUS   By his father's hand? Or was it by his own?   1250

MESSENGER   His own, against himself, in fury at his father for
        murder.

CHORUS   Oh seer! How rightly you fulfilled your prophecy!

MESSENGER   Since things are so, you must prepare for what's to
        come.

Unexpectedly, EURYDIKE—HAIMON'S *mother—comes out
the door of the royal house, alone.*

CHORUS   Yes, I see poor Eurydike nearby—
        The wife of Kreon. She comes here, perhaps,
        Because she heard about her son—or by chance.

EURYDIKE Men of the city!—as I was at the door,
To go in supplication and in prayer
To the goddess Pallas, I overheard some talk,
And when I chanced to loosen and pull back   1260
The bolts of the outer door to open it,
Word of dire harm to this house struck my ears,
And I fell against my women slaves, afraid,
And fainted. But no matter what report
Has come, tell it again! And I will listen
As one who has lived through adversity.

MESSENGER I myself was nearby, my dear mistress,
And will tell you, and won't hold back a word
Of the truth—for why should I soften for you
What would show me to be a liar, later?   1270
Always, the truth is the right thing.
                                        I went
As guide with your husband to the highest place
On the plain, where the body of Polyneikes
Still lay, unpitied and torn apart by dogs.
We prayed to the goddess of crossroads and Pluto
To restrain their anger and to be benign,
Then we washed the body with pure water,
And what was left of him we put with young,
Freshly broken branches and burned, and then
With earth of his own land we built a mound   1280
For burial, straight and true, and afterward
We went toward the young girl's hollowed-out
Bridal crypt of Hades with its floor of rock.
And near that chamber without funeral rites,
One man hears a shrill wailing that sounds
Far off, and he comes rushing up to tell
My master Kreon—who, as he creeps nearer,
Hears all around him pitiful shouts that cannot
Be understood, and he groans aloud and cries
These anguished words of grief: "Oh miserable me,   1290
Am I a seer? Am I traveling along
A path that's more unfortunate than all
The roads I've taken? What greets me is the voice

Of my son. You men! Come here quickly! Closer!
Go to the tomb! Go look inside the mound,
There where those fitted stones have been torn out,
Go right up to the mouth of it to find
If what I'm hearing is the voice of my son
Haimon—or if the gods are tricking me!"
    At these commands from our despairing master,   1300
We looked. And at the back of the tomb we saw
The girl there, hanging by her neck in a noose
Tied of fine-woven linen, and the boy
Pressing against her, falling with his arms
Around her waist and moaning because the bed
Of his bride had been despoiled, down below,
And because of his father's actions and his own
Ill-fated marriage. When Kreon sees them, he goes
Inside toward him, moaning sadly, then
With wailing cries he shouts, "You desperate boy—   1310
What a thing you've done! What was in your mind?
What happened that spoiled your reason? Come out,
    son!
I beg you, like a supplicant!" But the boy
Looks wildly at him with fierce eyes and spits
In his face and without giving him an answer
Draws his sharp, two-edged sword, but as his father
Fled rushing out, the blow missed. Instantly
The boy, ill-fated and furious at himself,
Leaned over his sword, pushing it half its length
Into his side, and still in his senses, he wraps   1320
The girl in the weak crook of his arm, pulling
Her close, and gasping he spurts a quick stream,
Blood-red drops on her white cheek.
                            One corpse
Atop another corpse, he lies there now,
Desolate boy, who in the end has had
His wedding ceremony—but in the house
Of Hades, having shown to all men that
Sheer folly is much the worst of all man's evils.

         EURYDIKE *turns and goes into the royal house.*

CHORUS What do you think this means? The lady has gone
      back
    Inside again, without a word, either good or bad.   1330

MESSENGER I too am amazed. I cherish, though, the hope
    That having heard of her son's pain, she will
    Not wail her cries in public in the city,
    But in the shelter of her own house she
    Will lead the private grieving among her servants.
    She's not without good judgment, and won't do
      wrong.

CHORUS LEADER I do not know. But too much silence seems
    To me as weighty as loud pointless weeping.

MESSENGER But I will learn, once I am in the house,
    If she is keeping hidden some close secret   1340
    In her raging heart. You speak well—too much
      silence
    Also can point to what weighs heavily.

FINAL EPISODE / SCENE VIII

The MESSENGER *goes into the house, while from the
side that leads in from beyond the city,* KREON *and
some of his attendants arrive with the body
of* HAIMON.

CHORUS   *Chanting.*

And here is our Lord
        Himself, arriving
With a conspicuous sign
        In his arms, a memorial,
His own ruin—
        No one else's (if it is
Lawful for us to say so),
        Having himself done wrong.

KREON   *Singing.*

Oh!   *strophe a*
The stubborn wrong-
        Doing and death-
Dealing of mistaken
        Thinking!
Here you see
        Kindred who have   1350
Killed and been
        Killed! Oh my
Foolish heedlessness!
        Oh my young
Son, dead
        So young,
Aiee!
        Aiee!
You died, you were
        Torn away from us
Because of my
        Foolishness, not yours!

CHORUS   *Speaking.*

Ah, you seem to recognize what justice is, too late!

KREON   *Singing.*

Oh!   *strophe b*
In my desolation, I have
        Learned! Then, then, some god
Leapt with all his heavy
        Weight and struck me in the   1360
Head and sent me spinning
        Down savage roads, over-
Turning my joy, to be trampled
        On! Oh no! No!
The burden of being mortal—
        The sad, exhausting burden!

The MESSENGER *returns from within the house
and sees* KREON.

MESSENGER   *Speaking.*

Master, the woes that you come bearing in
Your arms belong to you, and yet I think
You will see even more inside the house.

KREON   *Speaking.*

What worse woe is there, following on these woes?

MESSENGER   *Speaking.*

Your wife, poor woman—the mother absolute
Of this corpse—is dead of knife wounds just inflicted.

KREON   *Singing.*

Ah!   *antistrophe a*   1370
Ah, Harbor of Hades
          Never to be purified!
Why, why do
          You destroy me?

                                              To MESSENGER.

You bringer of bad
          Tidings for me—what
Words are you saying?
          Aiee! You have killed
A destroyed man
          Twice over! Speak,
Boy! Of what new
          Killing do you tell me?
Aiee!
          Aiee!—

A woman's
         Sacrificial
Death piled on
         Top of death?

SERVANTS *open the palace door, revealing the body*
                                   of EURYDIKE.

CHORUS   *Speaking.*

See her! She is no longer hidden deep within.   1380

KREON   *Singing.*

Ah!   *antistrophe b*
Miserable me, I see this
         Second horror! What fate,
What fate, is waiting for me still?
         Only now I held my
Son in my arms,
         Miserable me, and now
I see her body before me.
         Ah! Ah!
Pitiful mother!
         Ah! My son!

MESSENGER   *Speaking.*

At the altar, with a sharp-edged, pointed blade
She stabbed herself with sudden force and allowed
Her eyes to close on darkness—after she wailed
For the empty bed of dead Megareus   1390
And for this son, too; and last, she chanted hymns
Of evil curses on you, killer of sons.

KREON   *Singing.*

Aiee! Aiee!   *strophe c*

I shake with dread!
               Why has no one
Stabbed straight
               Into my chest with a two-
Edged sword?
               Desolate me, aiee!
Desolate the anguish
               That is now mixed into me!

MESSENGER   *Speaking.*

Yes—you were charged by the dead woman here
With blame for this death and the other one.

KREON   *Speaking.*

How was she torn away from us so bloodily?   1400

MESSENGER   *Speaking.*

With her own hand, she struck herself below her liver,
When she learned of her son's bleak end, that brought
               sharp wailing.

KREON   *Singing.*

Ah me! Because of my   *strophe d*
               Guilt, these things will
Never be fitted to
               Any other man. It was
I, I who killed you,
               In my useless misery!
I speak the truth.
               You servants! Lead
Me quickly, lead me
               Away from everything,
I who am no more
               Than nothing!

CHORUS   *Speaking.*

If woes bring profit, then you advise what's profitable.
When woes are in our path, the briefest are the best.   1410

KREON   *Singing.*

Let it come! Let it come!   *antistrophe c*
May it appear to me —
            That best of fates
That brings my
            Final day,
The most perfect!
            Let it come! Let it come!
So that I will not
            See another day!

CHORUS   *Speaking.*

That's in the future. We must do what lies before us.
Those who take care of these things will take their
        care.

KREON   *Speaking.*

But I have prayed for everything I long for.

CHORUS   *Speaking.*

Don't pray for anything — for from whatever good
Or ill is destined for mortals, there's no deliverance.   1420

KREON   *Singing, as he looks from* HAIMON's *body
                              to* EURYDIKE's.

Lead me away   *antistrophe d*
            From everything, a useless
Man, who killed you,
            My child! — although not

115

By my intent. And I killed
                    You, also. Ah, my helpless misery!
I do not know which one
                    To look at or where to
Lean now to find support.
                    Everything is twisted in
My hands, while onto my head
                    Unbearable fate has leapt down!

                              KREON's MEN *lead him away.*

CHORUS   *Chanting.*

Good sense is the
                    First principle
Of happiness. We
                    Must not act
Disrespectfully
                    Toward the gods.
Grand words of arrogant
                    Men, paid back with   1430
Great blows, in old age
                    Teach good sense.

NOTES ON THE TEXT

I [Charles Segal] have profited from the commentaries of Andrew Brown, *Sophocles: Antigone* (Warminster, 1987), Mark Griffith, *Sophocles: Antigone* (Cambridge, 1999), and Richard Jebb, *Sophocles, The Plays and Fragments*, III (Cambridge, 1900); and also from R. D. Dawe, ed., Sophokles, *Tragoediae*, vol. 2 (Leipzig, 1985); from J. C. Kamerbeek, *The Plays of Sophocles, Commentaries, Part III, The Antigone* (Leiden, 1978); and from H. Lloyd-Jones and N. G. Wilson, *Sophoclea* (Oxford, 1990).

Line numbers are given in this order: translation (bold type) / Greek text. Quotations from the translation are in italics; paraphrases or other renderings are in quotation marks.

CHARACTERS

ISMENE: probably a little younger than Antigone, as the latter is to be married first, but the play gives no clear indication.

THE CHORUS: Sophokles has chosen a chorus of elderly citizens, men of stature and importance, to emphasize the civic and political aspects of his theme. One should keep in mind that classical Athens also contains a large population of resident aliens ("metics") and slaves, and that neither are citizens. Freeborn Athenian women, though they have many rights, do not have the right to vote, hold public office, or own property in their own names. They are expected to remain primarily in the house and to be concerned with the rearing of children and the management of domestic affairs. They do, however, have important religious functions (many cults had priestesses), particularly in the area of funerary ritual.

MESSENGER, and VARIOUS MALE ATTENDANTS; SERVANTS; SLAVES: Though the Guard is probably a lower-class citizen, the other minor figures on the stage are probably slaves. Slavery was an accepted part of Athenian life and an essential part of the ancient economy. Slaves did much of the menial work in the household and were often the manual workers in agriculture, the various trades, and mining. Slavery is not particularly an issue in the play, except in those cases in which it appears as an insult in angry exchanges between characters (e.g., 527–28 / 479, 568 / 517, 816 / 756).

1–2 / 1 *Ismene, my own true sister . . . sharing our common bond of birth* Antigone's dense opening first line addressing Ismene suggests both her intense involvement in kin ties and the disastrously involuted nature of these ties within the house of Oidipous. The English can only approximate the effect of what in the Greek is, literally, "common self-sistered head of Ismene," i.e., my very own sister. This formulation, "head of" someone, is fairly common in tragedy and is a somewhat more emotional, loftier, and more dignified form of address than the ordinary. The phrasing is significant, for the words "common" and "self-" (in various compounds, or sometimes translated in such form as "with their own hands," 192 / 172), recur throughout the play to describe the incest and self-blinding of Oidipous and the mutual fratricide of the two brothers; see note on 61–71 / 49–57.

3 / 2 *one evil left to us by Oidipous* The play at once reminds us of the sufferings of the house of Oidipous, which include King Oidipous' murder of his father, Laios, and his incestuous marriage with his mother, Queen Iokaste, from which have been born Ismene and Antigone and their brothers Polyneikes and Eteokles. In many versions of the myth, the death of the two brothers at one another's hands results from Oidipous' curse on them. In *Antigone*, Oidipous has presumably died at Thebes; in *Oidipous at Kolonos*, composed some thirty-five years after *Antigone*, Oidipous wanders for many years in exile, blind and impoverished, attended by a devoted Antigone, until he arrives at Athens, where he curses the brothers shortly before his death. The curse is to be fulfilled soon afterwards at Thebes, and the play ends with Ismene and Antigone returning to Thebes, the point where *Antigone* begins. In Euripides' *Phoinikian Women* (409 BCE) Oidipous is still alive at the time of the brothers' quarrel and death. Also see Appendix 2.

7–8 / 4 *nothing that's not weighed down by ruin* The reading of the manuscripts here is uncertain. We adopt a widely accepted nineteenth-century emendation.

10 / 8 *the general* Throughout the play Antigone avoids calling Kreon, "the new ruler of Thebes," "king," or "lord." For an Athenian audience, the term "general" could also suggest one of the ten generals elected each year, who had broad powers in the field. Most Greek tragedies are set in the remote time of Mycenaean kingdoms, with their mythical atmosphere, but allow anachronistic references to Athenian political institutions. See note on 680 / 632.

13–14 / 10 *evils of our enemies . . . against our friends and dear ones* Antigone ends her speech with the two terms whose definition becomes a central issue in the play. "Friends," *philoi* (which we translate as "dear ones," also), is a particularly important term. It can include loved ones in the intimacy of the family, or "friends" in our broader and looser sense, or those on one's side in politics, one's "allies." The play exploits this range of meanings very fully. The connotations of intimacy are especially strong, as the underlying meaning of *philos* is what lies in the realm of one's own, in contrast to the other or the outsider. "Evils of our enemies" here can mean either the evil that Kreon intends for one of Antigone's "friends" or "dear ones," i.e., her brother Polyneikes, or the sufferings appropriate to her family's enemies, including perhaps the Argive attackers.

18–19 / 13–14 *two brothers . . . twin blows* The repeated numerals emphasize both the pathos and the horror of the mutual fratricide and recall the dark background of the kin ties in this accursed house. Similar collocations recur later: 62–72 / 49–57, 190–91 / 170–71.

21 / 16 *This very night* It is presumably just before dawn, after the night battle. See note on 118–81 / 100–61.

28–29 / 23–24 The manuscript text of these lines is probably corrupt; we have followed a widely accepted emendation.

33–38 / 27–30 *proclamation . . . left unmourned, unburied . . . their greedy joy* Here and elsewhere in the play Sophokles echoes Homeric language for the exposure of a warrior's corpse. Whether Kreon is legally justified so to maltreat the body is left open, and this gray area enables the tragic conflict to develop. Homeric warriors often threaten to maltreat an enemy's body (as Achilles, notably, does to that of Hector at the end of the *Iliad*), but in fact do not often do so. In the fifth century each side was generally allowed to gather and bury their dead, but in Athens the bodies of traitors could be denied burial within its borders. We learn of Kreon's treatment of the body first from this description by Antigone, which of course puts his behavior in the worst light. She stresses the two major components of proper burial, the keening or lament over the body and covering it in a tomb or grave (see notes on 472–76 / 427–31, 962–65 / 900–903, and 1275–81 / 1199–1204). Her vivid language depicting its violation by birds of prey, the most horrible fate a Greek can imagine for a corpse, conveys at once her intense emotional involvement. Kreon's announcement of his decree in 230–35 / 203–6 echoes the language of Antigone here, but adds *dogs* to her *birds* and omits her vivid image of the *sweet-tasting treasure*. See note on 1080–81 / 1016–18.

40 / 31 *The noble Kreon* Antigone's irony, following immediately on her description of the exposed body of Polyneikes, intimates her hatred of Kreon that will emerge increasingly in the course of the action.

46–47 / 35–36 *by public stoning murdered* This is the punishment for traitors in Athens. Kreon's decree later, however, refers only to Antigone's underground burial, with its many thematic and poetic advantages for the play. Although our sources for the myth of Antigone are very scanty, it is possible that her underground burial is Sophokles' invention. See note on 944–50 / 885–90.

48–49 / 37–38 *whether you are noble . . . cowardly* Antigone espouses what are traditionally male heroic values of nobility or honor: see notes on 87–90 / 72–74 and 114–15 / 96–97.

52 / 41 *joining in my action and my burden* Antigone's repetition, in the Greek, of two verbs beginning with the prefix *sun-* (or *syn-*), "together with," expresses her sense of family solidarity (which, however, will soon fracture). "Burden," *ponos*, means "suffering" as well as "work," "toil," or "effort." That meaning recurs emphatically at the end of the play in Kreon's outcry at the magnitude of his "burden," 1363 / 1276. The burden/suffering that Ismene here refuses but later will attempt to share proves greater than either sister can anticipate in this opening scene.

53–60 / 42–48 *What sort of dangerous act . . . not for him to keep me from my own* This exchange at once depicts the contrast between Ismene's timidity and Antigone's defiance of authority.

61 / 49 *Oh!* These exclamations recur throughout the play and are part of the conventionalized language of emotional expression here and in all of Greek tragedy. The Greek interjection, as here, is often *oimoi*, which has no easy English equivalent. It is often rendered "alas" but may express a wide range of emotions, including sorrow, annoyance, impatience, or anger. It is possible that these words in our text may have been merely a shorthand indication to the actor of the need for an emotional cry of some sort whose exact tone he would indicate by gesture and inflection of voice. We have rendered these terms differently as the various contexts seem to require.

61–71 / 49–57 *But sister . . . shared a doom in common* See note on **1–2 / 1**. The vocabulary of "self," "each other," "common," etc. recalls the crimes and pollutions that mark the misfortunes of Oidipous' family. The phrase "self-striking hand" is echoed several times later in the play for violence directed against the self (**192 / 172, 350/ 306, 1249 / 1175, 1401 / 1315**, and compare also **62–65 / 51–52** here), thus suggesting the continuation of the sufferings of the accursed family into the next generation. This turning of the family against itself is also the subject of the second stasimon (**633–77 / 582–630**). The language here, recalling Antigone's opening lines, associates the suffering of the two living sisters with the too closely intertwined dooms of the dead incestuous parents and the fratricidal brothers.

62–68 / 49–54 *Our father, after beating out his eyes . . . mother and wife . . . violently disfigured her own life* Sophokles is referring to the familiar story of Oidipous and Iokaste, the subject of his *Oidipous Turannos* (written at least a decade later). Oidipous discovers that he has unwittingly killed his father, Laios, and married his mother, Iokaste. After this discovery, he blinds himself and Iokaste hangs herself. Sophokles will repeat some of his language for the hanging and blinding in the *Oidipous Turannos* (**1266–78**).

74–75 / 59–60 *rulers' vote and power* The Greek word for "vote" suggests analogies with fifth-century BCE Athenian political institutions; see note on **680 / 632**. The word for "rulers" is *turannoi*, which does not mean "tyrant" in our sense but nevertheless may carry a pejorative association of autocratic and illegitimate power; see note on **556 / 506**.

76–77 / 61–62 *born as women . . . war with men* Ismene introduces the conflict of genders that is developed further in Kreon's obsession with being defeated by a woman.

87–90 / 72–74 *For me it's noble . . . tied by love . . . holy crime* Noble (*kalos*) is an important value term in classical culture. It includes physical beauty, but also denotes what is beautiful, admirable, or (in an earlier idiom) fine. Antigone here reveals some of the principal springs of her actions. She combines her concern with the heroic values implicit in *kalos*, beautiful or noble, with her commitment to the bonds of family love (*philia*) and her paradoxical situation of committing what she regards as a justifiable crime. As a woman who espouses masculine heroic values and defies male authority to commit *a holy crime*, she at once defines herself as a paradoxical figure, and hence as tragic. See notes on **53–60 / 42–48** and on **114–15 / 96–97** and **345 / 301**.

91–92 / 75–76 *those down below . . . those up here . . . forever* This is the play's first statement of the contrast between upper and lower worlds, and it comes appropriately in the context of Antigone's devotion to the dead. This contrast recurs in her important speech of defiance to Kreon in **495–518 / 450–70**, in her lament in **910–12 / 850–53**, and in Teiresias' warning in **1135–43 / 1066–73**.

105 / 88 *heart that's hot for what is chilling* Ismene's reproach implies Antigone's eagerness for actions that should make one "chilled" with fear. In *Oidipous at Kolonos* 621–22 the aged Oidipous predicts that his "chill corpse" will drink the "warm blood" of Athens' enemies. The association of "chilling" with death reinforces Ismene's repugnance to Antigone's plan.

110–12 / 93–94 *hated by me . . . to the dead man . . . a hated enemy* These words indicate the harsher side of Antigone, in sharp contrast to her devotion to the ties of family love or *philia*.

113 / 95 *ill-considered plan* The contrast of supposed good sense and Antigone's "foolish" sacrifice of her life to bury her brother becomes a major motif in the conflict between Antigone and Kreon and a major component of her tragedy. Compare also Ismene's objection in **83 / 68**, that Antigone's intended act *makes no sense*. When Ismene exits, the scene ends, in fact, with the contrast between Antigone's "foolishness" and love or *philia* within the family (**116–17 / 99**).

114–15 / 96–97 *suffer nothing so bad as to deny me a death with honor* The accumulation of three negatives in a single line in the Greek syntax perhaps expresses Antigone's passionate determination to overcome the obstacles on which Ismene has insisted. *Death with honor,* Antigone's last words in the prologue, reaffirm the heroic ethos of the male warrior that she has espoused. See note on **53–60** / 42–48.

117 / 99 *rightly dear to your dear ones* The motif of family love (*philia*) ends the scene, along with a contrast of "love" and "death" (**115** / 97). See note on **113** / 95.

118–81 / 100–161 Parodos (first ode) The chorus of elderly Theban citizens enters the orchestra singing what is essentially a hymn of celebration for the victory over Polyneikes and his Argive army. It begins with the Sun and ends with Dionysos, one of Thebes' major divinities. In between it mentions Zeus, whose fiery lightning wards off the fire of the attackers (**148–49** / 131; compare **140** / 122–23, **154** / 135), Ares, god of war, and Victory. Choruses of citizens regularly sang and danced in such civic rituals, and the ritual character of the ode is clearly indicated by the exhortation in **171–72** / 152–54 to visit all the temples of the gods in thanksgiving. The chorus's opening words mark the new dawn (see note on **21** / 16), and the sun's radiance symbolically expresses the joy of the city's new lease on life. The chorus depicts the attackers both as bloodthirsty birds of prey and as furious madmen, seething with the wildness of the followers of Dionysos (**153–54** / 135–36). By contrast, the ode ends with the city's celebration of Dionysos, born in Thebes and a major protective divinity (**174** / 154). The ode introduces a perspective very different from Antigone's in the opening scene, revealing the terror of the threatened city and the anxiety of the citizens about their very survival. It thus helps frame the play's fundamental conflict between loyalty to family and loyalty to the city. Appropriately, the ode introduces Kreon, the new ruler of the city (**175–81** / 155–61). The ode contains a number of verbal echoes of Aiskhylos' *Seven against Thebes* (467 BCE), probably Sophokles' most influential predecessor in dramatizing the myth. That play became famous for its depiction of martial valor in defense of the city.

119–20 / 101–2 *seven-gated Thebes* The struggle over the city focuses on the defense of its seven gates. See note on **160** / 141.

124 / 106 *Argive warrior* The reading is not completely certain. If it is correct, it is probably to be understood collectively as the Argive army that Polyneikes is leading against his native city. In **148ff.** / 131ff. the enemy is individualized in the ferocious attacker, Kapaneus.

127 / 108–9 *sharp bit stabbing him* The metaphor of the bit is common in Greek tragedy and recurs later in the play. Although riders today use the bit to restrain the horse, the metaphor here seems to imply its use to drive the animal forward with greater urgency, as the Argive warrior is rushing in headlong flight.

128–34 / 110–16 *Chanting* After the highly lyrical meters of the preceding lines, the chorus changes to anapests, the marching meter that often accompanies their entrance. They continue this alternation of anapests and lyrical meters throughout the ode. Here and elsewhere we have used the term "chanting" to indicate the anapests.

129 / 110 *Quarrels of divisive Polyneikes* The phrase in Greek plays on the second part of Polyneikes's name, *neikos*, "quarrel." The reading of the manuscripts presents problems, and we here adopt a widely accepted emendation.

140 / 123 *fire-god* Hephaistos is the god of fire, here mentioned metonymically.

144 / 126 *the Theban Serpent* Kadmos founded Thebes by slaying the serpent or dragon that guarded its spring, Dirke. He then sowed the creature's teeth in the ground, and from these sprung the original warrior-race of Thebes, the Spartoi (Sown Men or Planted Men). They immediately fought one another, anticipating the internal conflicts of Thebes' royal house, and only five survived to become the first citizens and founding race of Thebes. In the background may be the Homeric image of an eagle fighting a serpent, but a metaphorical wrestling is also implied. The text is not entirely certain. Variant readings would give the sense "a hard-won victory of his (the Argive's) snake antagonist" (Griffith) or "the attack of the Serpent antagonist against which the Argive could not prevail" (see Jebb).

152 / 134 *tumbled crashing to the hard ground* This attacker is probably to be identified with the fiercest of the attackers, the boastful Kapaneus, who, however, stands for the fury and savagery of the enemy army as a whole.

153 / 136 *Bakkhic fury* Though not referring specifically to Dionysos, the phrase draws on the image of the ecstatic wildness and madness of the devotees of this god in their dances and processes. The language recurs in the last ode with much more specific Dionysiac associations: see notes on 1196/ 1121 and 1221–24/ 1149–52.

157–58 / 139–40 *the great war god . . . lead horse* Ares, god of war, is compared to the horse on the right-hand side of a team of horses, the position given to the strongest horse.

160 / 141 *Seven captains* One opponent is matched to each of the seven gates of Thebes. Sophokles here (as elsewhere in the ode) may have in mind the celebrated description of the attack in Aiskhylos' *Seven against Thebes*, 375–676, where Eteokles, in a long speech, appoints one captain to guard each gate against his adversary, keeping the seventh post, tragically, for himself against his brother, Polyneikes. See note on 118–81 / 100–161.

162 / 143 *battle-turning Zeus Zeus Tropaios* receives the dedication of the "trophies," the enemies' armor or weapons that the victors set up on the field, at the place where the enemy made their "turning" (*tropê*) in flight.

163–66 / 144–47 *two doomed, cursed men . . . one father . . . one mother . . . one death in common* Sophokles again uses the contrast of one and two and the language of mutuality to interweave the death of brother by brother with the incestuous union of Oidipous and Iokaste. The density of the language itself in Greek represents the disastrously introverted nature of the kin ties in this family. See note on 18–19 / 13–14.

170 / 150–51 *Forget this war* Sophokles may be alluding here to the ancient motif of song as bringing forgetfulness of grief: e.g., Hesiod, *Theogony*, 54–55, 99–103.

174 / 154–55 *Dionysos, Earth-shaker of Thebes* Dionysos, one of the major divinities of Thebes, often manifests himself by earthquakes. His appearance as a savior here contrasts with the Dionysiac madness of the attackers in 153–54 / 135–36.

182–240 / 162–210 Kreon's first speech reveals the basic lines of his character, his concern with the state, authority, and power. His emphasis on the safety of the city in a time of danger would probably win him the sympathy of the audience of Athenian citizens. At the same time his vehement insistence on his own authority (conveyed by his repeated use of the first person) and his reference to *all the power and the throne* (194/ 173) are disquieting hints of the authoritarian mood that will become increasingly visible later and so cast at least a shadow of doubt on the full justice of exposing Polyneikes' corpse. His sententious language, though appropriate to a political figure, contains more than a hint of self-righteousness.

193 / 172 *own polluting murder of one another* Pollution, an important theme in the play, is often caused, as here, by the shedding of blood between kin. Sophokles again uses the language of "self-" for this intra-familial bloodshed: see notes on 1–2 / 1, 61–71 / 49–57, 944–50 / 885–90, 1078–79 / 1015, 1107–12 / 1040–43, 1153–58 / 1080–83, and 1371 / 1284.

204–5 / 182–83 *any man who feels that someone close to him* Kreon's word here is *philos*, which can mean "loved one," "personal friend," or political ally. For the multiple meanings of *philos*, see note on 13–14 / 10. Here, as a few lines later in 210–11 / 187, Kreon defines *philos* wholly in terms of loyalty to the city. The strong contrast to Antigone's definition in the prologue sets up the conflict between them in the next scene.

214–15 / 191 *These are the laws . . . make our city grow strong* It turns out that Kreon's view of the "laws" has just the opposite effect on his city. See note on 495–518 / 450–70.

230–35 / 203–6 *It has been proclaimed . . . for anyone to see* See note on 33–38 / 27–30. Whereas Antigone in the prologue is emotionally involved in the proper burial of a brother's body, Kreon is concerned with the assertion of his authority.

244–45 / 213–14 *use any law in dealing with the dead* This proposition is exactly what Antigone challenges in the name of a different law, particularly about the dead. See note on 495–518 / 450–70.

246–47 / 215–16 *Make certain . . . some younger man* The chorus initially understands Kreon's "watch over" literally, as if they were to guard Polyneikes' corpse.

252–53 / 221–22 *And that will be the price . . . hope for profit* Kreon characteristically reasserts his power to inflict the death penalty. This statement about *profit* is the first of many such remarks and indicates his obsession with plots against him and the material gain that allegedly motivates them.

254ff. / 223ff. *Guard* Greek tragedy occasionally gives a vivid personality to minor figures, for example, the Nurse in Aiskhylos' *Libation Bearers*. The Guard's breathless entrance prepares us for something unusual. He might be a slave, but his freedom of expression suggests rather that he is a free citizen, perhaps an example of the independent Athenian of the lower classes. A practical man, he is wary of Kreon's authority but is not completely intimidated. In any case, his elaborate garrulousness, in counterpoint to Kreon's self-important urgency, injects an element of humor into the scene, while his earthy and canny frankness about saving his own skin contrasts with Antigone's idealistic readiness to die.

276 / 241 *You take aim at me* Some take this line to mean "aiming at me," in the sense of "trying to figure me out" or "trying to confuse me." Others take the word to be a metaphor from hunting.

290 / 255 *not covered with a mound* The phrase can also mean "buried in a tomb," but so elaborate an interment cannot be in question here. The same root can denote a tomb. Kreon uses it for Antigone's underground *tomb* in **944 / 886**, and she soon after begins her last iambic speech by addressing her *tomb* (**951 / 891**). When Kreon does finally bury Polyneikes at **1280 / 1203**, the messenger uses this word to mean *mound*.

292–93 / 256 *as if by someone trying to avoid pollution* Anyone who passed an unburied corpse without covering it with dust was considered polluted and so could bring a curse on himself, his family, and his city. Pollution will prove to be a major concern of the play: see notes on **193 / 172** and **467 / 421**. The guard, of course, has no idea that the actual perpetrator had motives rather different from what he here supposes.

319–20 / 278–79 *my own thoughts . . . directed by the gods* The chorus's mild suggestion raises the question of possible divine intervention in the first burial of Polyneikes, the problem of the so-called "double burial." The absence of marks on the ground, according to the Guard's description (**284ff. / 249ff.**), might lend credence to the chorus's suggestion. It has also been suggested that the reference to *the first man of the day-watch* (**288 / 253**) points to the gods, for Antigone is still speaking to Ismene before dawn (*this very night,* **21 / 16**) and so presumably cannot yet have buried the body. The gods' burial of Niobe's slain children in *Iliad*, 24.610–12 is a famous example of divine intervention of this kind. If Antigone did bury the body the first time, she has returned to cover it up again, as the next scene shows, and one must ask why she returns a second time, for the previous sprinkling of dust (as the Guard implies) would presumably have sufficed for the ritual. But it is easy enough to supply Antigone's motives for returning to the body a second time, although there is no explicit evidence for these in the text: she may have felt that the guards' uncovering of the body was an indignity to the corpse that she would not tolerate, or, as some have suggested, she actually wants to get caught. Some have objected that the questions suggested by the mention of the two burials would not have been noticed by an audience in live performance. The controversy remains open. The chorus's remark here, however, indicates how a spectator might feel: at the very least, the gods *might have* buried the body the first time. Perhaps it suffices for the play that the possibility is raised, if not decided. Kreon's angry reply to the chorus's suggestion is the first of many indications of his arrogant assumption that the gods are entirely on his side and that his will coincides with theirs, see **321ff.** / 28off.

321ff. / 28off. Kreon's somewhat grandiose language stresses the enormity of the attack and so of Polyneikes' crime. Kreon's gods are the visible, public gods of the city, who are worshiped in *temples with columns around them,* in contrast to the less visible gods of the underworld and of family cult, to whom Antigone primarily looks. And he increasingly identifies these civic gods with his own authority.

333–38 / 289–92 *Yet for a long time . . . raised a secret uproar . . . been content with me* Kreon expresses his obsession with plots against his authority in terms of the imagery of subduing animals characteristic of his concern with hierarchy and control. The recurrence of this theme in the first stasimon (**393–96** / 347–51) links that ode with issues of human authority, power, and autonomy in the play as a whole. Sophokles is rather vague about the time it took for this dissatisfaction to develop and find expression in the city, as the edict has only recently been proclaimed (see **28–49** / 23–38). For dramatic effect, Sophokles obviously has to condense the sense of time, as he does later in Haimon's remarks about popular sentiment in favor of Antigone (**747–55** / 692–700). What exactly Kreon has in mind is also somewhat vague. Some interpreters think that the Thebans' dissatisfaction is at Kreon's recent edict about the exposure of Polyneikes' body; others suppose the reference is to his regency in general, about which the play is also vague. Kreon's assumption that there are supporters of Polyneikes within the city who may still cause trouble is in keeping with the internal politics of Greek city-states in the fifth century.

340–45 / 295–301 *For nothing current . . . silver . . . all kinds of irreverence* Kreon characteristically focuses on material gain as the main motive for wrongdoing. His words would resonate with an audience accustomed to accusations of bribery in civic affairs, but they also indicate the narrow

rationalism and materialism with which he views the world. He will
be stymied by the very different motivations of Antigone's actions.

345 / 301 *All crimes . . . all kinds of irreverence* The Greek word, *panourgia* (from
pan, "every," and *ergon*, "act" or "deed"), means an unscrupulous disregard for the laws and for the rights of others that would lead one to
do "any and every act." The word carries unsavory associations of the
meanness of a common criminal: see Bernard Knox, *The Heroic Temper* (Berkeley, Calif., 1964), 93. Kreon further emphasizes his law-and-
order point of view by repeating the constituent parts of the word in
"every act" (*pantos ergou*) in the next line. The verbal form of *panourgia* is also Antigone's word for her *holy crime* or "holy villainy" in
90 / 74 (*hosia panourgêsasa*), combining the verb with its opposite,
hosia, "holy."

348 / 304 *If Zeus gets any reverence* Kreon appeals self-righteously to Zeus. This
elaborate periodic sentence expresses the vehemence of his anger. *Reverence* for the gods becomes a major motif in the play, along with the
accusations of *irreverence* (see note on **345 / 301**). Kreon's reverence is
entirely for the Olympian gods of the public religion; Antigone has her
own *reverence* for the gods of the lower world.

355–59 / 310–14 *where to get your profit from . . . profiting . . . shameful earnings*
Kreon ends his tirade with more generalizations about the dangers of
profit, greed, and money.

362–65 / 317–20 *Would it be your ears . . . diagnose where I feel pain . . . born to
talk* There is a touch of humor here that both points up and undercuts
Kreon's passionate assertions of his authority.

372–76 / 327–31 *May he definitely be caught . . . owe the gods great gratitude* The
Guard's remarks are addressed to himself (and the chorus) and not
intended for Kreon's hearing. In any case, the Guard's practical concern with his own safety contrasts with Antigone's total disregard for
hers in the next scene (when, contrary to his expectations, he will
return). There are no stage directions in the manuscripts. It is probable,
though not absolutely certain, that Kreon exits immediately after **371 /
326**.

377–416 / 332–75 *At many things—wonders, terrors—we feel awe* The first stasimon
(second ode), one of the most celebrated choral odes of Greek tragedy,
is known as the Ode on Man. See the Introduction, 26–27. Sophokles

here draws on contemporary theories of the origins of civilization associated with Sophists like Protagoras and Presocratic philosophers like Democritus. But he also models the opening of the poem on the central ode of Aiskhylos' *Libation Bearers* (458/457 BCE), substituting a praise of human intelligence for Aiskhylos' accusations of the deadly lust of women. The ode has multiple levels of meaning. The conservative elders of the city chorus speak in pious generalities, separating themselves from any criminal who would be *outside any city*; but their words, like almost everything in the ode, carry meanings that reach beyond what they can know at this moment. Three words of the opening phrase in the translation, *awe, terror,* and *wonder,* translate the ambiguity of the single Greek word *deinon,* which may refer to both Kreon and Antigone and, more broadly, to the ambiguous capacities of human beings generally, who, as the ode says (and as the play shows) may move *both to evil and to good* (409 / 367). The echo of Aiskhylos can evoke the dangerous and destructive passions of women and so point to Antigone. Yet the praise of mankind's control of nature also points to Kreon, particularly because the ode's language of taming, trapping, and hunting resonates with the authoritarian language of Kreon and his will to power and domination. The warnings about mankind's impotence before Hades, or Death (403–5 / 361–62), also evoke the area of conflict between Kreon and Antigone that will, in fact, reveal Kreon's inability totally to control and dominate his world. The pointed rhetorical juxtaposition of *inventive in everything* and *without invention* (401–2 / 360) in these lines encapsulates the play's tragic ambiguity of human power. It is echoed in the similar syntactical pattern of *high in his city . . . outside any city* (412–13 / 370).

382–83 / 338 *Earth . . . highest of all the gods* Here *highest* has the sense of "supreme," "most revered," because, as the foundation of all being, Earth is the oldest: see Hesiod, *Theogony,* 117–18, 126–33. Nevertheless, the adjective may have a certain paradoxical ring, which may suggest the interplay between upper and lower realms that is so important to the play: see note on 737–38 / 683–84.

394–95 / 350 *harnesses the horse* The manuscript reading for *harnesses* is corrupt, and this is a plausible emendation. Other editors emend to "fetters" or "hobbles."

409–11 / 368–69 *Honoring the laws of the earth and the justice of the gods* We are reminded of Kreon's and Antigone's very different views of which laws and gods to obey and also of their very different ways of understanding "earth": for Kreon "earth" is the political territory of Thebes, defined by human laws; for Antigone it is the realm of the gods below, who protect the rites of the dead: compare her speech in the next scene, **495–518 / 450–70.** The manuscripts here read "weaving" or "threading in the laws," which is barely possible but unlikely, and so we have adopted the widely accepted emendation, *honoring*.

413 / 371 *he who dares to consort* This "dares" recurs to describe Antigone's transgression, in Kreon's view: **494 / 449, 979 / 915.**

420 / 379–80 *Oh unfortunate child of your unfortunate father* The chorus's address to Antigone again recalls the family misfortunes, which will also be the subject of the next ode.

422–23 / 382 *disobeyed the laws of the king* Antigone, of course, looks toward a different kind of law: see note on **495–518 / 450–70.**

425–632 / 384–581 The direct, on-stage conflict between Antigone and Kreon is the only scene in the play that requires the use of all three actors permitted by the conventions of Greek tragedy. The actor who plays the Guard exits at **490 / 445** and returns at **577 / 526** in the role of Ismene.

425–26 / 384–85 *Here's who did the deed* The Guard's clipped phrasing expresses his eagerness to exculpate himself, which he expresses again at the opening of his speech to Kreon (**429–43 / 388–400**).

434–35 / 392 *Happiness . . . beyond one's very hopes* The manuscripts read "happiness outside and beyond one's hopes," but syntactical difficulties are in favor of the emendation, *for which one prays*, which is also in keeping with the Guard's elation at escaping blame.

450ff. / 407ff *Well, what happened was* As the Guard recounts the capture of Antigone, he becomes expansive. His narrative gives a vivid picture of the remote place, outside the city walls, where Polyneikes' corpse has been left to rot. The details of the *whirlwind* that *raised a pillar of dust . . . high as heaven* (**462ff. / 417ff.**) and *this supernatural plague* (**467 / 421**) suggest the mysterious powers of nature and the gods that are not as controllable as the previous ode has implied. The motif of dust thrown into the sky also continues a pattern of interaction between upper and lower worlds that runs throughout the play. The hints of supernatural intervention remain consistent with the possibility (never more than that) that the gods have had a role in the burial; see note on 319–20 / 278–79. The dust storm, in any case, has helped Antigone to achieve her aim and casts an aura of mystery about this event.

463–64 / 418 *trouble high as heaven* Literally, "a woe, or grief, in the sky." The phrase can also mean "a trouble rising to the sky" or "a trouble sent from the sky." Sophokles has probably left some deliberate openness to other meanings to suggest the possibility of divine intervention: see the previous note.

467 / 421 *this supernatural plague* The phrase can mean both "sent by the gods" or merely "supernatural," "marvelous." "Plague" or "disease," which the Guard here uses in a general sense, becomes much more specific later in the dangerous "plague" of pollution from the exposed corpse. The Guard's description here, along with the *storm of trouble high as heaven*, foreshadows that pollution carried into the sky by the carrion-eating birds in Teiresias' prophecy in 1079–86 / 1015–22. See notes on 1078–79 / 1015 and 1107–11 / 1040–43.

472–76 / 427–31 *she moaned . . . pours libations* Antigone fulfills two of the offices to the dead that Kreon has forbidden, the ritual lamentation and the covering of dust; see notes on 961–62 / 901, 1275–85 / 1199–1204. The language of lamentation here is echoed later in the laments of Haimon in 1305 / 1224 and of Eurydike in 1389–92 / 1302–5, which, like Antigone's lament here, are offstage events reported by a narrator. The simile comparing Antigone's lament to the cries of a bird whose fledglings have been taken conveys her emotional intensity and also underlines her involvement in the traditional female role of lamenting the dead. It may also suggest some sympathy for her on the part of the narrator, the Guard, in contrast to Kreon's harshness; see note on 481 / 436. The comparison to the bird also suggests her identification with the subdued natural world of the Ode of Man, whose first antistrophe begins with the netting of birds (387ff. / 342ff.). Note too the Guard's metaphor of "hunting her down" in 477 / 433. His use of the passive, *this wailing child is seen*, in 468 / 423 also adds to the pathos of Antigone's helplessness. In his eagerness to recreate as vividly as possible an event that is so important to him (and to us), the Guard switches from past to present tense and back again.

479–80 / 434–35 *what she'd done, before, and what she now was doing* While the Guard emphasizes the two separate acts of defiant burial, he does not explicitly say that Antigone performed both acts, only that she made no denial. The careful phrasing still leaves open the possibility of divine agency for the first burial.

481 / 436 *both satisfaction and pain* Despite his joy for himself, the Guard still pities Antigone—the first expression of sympathy for her, and from an unexpected quarter.

484–85 / 439–40 *all of these things are less to me than safety for myself* The Guard's attitude contrasts with Antigone's defiant lack of concern for her personal safety.

486 / 441 *turning your head away, to the ground* Here Sophokles implies a stage direction to the actor playing Antigone. Antigone's gesture expresses defiance: she refuses to look at Kreon.

495–518 / 450–70 *It was not Zeus . . . to being charged as foolish by a fool* In contrast to her silent entrance and clipped answers to Kreon just before, Antigone now bursts forth in a torrent of high idealism. In this important speech she frames her motives in the largest and most general terms, expressing her defense of principles of justice and behavior. She identifies these both *with the gods below the earth* and with *laws of the gods, that are unwritten and unfailing*, in contrast to the manmade *proclamation* of Kreon. She thus raises the question of whether a "good" citizen has the right to disobey what she or he perceives as unjust authority, in the name of higher, more universal laws. She has in mind both the universally recognized right of the dead to burial (her "unwritten laws") and the particular rights of the gods beneath the earth, the chthonic divinities, like Hades and Persephone, who are concerned with the proper burial of the dead.

508–10 / 461–62 *But if I die before my time, I count that as my profit* Antigone's defiance of death and her notion of *profit* contrast with and undercut Kreon's views of the power of both.

513–15 / 466–67 *But if I let the son of my own mother lie dead and unburied* Here Antigone cites her intimate family ties as part of her motivation, parallel to the more abstract statement of principle at the opening of her speech. The former reasoning will dominate her last speech (967ff. / 905ff.).

517–18 / 469–70 *foolish . . . to being charged as foolish by a fool* Antigone ends her speech with the recurrent motif of sensible behavior, but her notion of good sense again contrasts with Kreon's narrowly materialistic and rationalistic view of human behavior.

519–20 / 471–72 *fierce child is the offspring of her fierce father* The chorus returns to Antigone's heredity from Oidipous to account for her behavior, harking back to their same point earlier (see note on 420 / 379–80). Despite the chorus's repetition of this idea in the next ode, it would be an oversimplification to regard family heredity or the family curse as the sole key to the meaning of the tragedy. It is a contributing factor, to be sure, but one must keep in mind that the chorus functions as an actor among actors; their hypotheses are on the same level as those of the other characters' attempts to account for the suffering. *Offspring* here is the reading of most of the manuscripts. It is also the word that the chorus uses to introduce Haimon at 673 / 627. Here some editors amend to a word for "spirit" or "temper": Antigone shows "the fierce temper of a fierce father."

521–28 / 473–79 *rigid wills . . . hardest iron . . . a small sharp bit . . . someone who's the slave of others* Kreon characteristically responds to the challenge to his authority with harsh images of technological mastery and taming animals, both of which hark back to the Ode on Man. His references to slavery and, sarcastically, to Antigone as *the man* (534 / 484) are also typically vehement assertions of hierarchy and increasing indications of his authoritarian views.

535–38 / 486–87 *no matter if she is my sister's child . . . our household shrine to Zeus* Kreon's dismissal of family ties takes the form of rejecting *Zeus Herkeios*, "Zeus of the courtyard," one of the gods who presides over and protects the family. The defiance of Zeus is part of a pattern in Kreon's speeches (see notes on 348 / 304 and 1107–12 / 1040–43), and in this case verges on a dangerous impiety. In fact, Kreon's statement sounds even more blasphemous than the translation can convey, for *Zeus Herkeios* stands as a metonym for the family that Zeus's altar sanctifies and protects. Literally, he says, "not even if she is a closer relation than *Zeus Herkeios* entire."

544–45 / 493–94 *plan in the dark . . . as a thief* Kreon returns to his favorite idea of secret plotting and wrongful gain.

550–54 / 499–504 *Then why delay . . . what greater glory . . . my own true brother* Antigone defies Kreon's greatest token of power, the ability to put her to death. She again claims the traditionally masculine heroism, or glory, that she had looked to in the prologue (see note on **48–49** / 37–38).

555–56 / 505 *if fear did not lock up their tongues* Compare Kreon's denunciation of anyone who *is afraid of speaking and locks up his tongue* in his opening speech, **202–3** / 180. Antigone's point is just the reverse of Kreon's — she accuses him of silencing, rather than encouraging, the citizens to speak out.

556 / 506 *one-man rule* Antigone's word, *turannis*, though it does not carry the fully pejorative notions of "tyranny" that develop with Plato, nevertheless associates Kreon with "tyrannical" behavior, that is, with the arbitrary exercise of power that lacks the full, legitimate authority of endorsement by all the people. "Tyrannies" developed in many Greek cities in the course of the sixth century, as influential men allied themselves with the people and took over power from the dominant aristocratic families. They often promoted large building programs and expanded religious and cultural institutions, such as festivals and public cults, to ingratiate themselves with the people, and were not necessarily seen as "tyrannical" in the modern sense. Peisistratos in Athens and Polykrates of Samos were particularly successful and noteworthy examples. Kreon has succeeded to his rule through the ties of kinship, as he says (**194–95** / 173–74), but as a new ruler he is still insecure and afraid of conspiracies, a common concern of "tyrants." See note on **74–75** / 59–60.

559–74 / 508–23 The line-by-line exchange, or stichomythia, sharply sets out the diametrically opposed viewpoints of Kreon and Antigone, particularly with regard to their valuing of family ties (*philia*) versus the demands of the city. In connection with the former, Antigone also asserts the importance of the laws of Hades (**570** / 519), that is, the rights of burial that belong to the gods of the lower world (see note on **495–518** / 450–70).

559 / 508 *alone among the Thebans* Kreon emphasizes Antigone's isolation, but his view will be challenged later by Haimon, who suggests that Kreon's position is the isolated one: **793–99** / 733–39.

563 / 512 *he who died against him* Kreon is referring to Eteokles.

567 / 516 *honor him the same as the irreverent one* Here, as throughout this debate, Kreon insists on *differentiating* the two brothers on the basis of their opposite loyalties to the city, whereas Antigone insists on their *equality* in terms of the bonds of family and the rights due to the dead.

568 / 517 *my brother who died* Antigone means Polyneikes, although, of course, both brothers have died.

570 / 519 *these laws* A variant reading has "Hades wishes equal laws," which some editors accept, although it has weaker manuscript authority.

574 / 523 *not to join in hate but to join in love* Sophokles gives Antigone's response great rhetorical force by apparently coining two new words for her, *sunekthein* and *sumphilein*. Antigone reasserts her commitment to family ties, her "friends" or "dear ones," *philoi*, but she does so with a particular emphasis on "sharing" or "joining in" the relationship of kin ties (*sum-philein*), in contrast to Kreon's sharp differentiation of "friends" and "enemies." For her, the supreme value is her bond of "joining with" those she regards as her "friends" or "loved ones," and she rejects Kreon's concern with separating her loved ones (*philoi*) as political "enemies" (*ekhthroi*). Knox, *Heroic Temper*, 82, catches this point well in his paraphrase, "I was born to join not in their political hatred for each other but in their love for each other as blood brothers"—to which one must add also her own bond of family love (*philia*) to both brothers. Karl Reinhardt, *Sophokles* (1947), trans. H. and D. Harvey (Oxford, 1979), 78–79, paraphrases, "I was not born into the circle which believes 'Hate your enemy,' but into the one where love between blood relations knows itself to be in harmony with its like." And he comments, "Not that Antigone is the personification of love, but her hate and love spring from a different level from that which produces Creon's friendships and enmities." Lloyd-Jones, in his Loeb edition, also calls attention to the importance of birth, rather than on "inborn nature," in Antigone's verb, *ephun*, and translates, "I have no enemies by birth, but I have friends by birth." While it is important to keep in mind the specific reference of *philein* to the ties of family and so not make Antigone indulge in a saccharine declaration of a universally loving nature, Lloyd-Jones's interpretation seems to give insufficient force to the repeated *sun-*, "sharing in" love or hate.

575–76 / 524–25 *Then go down there . . . a woman will not rule!* Kreon impatiently and sarcastically dismisses Antigone's concern with the gods of the lower world. He treats her with increasing cruelty and callousness, which probably contribute to our declining sympathy for him in the middle third of the play.

584–85 / 533 *I raised a double ruin to bring down the throne* Kreon again focuses on maintaining his power, which may, in turn, reflect his insecurities about his new position.

587ff. / 536ff. The exchange between the two sisters, which has many echoes of their dialogue in the prologue, exhibits the fierceness of Antigone's commitment to her independence of action and her devotion to the dead and the realm of the dead (e.g., **610f. / 559f.**).

600 / 549 *Ask Kreon . . . whose side you take* The last phrase uses a word that means both "kin" and "mourner" of the dead, implying perhaps Antigone's view of herself as the only one entitled to mourn Polyneikes, but also harshly insulting Ismene, as if Ismene regarded only Kreon as her "kinsman." So devoted to the bonds of kinship, Antigone is cruel and ungenerous to the last of her living kin.

602 / 551 This dense line has a number of possible meanings, as the verb can mean both "laugh" and "mock," and Antigone may be referring to "mocking" Ismene or "mocking" (laughing at) Kreon. Some have assumed that a line or two has dropped out.

619 / 568 *kill your own son's bride-to-be* This is the first allusion in the play to Haimon, and it comes from Ismene, not Antigone. The latter never speaks directly of Haimon, although, in her last scene on the stage, she laments the loss of marriage. See note on **623 / 572**.

620 / 569 *other furrows he can plant* The crude agricultural metaphor may allude to the Athenian marriage formula, which stipulates "the sowing of legitimate children." In *Oidipous Turannos*, Sophokles makes heavy use of such agricultural metaphors for the incestuous union of Oidipous and Iokaste. At the same time, the metaphor reveals Kreon's tendency to depersonalize and devalue intimate emotional ties by objectification, generalization, or cliché.

621 / 570 *Not the way he and she were fitting for each other* The word "fitting" belongs to the language of betrothal and so may imply the "appropriateness" of this marriage between first cousins, which is considered highly desirable when the girl's father has died without male heirs and so leaves only daughters to inherit the property. Her marriage to her uncle's son (or even to the uncle himself, if he is unmarried) keeps the property in the family. "Fitting" can also mean that Haimon and

Antigone are particularly "well suited" to one another, a "good fit." Both meanings may be present simultaneously.

623 / 572 *Dearest Haimon* This line has provoked considerable controversy. The manuscripts attribute it to Ismene, which we believe to be correct, as Ismene is the first to introduce the subject of Haimon. Having failed to soften Antigone, she now brings up the marriage in the hope of softening Kreon. Antigone, resolved to die for her devotion to her family of origin, shows no interest in Haimon and, as we have noted, never mentions him. By *your marriage-bed* in the following line, Kreon then means, "the marriage that you, Ismene, speak of," referring to her words immediately preceding. Attributions of speakers in the manuscripts, however, are not always reliable, and the first printed edition of Sophokles, the Aldine text of 1502, attributes the line to Antigone, and some editors have accepted this.

627–28 / 576–77 *Ismene: It seems decided, then, that she will die—Kreon: By you and by me!* The Greek word for "decided," which can also mean "decreed," has the sense of a political decision. Some interpreters take Kreon's reply to be in an ironic tone, which also reflects his tyrannical nature. Others think that Kreon understands Ismene's verb in an alternative sense, "it seems good," and, again, replies in an ironic tone of voice, but this meaning seems less probable, given the perfective verb form that Ismene uses. Some manuscripts attribute **627 / 576** to the chorus leader, and some editors accept this. If this is so, then Kreon would be including them in his decision ("Yes, it has been decided by you [chorus leader] and by me"), which seems less likely. Kreon's remarks in the rest of the scene are also sarcastic and callous. He adopts the same tone later in **942–43 / 883–84**.

633–77 / 582–630 Second stasimon (third ode) Coming directly after the condemnation of Antigone to death, the mood of this ode is darker, in every sense, than that of the previous two odes. This mood, along with the emphasis on the gods of the lower world and the remote power of Olympian Zeus, leads into the next phase of the action, where the tragic catastrophe begins to unfold. The chorus here develops its earlier explanation of Antigone's imminent death in terms of the accursed house of her ancestors, the Labdakids. Labdakos is the father of Laios and so the great-grandfather of Antigone and Ismene.

635–36 / 585 *creeps over a multitude of generations* The chorus's allusion to the family curse working over many generations recalls Antigone's opening lines of the play, about the sufferings of Oidipous that have now afflicted his daughters.

636–41 / 586–92 The image of the stormy, turbulent northern sea contrasts with the tamed sea of the first stasimon, the Ode on Man; this difference is indicative of the growing sense of disaster.

642–44 / 594–95 *afflictions . . . yet earlier afflictions of the dead* The chorus means that the woes of the living Labdakids, i.e., Antigone and Ismene, are being added to those of the already dead members of the family, from Laios through Eteokles and Polyneikes. It is also possible to construe these dense lines to mean that the woes of the dead Labdakids are being added to those of their living kin, but this is rather less likely.

647–50 / 598–603 *rootstock of the House of Oidipous . . . reaped by blood-red dust of the gods under the earth . . . a Fury in the mind* These are among the most difficult and controversial lines of the play. The image of the bloody dust "reaping" or "mowing down" the root of Oidipous' house is bold, too bold for many editors, who emend the word "dust" (*konis*, the reading of all the manuscripts) to "knife" (*kopis*). But the manuscript reading is in keeping with the play's emphasis on the powers of the lower world; and the bloody dust evokes the death of the two brothers, the continuing doom of the house in Antigone's sprinkling of dust over Polyneikes' body, and perhaps also the dust storm in which she performs that burial (see **291 / 256, 451–52 / 409, 474 / 429**). The emendation *kopis*, moreover, would refer to a "chopper," or sacrificial knife, which does not seem particularly appropriate here. Further support for the manuscript reading comes from Aiskhylos' *Seven against Thebes*, which focuses on the death of the two brothers and is almost certainly in the background here. Aiskhylos' chorus describes how, at the mutual slaughter of the two brothers, "the earth's dust drinks the red clotted blood" (*Seven*, 734–37). In the next strophe Aiskhylos' chorus goes on to describe Oidipous' patricide and incestuous marriage, in which he "endured the bloody *root*" (referring to the incest and its consequences). That strophe ends with "the madness of *mind*" that "brought together" Oidipous and Iokaste as bride and bridegroom (*Seven*, 756–57), and Sophokles may also be referring to that passage in Aiskhylos' antistrophe here, *foolishness of speech and a Fury in the mind* (**650 / 603**). The Furies, or Erinyes, are the avenging deities of the lower world who typically punish the crime of bloodshed within the family. In this function they are also often the instruments that fulfill a family curse. They typically bring madness upon their victims. Thus, Antigone's *Fury* *in the mind* here seems to refer to her ritual burial of Polyneikes and its aftermath where (as the chorus sees it) reason and good sense give way to the destructive madness and folly that persist in the house of Oidipous as the result of the inherited curse (e.g., 420 / 379–80, 612–13 / 561–62, 913ff. / 853ff.) The reference to a Fury also picks up the motif of the dangerous power of the gods of the nether world who will eventually punish Kreon; see note on 1145–46 / 1074. Sophokles' moralizing use of the agricultural imagery here also recalls Aiskhylos, *Persians*, 821–22, where King Dareios accounts for Xerxes' fall in similar terms: the latter's "outrage" (*hubris*) against Greece "mows down (*ex-amâi*) the much-lamenting harvest" that sprang up from the excessive overgrowth of his destructive folly (*atê*).

651ff. / 604ff. The second strophe contrasts the remote, eternal power of the gods with the sufferings of human beings and the mortal generations of the family and its sufferings. The chorus gives particular prominence to Zeus, and we may recall Kreon's dangerous dismissal of Zeus's power at various points in the play; see notes on 495–518 / 450–70 and 708–9 / 658–59.

652–53 / 606 *sleep that catches everyone in its nets* This epithet of "sleep" is an emendation of the manuscript reading, "sleep the all-aging," which makes little sense here and is regarded as corrupt by most editors.

659–661 / 613–14 *only one law . . . beyond the reach of ruin* This divine law contrasts with Kreon's insistence on the human law of the city that he sees himself as representing. The text of this passage has some uncertainties, and we adopt a plausible and widely accepted emendation.

664 / 617 *desires light as air* Sophokles also uses this adjective of the birds trapped by human cleverness in the Ode on Man (387 / 342), perhaps signaling here two opposite possibilities of human behavior. *Desires* also points ahead to the next ode, in which the force of erotic desire will emerge as one of the ingredients of the tragedy.

665–67 / 618–19 *he cannot see clearly until already he has burnt his foot* Sophokles seems to be adapting two traditional sayings—knowing one's disastrous situation only when it is too late, and walking on ashes as a metaphor for dangerous and foolish behavior.

668 / 622 *famous saying* The chorus refers to a sentiment that occurs in various forms in early Greek literature and tragedy, that the gods destroy the judgment of the person bent on evil and destruction. As we might phrase it in our more psychologizing terms, the gods collaborate with the evil tendencies of the prospective criminal to lead him to his ruin. We would probably understand "god" as standing for all the invisible forces that twist a person's mind to destructive and self-destructive crimes.

671–72 / 624–25 The ode ends with a strong repetition of the word *ruin, atê,* which can also mean the folly or infatuation that leads to ruin. The same word also ends the previous strophe (661 / 614). See also notes on 1344–45 / 1258–60 and 1345 / 1260.

673 / 626–27 *last and youngest offspring* The phrase hints at the dark motif of family ties in the background and also at the death of Kreon's other son, Megareus, mentioned in 1390 / 1303 (see note on 1387–92 / 1301–5). The ominous associations of the phrase are also suggested by the use of *last* for the doomed race of Antigone's family in 647 / 599 and her *last road* in 867 / 807.

678–842 / 631–780 The scene between Haimon and his father comes at roughly the midpoint of the play and marks a major shift of emphasis. It confirms the autocratic side of Kreon, introduces a new perspective on Antigone, and exposes the vulnerable area of Kreon's life, his own family ties. It also reflects his insensitivity in this area of family ties, for Kreon misunderstands his son's genuine concern for him and gradually allows his suspicion of Haimon's devotion to Antigone to overshadow his son's filial loyalty. Hence the brutal ending of the scene, with Kreon's further misunderstanding of Haimon's threat at his exit; see note on 811–12 / 751–52, and also Introduction, 10, 16–18.

678 / 631 *better than the seers* Sophokles is adapting a proverbial phrase indicating direct and immediate knowledge, but he may also be foreshadowing the importance of seers in the ensuing action.

680 / 632 *final vote* This is another term, like *general* in 10 / 8, that would resonate with the contemporary Athenian audience, for whom voting is an important part of the democracy. See note on 74–75 / 59–60.

682 / 635 *Father, I'm yours* Haimon, knowing his father's temperament, wisely begins with an affirmation of total allegiance, which he will totally reverse by the end of the scene. Here he encourages Kreon to expatiate, characteristically, on some of his favorite themes: obedience, hierarchy, the

analogy between authority in the family and in the city, the dangers of subjection to women, and total commitment to the city.

699–700 / 650 *that soon enough grows cold wrapped in your arms* This striking phrase consists of only two words in the Greek, literally, "a cold embracing." The tragic irony in the phrase is that Kreon unwittingly foresees the way in which Haimon will, finally, wrap his arms about Antigone's corpse in **1320–21 / 1237**; and this irony is made more pointed by Kreon's having expressed an expectation of knowing *better than seers* what his son would do (**678 / 631**).

707 / 658 *I'll kill her* Kreon's phrase, as brutal in the Greek as it is in English, is not only tactless, addressed as it is to Antigone's betrothed, but also shows his cruelty and his tendency to associate the rule of law in the city with his personal authority; compare his similar first-person statement in **833 / 773**, *I'll lead her out.* (But see note on **833–34 / 773–74**.) We may contrast the emphasis elsewhere on her execution as the action of the entire city; compare **46–47 / 36, 837–38 / 776**. Haimon's restraint in the light of this brutal announcement is remarkable. Only at the end of the scene does he lose patience.

708–9 / 658–59 *let her sing her hymns in praise of Zeus the god of bonds of blood!* Kreon's dismissal of family bonds in favor of absolute obedience to the city once more takes the form of a dangerous defiance of Zeus; see notes on **348 / 304, 535–38 / 486–87, 651ff. / 604ff.** We are reminded particularly of his scorn of *Zeus Herkeios* in **535–38 / 486–87**. His scorn of women's lament recurs in his taunts to Antigone later; compare **942–43 / 883–84**. It is perhaps part of the tragic irony that the Greek word for "sing her hymns" recurs in Eurydike's "hymn" of curses against Kreon at the end (**1391–92 / 1305**)—a lament that he cannot dismiss this time; see note on **1387–92 / 1301–5**.

714–23 / 663–71 *A man like that . . .* With many editors since the nineteenth century, we accept the transposition of some of these lines (especially **718–23 / 663–67**) to a later place in the speech. The problem, however, may lie more with Kreon than with the manuscripts. After his peremptory resolution to kill Antigone in **707 / 658**, he can still go on with his gnomic generalizations, oblivious to the devastating effect that it must have on Haimon.

722–23 / 666–67 *must be obeyed in everything . . . what's just, and the opposite* Some editors have suspected that these lines are spurious and deleted them.

Yet they are in character, and they come at the point when Kreon, warming to his favorite subject, is carried away to excess. If they are authentic, they are revealing of Kreon's absolutist notion of "law," which for him is to be identified with obedience to authority, not justice. Contrast Antigone at **495–518** / 450–70.

731–34 / 679–80 Kreon ends with a restatement of another of his favorite themes: not being subject to women (compare **696ff.** / 648ff., also Ismene at **76–77** / 61–62). His last three lines contain a word play hard to render into English, for to be "defeated by" and "weaker than" are both from the same root (*hêttôn*, worse than, inferior to), so that to be "defeated by a woman" is also to be "weaker than a woman" or "inferior to a woman." On this note he ends his speech. See also **806** / 746.

737–83 / 683–723 Haimon again begins moderately, with neutral generalizations, but is soon on more delicate ground with his report of the city's secret praise of Antigone (**747ff.** / 691ff.), which, for the first time, offers a public perspective on Antigone contrary to Kreon's. Haimon is careful to phrase these views as the city's, not his own; but his remarks here endorse what Antigone herself, in her defiance of Kreon at **555–56** / 504–5, had said about other, hidden voices in the city and what Kreon had himself said about voices of dissatisfaction among the citizens (see note on **333–38** / 289–92). Haimon also indirectly validates Antigone's claims to "glory" or "honor" in the prologue (compare **87ff.** / 72ff., **114–15** / 96–97, **552–54** / 502–4, and see note on **550–54** / 499–504).

737–38 / 683–84 *good sense — highest of all the things that we possess* Haimon's *highest* echoes the epithet of Earth in the Ode on Man (**383** / 338). May there be some tragic irony in this exaltation of the two things that Kreon, as it proves, scorns?

742–44 / 688–89 A variant reading, which has weaker manuscript support, would make Kreon the subject and give the sense, "You are not naturally disposed to foresee everything that people say or do or have (as reasons) for blame." But, aside from the stronger manuscript support for the first reading, it seems more appropriate for Haimon at this point to speak of his own limitations rather than those of his father, whom he still hopes to win over by persuasion.

745–47 / 690–91 *to the common citizen . . . your eye becomes a terror* The syntax of the Greek is slightly harsh, and some editors have supposed that at least one line has dropped out. But the syntax, though awkward, is within the realm of possibility.

766–67 / 708–9 *when men like that show what's inside them . . . empty* The metaphor here refers to a folded writing tablet that would be read on being un-folded or *opened up*. The figure of "opening" the interior of a person so as to reveal the hidden truth of character recurs frequently in clas-sical Greek literature and tragedy.

771–83 / 712–23 The metaphors of pliancy and yielding to nature recall Kreon's warnings to Antigone in terms of the hardness of metals, **521–24 / 473–76**. The sailing metaphor recalls Kreon's very different use of the same figure in his opening speech (**212–13 / 189–90**). But the son's plea for a hearing from the father despite his youth upsets Kreon's emphasis on hierarchy and obedience. Nor is Kreon, who prides himself on his "good sense," likely to welcome Haimon's closing suggestion that wis-dom might reside in someone other than his father.

784–842 / 724–80 The chorus, as often in such debates, attempts a compromise position, but the division between father and son is now out in the open, and the set speeches give way to the tense line-by-line conflict (stichomythia), like that between Ismene and Antigone in the prologue and in **599–609 / 548–58**, or between Antigone and Kreon in **559–74 / 508–23**.

810 / 750 *never marry this girl while she's alive* Another instance of Sophoklean tragic irony: Haimon will in fact "marry" Antigone when she is no longer alive (**1322–28 / 1234–41**). See note on **699–700 / 650**.

811–12 / 751–52 *destroy—someone else . . . attack me with threats* Kreon understands Haimon's words as a threat against his own life, whereas what follows indicates that here Haimon (despite his later attack on his father) is probably thinking already of his own suicide.

824 / 765 *rave on* The motif of "raving" or madness becomes prominent in the next two odes (**851 / 790, 1027–28 / 960**), but it has already appeared in the rage of the attackers in the parodos and in the *Fury in the mind* in the second stasimon (**650 / 603**).

827 / 767 *weighed down by grief* An echo (in English, *weighty*) will sound for Eu-rydike at her silent exit near the end (**1338 / 1251**).

828–29 / 768 *grand thoughts too big for a man* A similar warning about mortal presumption recurs in the chorus's final lines, but with reference to Kreon—another of the reversals in his situation.

831 / 771 *did not touch* Although the Greek verb for "touch" is used in a general sense and has no expressed direct object in the original, it might imply actual contact with the forbidden corpse, as in 598 / 546–47.

833–34 / 773–74 *I'll lead her out . . . and seal her up* Although Kreon says that he himself will lead Antigone to her cave, he later delegates this task to his attendants at 944 / 885.

838–42 / 777–80 *where she can pray to Hades . . . pointless waste . . . to worship what is down below with Hades* Kreon's repetition of Hades reflects his scorn of Antigone's involvement with the gods of the lower world (compare her *Justice, who resides in the same house with the gods below the earth* in 496ff. / 451ff.). Teiresias' prophecy in the next scene ominously answers Kreon's taunt (1133–48 / 1064–76).

843–65 / 781–805 *Third stasimon (fourth ode)* This ode on the invincible power of passion or desire (*eros*, here personified as the god Eros), following directly on the conflict between father and son, marks the rising tide of emotional violence in the play. It suggests Haimon's erotic motivations, even though he only hinted at these in his previous exchange with his father. His anger there offers a glimpse of a passion that (in retrospect) the chorus seems to see as fueled by *eros*. Nevertheless, *eros* is kept in the background of the play. Antigone's love for Haimon is never made explicit, although Ismene's remarks on the betrothal might be construed as implying it. It is probable, though not certain, that Kreon exits just before the ode, at 842 / 780, which sounds like an exit line. It is easier to envisage Antigone's lyrical lament with the chorus at 861–941 / 801–82, following the Eros ode, without Kreon's presence on the stage. Kreon then reenters no later than 942 / 883 for his last scene with Antigone, and gives the final command to have her led away to her death (999–1004 / 931–36). There is, however, considerable disagreement about Kreon's presence during the odes, especially the third and fourth stasima: for discussion see R. P. Winnington-Ingram, *Sophocles: An Interpretation* (Cambridge, 1980), 136–37, with n. 58; H. D. F. Kitto, *Form and Meaning in Drama* (London, 1956), 146–47.

843–44 / 782 *that leaps down upon the herds* We have adopted the widely accepted emendation *herds* for the manuscripts "possessions." The destruction of "possessions" or wealth by Eros seems less plausible here than its universal power over beasts, human, and gods.

848–50 / 787–88 *neither the immortals nor man, who lives only a day, can escape from you* The language here recalls the inescapable power of death in the Ode on Man (403–5 / 361–62) and so reminds us of forces in human life that intelligence and technology cannot overcome. In contrast to death in the Ode on Man, in this ode it is desire that rules both gods and mortals. Sophokles here alludes to the numerous myths of gods and goddesses mating with mortals, familiar from the poetry of Homer, Hesiod, Pindar, and others.

857–58 / 795–97 *love in the gaze . . . wedding joy* The dense language of this passage permits several different interpretations. It can refer to the Greeks' belief that desire is an active force that emanates from the eyes of the loved one, in this case the new bride, and inspires desire in the beholder. Or it can refer to the lover's desire for the bride's beauty, or to the eyes' desire for the bride. It is possible that aspects of all three meanings are present simultaneously. In any case, these lines emphasize the erotic side of marriage, over which Aphrodite presides (860 / 800), preparing for the eroticized death of Haimon in his *Liebestod* later.

858–59 / 797–98 *rules equally with the great laws* Editors have suspected a corruption because the claims for Eros seem exaggerated and because there is not a full metrical correspondence with the relevant line in the strophe. A more serious problem is that one would expect Eros to be the destroyer or transgressor of these "laws." Yet such grandiose claims are appropriate to the hymnic style, and no satisfactory emendation has been suggested. We keep the manuscript text. The word for "laws" here, *thesmoi*, is different from the "laws" of the city (*nomoi*) that the play uses elsewhere. It has a more solemn ring and suggests the existence of a divine power that cannot be controlled or legislated by human structures. The play uses it only here and at 862 / 801.

860 / 799–800 *Aphrodite at her play* "Play," which one perhaps does not expect at this moment of approaching crisis, is frequently associated with the lighter side of love, the "game" of seduction and persuasion over which Aphrodite, as goddess of love, presides. In this sense, it is common in lyric poets like Anakreon (middle of the sixth century BCE) and contrasts with the more dangerous aspect of the "invincible" power of desire that is the ode's main subject.

861–65 / 801–5 The chorus's brief description of Antigone, in the marching meter of anapests, marks the transition from the formal ode on Eros to the lyrical exchange with Antigone that follows.

861–62 / 801–2 *I myself . . . swing wide off the track . . . what the Laws allow* The reference to the *Laws* harks back to the power of desire a few lines before (858–59 / 797–98). Although the men of the chorus for the most part identify with the city and are, besides, intimidated by Kreon, they are moved by sympathy for Antigone, whom they see now led in for immuring in the cave, and so emotionally they veer beyond what they consider permitted by the laws. In describing the cave where she will be walled up to die as her *bridal chamber*, the chorus harks back to previous ode on the power of desire and the bride and also prepares for its lyrical exchange with Antigone, which is much concerned with her figurative "marriage" to Hades, god of the underworld.

866–941 / 806–82 This long lyrical exchange between Antigone and the chorus, technically known as a *kommos*, is one of the most emotionally intense passages of the play. Antigone sings in lyric meters, and the chorus replies in anapests and then changes to the more emotionally expressive lyric meters at **913–16 / 853–56** and **931–34 / 872–75**. Antigone, hitherto firm and courageous in her resolve to die for her loyalty to family, now expresses her grief at the prospect of death in her rocky tomb, which she describes as a negated bridal chamber. The contrast with the preceding ode on the power of desire, with its fleeting allusion to the "playful" side of love at the end, enhances the pathos of her situation. We are here reminded of the youth and vulnerability of Antigone as an orphaned young girl on the verge of marriage. Even the stern, civic-minded elders of the chorus are moved to pity (see note on **861–62 / 801–2**).

866 / 806 *Look at me, citizens of my native land* Characters in Greek tragedy often call attention to the way they are viewed by others, in part because of a self-consciousness of the play itself as spectacle, in part because of a sensitivity to being exposed to public humiliation in a "shame culture" in which one's appearance in society defines one's rank and the respect one has (compare our "saving or losing face," or the Italian "bella/bruta figura"). Close parallels occur at the beginning of Aiskhylos' *Prometheus Bound* and Sophokles' *Aias*. Antigone turns to the chorus as members of the city (*polis*), from which she now feels totally isolated. Here, as in her cry to the *polis* and its powerful citizens in **902–3 / 842–43** and in her final address to the chorus in **1005–8 / 937–40**,

Antigone can still regard herself as belonging to and having legal rights in the *polis*—another indication that the absolute dichotomy of individual and "state" does not completely fit her situation. It enhances the pathos that, despite this appeal to the citizens, she has not heard Haimon's report of their sympathy (747–55 / 692–700).

873–76 / 813–16 *I have no share . . . hymn of marriage . . . Akheron* Throughout her lyrical lament Antigone contrasts her "marriage to Death" with the marriage of which she is being deprived. Her present song of lamentation makes a poignant contrast with the songs that would have been sung at her wedding. Girls who died before marriage were said to be "brides of Hades," and Akheron, the river that leads to the underworld, here stands for Hades' realm in general. In fact, Greek tragedy often exploits an association between marriage and death, in part because of the pathetic contrast, in part because the young girl's removal from her house of origin to the house of her husband in this virilocal marriage system was perceived as separation and loss both to the girl and her family and so could be the occasion for lament. For extensive discussion of this motif, see Gail Holst-Wahrhaft, *Dangerous Voices: Women's Laments and Greek Literature* (London and New York, 1992) and Rush Rehm, *Marriage to Death* (Princeton, 1994). *Hymn of marriage sing me to my wedding* in 875–76 / 815–16 emphasizes the ritual songs of marriage that Antigone will never hear. In this play hymns of marriage are replaced by funeral "hymns" and by the chanting of curses, the latter in Eurydike's "hymns" of imprecation against Kreon as she dies in 1391–92 / 1305. See notes on 708–9 / 658–59, 1309–10 / 1226–27, and 1387–92 / 1301–5.

877–79 / 817–18 *Do you not go with glory . . . hidden?* The chorus harks back to Antigone's own earlier reasons for burying Polyneikes, but the glory she had hoped to win in the opening scene (see notes on 48–49 / 37–38, 87–90 / 72–74, and 114–15 / 96–97) seems less satisfying to her when she is on the point of death. Instead of looking to masculine, heroic values, she will reply with the example of a pitiable, maternal women. The shift to this more vulnerable and feminine mood increases the pathos and sense of tragic loss surrounding her. The chorus itself here vacillates between sympathy and disapproval. Hence, while it recognizes her claim to honor, it also criticizes her as *answering only to the law of [herself], autonomos* (the first occurrence of this word in extant Greek literature), that is, disobeying the laws (*nomoi*) of the city, to which the chorus feel primary allegiance. But in her speech of 495–518 / 450–70, Antigone regards herself as the champion not of her "own laws" but of laws of the gods higher than those of the city. Note also her complaint about the "laws" under which she dies in her lament at 907 / 847.

883 / 824 *pitiable Phrygian stranger* Antigone here compares herself to Niobe, daughter of Phrygian Tantalos and wife of Amphion, an earlier king of Thebes. Comparing her numerous children boastfully to the two children of Leto, Niobe is punished by Leto's children, the gods Apollo and Artemis, who kill all of hers, whereupon in her grief she is transformed into the stony form of Mt. Sipylos in Phrygia (now western Turkey). This stony sleep of death harks bark to the epithet of Hades as making *us all sleep* in the previous strophe (871–72 / 810–11, and compare 865 / 804). There are numerous points of contact with Antigone's story—the lament and particularly the comparison of Niobe's petrification and her own enclosure in the stone prison of her cave—but Antigone, childless and unmarried, dies in a contrast of tragic irony with Niobe's fate. Homer has Achilles tell the myth of Niobe in *Iliad*, 24.602–17, and there is a more detailed version in Ovid, *Metamorphoses*, 6.148–312.

899 / 839 *Ah, I am laughed at* With her sensitivity to insult at this vulnerable moment, Antigone interprets pejoratively the chorus's qualification of her comparison of herself to Niobe, although the chorus also recognizes, again, the special honor that she gains by her death (895–98 / 836–38). The Greek word for *laughed at* is also used at 602 / 551 (see note) when Antigone acknowledges her own mocking of Ismene.

903 / 844 *springs of Dirke* Dirke is the fountain of Thebes closely associated with the origins and life of the city; it is mentioned first by the chorus in the parodos (123 / 104).

906–7 / 847 *unlamented by any friends* This absence of friends (which, as often, here translates the word *philoi*, the intimate relations of the family) is exactly what Antigone tried to avoid for Polyneikes, at the cost of her life. The tragic irony enhances the pathos of her lament.

907–9 / 848–49 *the high-heaped prison . . . dreadful grave* There is some uncertainty about the text of these intricate lines, but the sense is clear. The accumulating words for piling up the earth and rocks for a grave all suggest various forms of imprisonment and burial and reinforce Antigone's growing horror of being entombed alive. See also 1175–76 / 1100–1101.

913–16 / 853–56 *Stepping ahead ... the throne of Justice ... some torment of your father's* Despite their previous sympathy, the chorus continues to interpret Antigone's suffering as both a crime against the laws of the city and as the result of an inherited curse. Their lines reflect again the different views of "justice" in the play (compare Antigone in **495–518** / 450–70 and see note on **1357** / 1270). As before, the elders may still be intimidated by Kreon. Antigone never accepts these accusations of wrongdoing or moral failure or weakens in her initial resolve (see **114–15** / 96–97). In fact, she responds with another defense of her actions in her last speech (**967–91** / 905–24). Here, as in their final response at **931–34** / 872–75, the chorus moves from anapests to more intense iambic meters, indicating a heightening of emotion parallel to the increasing intensity of Antigone's lament.

918–19 / 858–59 *My father's doom — recurring like the ploughing of a field three times* The text here is uncertain. We have adopted the plausible emendation of Lloyd-Jones and Wilson's Oxford Classical Text, reading *oitou*, doom, for *oikton*, the reading of the manuscripts. The latter would mean something like "the pity" or "pitiful situation" of the Labdakids (or, possibly, "the much repeated lamentation for Oidipous and the Labdakids"). Many editors accept the manuscript reading, but the emendation gives more natural syntax and a more plausible Sophoklean diction. Dawe prints the manuscript reading but adds in a note, "The construction of the words is not easily understood." Antigone here harks back to the much repeated theme of the accursed past of her family, developed at length in the second stasimon. *Like the plowing of a field three times* (literally, "thrice plowed") is a common metaphor for something gone over again and again; here the agricultural metaphor may imply the incest and other intra-familial crimes of the three generations of Labdakids: Laios, Oidipous, and the children of Oidipous. See notes on **61–71** / 49–57 and **633–77** / 582–630.

926–27 / 868 *having no other home but theirs* Antigone here echoes her phrasing at the end of the previous strophe (**911–12** / 852), *having no home with either the living or the dead*. The repetition, almost a refrain, evokes her emotional suffering as she recognizes, more and more fully, her isolation. The word used by Antigone for *having no home* (literally, "changing her home") here, as in **911–12** / 852 and used later by Kreon in **950** / 890, is *metoikos*, whose primary meaning for most Athenians would be "metic," that is, a resident alien. This daughter of the ancient royal house of Thebes has been so completely cast out by Kreon that she is now a "metic." Her language in **925–26** / 867 also points up her anomalous position as a "bride of Hades": instead of leaving her ancestral house as the bride of Haimon, who would, in the normal practice of virilocal marriage, take her from her house to his, she remains bound to the house of her parents, with its incestuous marriage and its accursed past. See Introduction, 29.

928–29 / 869–70 *marriage that brought doom* This refers to the marriage of the exiled Polyneikes to Argeia, daughter of the Argive king, Adrastos, who then supplied the army that attacked Thebes.

931–34 / 872–75 *To show reverence . . . power, in him who holds power . . . self-willed temper* The chorus again qualifies its sympathy for Antigone. They acknowledge her *reverence* for the dead, but they are mindful of the overriding fact of Kreon's *power* or control, and they end with an accusation of Antigone's willfulness, echoing their earlier criticism of her as answering only to her own laws (**881** / 821). "Self-willed" takes up the negative associations of "self-" in sufferings of the house of Oidipous (see notes on **1–2** / 1, **61–71** / 49–57, etc.). *Temper* echoes the first stasimon, **398–99** / 355–56, *temperament for the laws of the town.* If we are meant to recall that ode, we may be reminded of the contrasts between the achievements of intelligence that it celebrates and the passions that may destroy or threaten those achievements.

935–41 / 876–82 Antigone returns to her grief at her isolation from the "friends" or "dear ones" (*philoi*) who have been the chief concern of her life. The repetition of the word *philos*, "friend" or "dear one," in her first and last lines creates the effect of a refrain, like that on *metoikos* in lines **911–12** / 852 and **926–27** / 868. The repetition of themes and language throughout Antigone's lyrics in this section of the play not only emphasizes her intense emotions of loss and suffering but is also a characteristic feature of the kind of ritual lament that she is performing.

939–40 / 879 *see this fiery eye of heaven* Seeing the light of the sun is a frequent metaphor in Greek poetry for being alive, and bidding it farewell is also taking leave of the life-giving natural world that we share with all living creatures. The metaphor has special poignancy here because the mode of Antigone's death will be a literal enclosure in a dark place where she will never again see the sun. Contrast the chorus's joyful invocation to the rays of the sun on behalf of the city to open their first ode (**118–19** / 100–101).

942 / 883 *Don't you know . . . stop singing* The text has some uncertainties, but the general sense is clear. Kreon presumably returns to the stage as Antigone sings the last part of her lament (935–41 / 876–82), which he overhears. His callousness will return bitterly on his own head at the end, when he is the one to sing a lengthy lament.

944–50 / 885–90 *Take her off! . . . We're pure . . . house up here* The contrast between Kreon's harshness and the pathos of Antigone's preceding lament is heightened by the fact that he echoes some of her words about burial underground, isolation, deprivation of her dwelling "above," and her house in the underworld. Kreon supposes that he can maintain his and the city's ritual purity by not actually shedding her blood (see 836–38 / 775–76). Hence the change from the initial punishment by public stoning (see note on 46–47 / 35–36). Teiresias, however, will soon warn him about just this pollution for the city (1079ff. / 1016ff. and compare 1215–16 / 1141), and at the end Kreon will experience the terrible blood pollutions in his own house. See note on 1078–79 / 1015 and 1371 / 1284.

945 / 886 *wrap arms around her* Continuing the inversion of marriage and death, Kreon metaphorically makes the cave of doom "embrace" the bride of Hades. That figurative embrace, however, will be answered by Haimon's literal embrace of Antigone in death (see note on 1320–21 / 1237) and will give a deep irony to Kreon's claim of "purity." See the previous note and also note on 699–700 / 650.

954 / 894 *Persephone* Goddess of the underworld and bride of its ruler, Hades, Persephone is carried off as a maiden to the realm of the dead to wed Hades; she is a mythical model for Antigone. See Introduction, 28–30, and note on 926–27 / 868.

955–56 / 895 *the last of them* Here, as elsewhere, Antigone forgets about Ismene.

959–61 / 898–99 *loved by my father, loved by you, mother, loved by you, my own dear brother* Repeating the word of family affection, *philos*, three times in the Greek, Antigone calls attention to the values to which she has sacrificed her life. At the same time, the direct address to mother and brother conveys her intense involvement in these emotions.

961–62 / 901 *washed and laid out your bodies* In describing the funerals of her family members, Antigone refers here to the full rituals of preparing the body for burial: the washing and dressing of the corpse (which was generally done by the women of the family) preliminary to its lying in the house, after which it was carried in a funeral procession to the grave, where libations were poured. In the case of her own burial of Polyneikes, however, she was not able to wash the body, but could only pour out libations and sprinkle a covering of dust. See **281–82 / 245–47** and **290–91 / 255–56** and the notes on **472–76 / 427–31** and **1275–81 / 1199–1204**.

962–65 / 900–903 *with my own hands and poured libations . . . recompense* Listing the dead members of her family, Antigone here defines her family love, or *philia*, in terms of her performance of the funeral rites for them. Her address to Polyneikes by name (**964 / 902**) is the rhetorical climax of this statement of her devotion to family; see the previous note. Her statement that she has buried her father, Oidipous, implies the version that he has died at Thebes, not in exile; see note on line **3 / 2**. The phrase *with my own hands* is the single word *autokheir* in Greek, another compound of "self." Earlier in the play this word describes the double fratricide (see note on **1–2 / 1, 61–71 / 49–57, 193 / 172**, etc.), which was the subject of Antigone's opening speech; and it is Kreon's accusatory term for the perpetrator of Polyneikes' burial (**350 / 306**). It recurs later for the suicides of Haimon and Eurydike (**1249 / 1175, 1401 / 1315**), thereby connecting Antigone's action with these disasters and linking the sufferings of the house of Oidipous to the house of Kreon.

965–66 / 904 *those who have clear thoughts.* Antigone returns to her view of "good sense" or "right thinking," so different from Kreon's.

967–79 / 905–15 These have been among the most discussed verses in the play. Many editors regard them as a later interpolation, perhaps by an actor's company for later performance, and so delete them. Strongly in favor of genuineness, however, is the fact that the passage was known to Aristotle, who quotes some of the lines (*Rhetoric*, 3.1417a), although the quotation does not eliminate the possibility that the lines were added sometime in the late fifth or early fourth century BCE. Among the internal reasons alleged for viewing the lines as spurious are the apparent illogic of Antigone's argument and particularly her change of motivation for the burial from a defense of principles in **495–518 / 450–70** to a highly personal and intimate connection with the family. But to these objections it may be answered that Antigone has her own very emotional sort of logic, which now, at the point of her being led to her death, comes forth in the most personal terms. Of the external objections, the most important is Sophokles' echo of a story in Herodotos' *Histories*, 3.119. Here the wife of Persian nobleman named

Intaphernes, who has been caught in a conspiracy against King Dareios, uses a similar argument for choosing to save her brother rather than a son or husband. Those who delete the passage argue that an interpolator modeled it on this passage. But Herodotos, who was a friend of Sophokles, was writing and giving readings of his work as early as the 440s. Stephanie West, "Sophocles' *Antigone* and Herodotus Book Three," in *Sophokles Revisited* (Oxford, 1999), 109–36, has recently pointed out additional evidence for the priority of Sophokles (see note on 1104–5 / 1038–39). Sophokles, moreover, has adapted the Herodotean material to Antigone's situation and character in significant ways. Intaphernes' wife would save a living brother; Antigone is going to die to bury a dead brother. Whereas the Persian wife (whose name is never given) in Herodotos has the approved female role of throwing herself on the king's mercy in her mourning and lamentation, Antigone is not only facing death, but is in the role of the transgressive and defiant tragic figure. And of course her own life is at stake, as that of Intaphernes' wife is not. Finally, it should be observed that Antigone does hark back to her initial rationalization of her motives in her emphasis on a "law" that she is following (971 / 908, 976 / 914), in the issue of the "Justice of gods" that she is accused of "transgressing" (987 / 921; compare 495–501 / 450–55, 913–15 / 853–55), in her "daring to do terrible things" (979 / 914–15; compare 283 / 248, 494 / 449; also 413 / 371) and in her *defying the citizens* (968 / 907; compare 74 / 59). This last phrase, in fact, exactly echoes Ismene's refusal in the prologue (95–96 / 79) and so at this point is the measure of how far Antigone's transgressive piety has taken her.

978 / 915 *my own dear brother* Antigone directly addresses Polyneikes for the second time (compare 960–61 / 899) and uses the same expression (literally, "head of my brother") that she had used to address Ismene in her opening line (1–2 / 1). Now the address is entirely to the dead, and the living sister is forgotten: see note on 955–56 / 895.

985–86 / 920 *still alive to the cave of the dead* Antigone repeats her lament about being between living and dead from her previous lyrics (910–12 / 850–52); see note on 926–27 / 868.

987 / 921 *Justice of the gods* Antigone harks back to her speech of 495–518 / 450–70 (see note) and her view of a Justice opposed to that of Kreon. See note on 995–96 / 927–28.

991 / 924 *charges of irreverence* Antigone reiterates the motif of her paradoxical *holy crime* or "holy wrongdoing" in **87–90 / 72–74** (see note); see also **931 / 872.**

993 / 926 *through suffering would know* Sophokles is alluding to the familiar tragic motif (in Greek, *pathei mathos*), made famous by Aiskhylos' *Agamemnon*, 176–78.

995–96 / 927–28 *May the evils that they suffer be no more than what they are unjustly doing to me* Antigone means, of course, that they should suffer at least equal justice, and there is a bitter irony in this understatement. "She can imagine no worse fate," remarks Jebb. In Greek, "justice" is her last word in the speech (in the form of an adverb, *ekdikôs*, literally "in a way outside of justice"), but we should recall that "justice" in Greek (*dikê*) also implies the law of retribution. She has been "outside of justice" (compare **913–15 / 853–55**) in the eyes of the authorities, but she hopes they will find themselves in the same position, as in fact proves to be the case. In her last lines of iambic trimeter, like the hero of Sophokles' *Aias*, 835–42, Antigone thinks of vengeance. For all that she describes herself as sharing in loving rather than in hating (**574 / 523**), hers is no sweet and gentle nature. Greek popular morality (at least before Plato), in contrast to Christian, strongly endorses vengeance against those who have done one wrong.

997–1011 / 929–43 The chorus, Antigone, and Kreon have a short, three-way exchange chanted in the marching meter of anapests as Antigone, escorted by Kreon's guards, exits to her underground cave in a slow, solemn procession. Kreon continues to speak with brutal, unpitying harshness. Antigone is alone and aware of her imminent death (**1001–2 / 933–34**). Kreon himself probably begins to exit into the palace after his final commands at **1003–4 / 935–36**, while Antigone sings her final lament (**1005–11 / 937–43**). Some have argued that Kreon remains on stage during the following ode, the fourth stasimon, but this seems to us less likely; see note on **1050–1165 / 988–1090.**

997 / 929–30 *The same storms of her spirit* The metaphor of the storm for Antigone's passion associates her, in the chorus's mind, with what is wild, savage, and outside the city. The chorus used the same metaphor for the fury of Kapaneus' attack on Thebes (**155 / 137**). Compare also *the storms and gales* of the North Wind, Boreas, in the following ode (**1046 / 984–85**).

1004 / 936 *are not final* Kreon's language here shows his rigid legalism and insistence on his authority.

1005–11 / 937–43 *Oh city of Thebes . . . last, solitary member . . . reverent toward reverence* Antigone makes her final appeal not to Kreon but to the land, gods, and lords of Thebes, which again emphasizes the pathos of the isolation of one who belongs to the royal house and has sacrificed her life to what she regards as part of the justice that the polis should recognize (495–518 / 450–70). See notes on 866–941 / 806–82 and 866 / 806. She reiterates that she is the last of her house (compare 955–56 / 895), once more forgetting Ismene and harking back to the motif of the destruction of the entire family. Her last words, however, look to the gods, rather than men, and to the *reverence* for them that has brought her death. See note on 991 / 924.

1012–49 / 944–87 Fourth stasimon (fifth ode) The problems of this dense, difficult ode are exacerbated by some uncertainties about the text. The chorus, in highly poetic language, tells three myths, which seem meant as some sort of consolation for Antigone but may also have some relevance to Kreon. Once more, the chorus may say or imply more than it knows. The first myth is that of Danae, daughter of King Akrisios of Argos, who imprisons her in a tower of bronze to prevent her from conceiving a child who is prophesied to kill him. Zeus, however, visits her in a shower of gold and sires Perseus, who eventually fulfills the prophecy. The second myth is that of Lykourgos, son of Dryas, king of Thrace, who, like Pentheus in Euripides' *Bakkhai*, opposes Dionysos when the god arrives with his new cult. In a fit of madness sent by the god, Lykourgos thinks his son, Dryas (named after his grandfather, as is customary) is the god's hated vine and cuts him into pieces with an axe. Lykourgos is then imprisoned in a cave. The third myth, told in a particularly dense and allusive style, is also set in Thrace, at Salmy-dessos, on the Bosporos. King Phineus has two sons by his first wife, Kleopatra, daughter of Boreas, god of the North Wind, and Oreithyia, daughter of Erekhtheus, one of the early kings of Athens. Phineus divorces, kills, or otherwise maltreats Kleopatra and marries a second wife, who, like Kleopatra, is unnamed in this ode but is generally called Eidothea or Idaia. She blinds her two stepsons with her shuttle, and the ode ends by commiserating with the unhappy fate of Kleopatra, which befalls her despite her lofty ancestry.

How these myths relate to one another and to the play is a subject of considerable controversy. Both the Danae and Kleopatra myths mention the power of fate, or Moira, (1019 / 951 and 1049 / 987), and some commentators have taken this as the link among the three myths. Fate does not, however, play a role in Sophokles' account of Lykourgos here. Both the Danae and Lykourgos myths involve divine punishment, but it is not particularly prominent in the third. Imprisonment is also an obvious link between the Danae and Lykourgos myths, but it is not explicit in the Kleopatra myth, although in one version the children and perhaps Kleopatra, too, are imprisoned. Sophokles does refer to a cave, but it is the cave of Boreas where Kleopatra was raised. While the Danae myth best fits the situation of Antigone, the tale of Lykourgos, angrily opposing the gods, seems more appropriate to Kreon, particularly in light of the warnings by Teiresias that soon follow. Kreon also, like Danae's father, Akrisios, tries to interfere with sexual union. Moreover, both the Danae and Lykourgos myths result in disaster for the father-figure. The two bloodily wounded children of the Kleopatra myth may also foreshadow Kreon's loss of his two sons and the bloody suicide of his wife, Eurydike, at the end of the play. All three myths, like that of Niobe in 883–93 / 823–33, emphasize the high birth of the sufferer and so are appropriate to Antigone: Danae is *of much-honored descent* (1017 / 948), Lykourgos is *King of the Edonians* (1023 / 956), and Kleopatra is descended from the royal line of Athens (1044 / 982) and is also a *child of gods* (1047 / 986). Thus, the ode takes up and answers Antigone's final lament that she is *the last, solitary member of the royal house* (1008–9 / 941).

All three myths also involve violent deaths within the family (particularly if the Lykourgos myth is taken to imply his insane killing of his son) and so would be relevant to the houses of both Antigone and Kreon. Conceivably, all three myths may also reflect different views that the chorus has of Antigone: she is cruelly imprisoned, like Danae; she is carried to violent excess, like Lykourgos; and she is a victim of human cruelty, like Kleopatra and her sons. But, more generally, the myths, taken together, exemplify the cruelty that family members can inflict on one another. Also, the agents and the victims include both men and women. In their concern with sexuality, anger, passion, and vengeance, moreover, all three myths are reminders of the violent and irrational forces in life that will soon break apart Kreon's apparently rational control of his world. The ode thus continues an undercurrent that runs through the previous two odes, on the curse on the house of Oidipous and on the power of Eros, respectively, and again contrasts sharply with the optimistic humanism of the Ode on Man.

1015 / 949 *Oh child, child* The chorus again expresses sympathy for Antigone but, as before, is careful to qualify this in their subsequent reference to *the power of fate.*

1019–20 / 951 *fills us with terror and awe* The chorus uses the same word, *deinon* (meaning both *terror* and *awe*) that described the ambiguous capacities of humankind in the first stasimon (377 / 332).

1029–31 / 962–65 *women quickened by the god . . . fire of Dionysos; that god's Muses* This refers to the maenads (literally "mad women") who are inspired by Dionysos and dance in torch-light processions in his honor. See note on 1221–24 / 1149–52. The Muses, nine daughters of Zeus and Mnemosyne (Memory), are goddesses of song, dance, and poetry, often closely associated with Dionysos.

1032–34 / 966–71 *indigo waters of two seas . . . neighboring land, Ares* The region described is the Thracian Bosporos, the narrow channel separating what is now European from Asian Turkey, connecting the Sea of Marmara (the ancient Propontis) with the Black Sea, which are the "two seas" here mentioned. Salmydessos is a Thracian city on the Black Sea, on the European side of the Bosporos and slightly to its northwest. The area is Ares' *neighboring land* because Ares, god of war, is often associated with Thrace and the warlike Thracians. There are some textual corruptions in the opening lines here. The manuscripts contain the problematical word "rocks," which, with many editors, we delete. Editors who retain "rocks" in some form take it to refer to the so-called Dark Rocks in this area, mentioned by Herodotos. They are traditionally identified with the "Clashing Rocks," or Symplegades, guarding the entrance to the Black Sea, through which Jason and the Argonauts had to pass.

1038 / 975 *Beaten blind* The chorus here uses the same verb that described Oidipous' self-blinding in the prologue (62 / 52) and in the self-blinding of Oidipous himself in the *Oidipous Turannos.*

1044 / 982 *Erekhtheids* This ancient family of the kings of Athens is named after their ancestor, Erekhtheus, who is the father of Kleopatra's mother, Oreithyia.

1046 / 985 *Boreas* As the god of the north wind, Boreas is associated with Thrace. He sweeps Kleopatra's mother, Oreithyia, off to Thrace, where Kleopatra is then raised in his cave dwelling.

1048–49 / 986–87 *on her, too, the Fates . . . pressed hard, Oh child* As in the case of the Danae, above, the chorus expresses sympathy and consolation to Antigone by invoking the inevitability of fate and by calling her "child."

1050–1165 / 988–1090 The scene between Kreon and Teiresias, the old prophet of Thebes, brings into the foreground the gods and the forces of nature through which the gods act on the human world. Gods and forces of nature have hovered in the background, but now move more threateningly into the foreground. Kreon presumably reenters abruptly from the palace at the news of Teiresias' arrival, although (as with all the details of staging) this is not completely certain. He says nothing about having come out from the palace at **1053 / 991**, but this first, sharp question, *What news do you have?*, can also indicate his arrival just when the seer's sudden presence makes the new situation seem urgent. This scene closely parallels the three previous scenes. Each one contains a test or trial that challenges Kreon's authority. After the obsequiousness of the chorus at his entrance, Kreon first confronts the Guard, with the first news of the burial; then Antigone, who immediately defies him, and, third, Haimon, who starts out by professing obedience but ends in bitter hostility. Teiresias' entrance marks the first time that Kreon confronts an older man and one who can claim an authority equal to or greater than his.

1054 / 992 *and you will obey the seer* Like other old men in Sophokles, notably the Teiresias of the *Oidipous Turannos*, the aged Oidipous of the *Oidipous at Kolonos*, and Telamon, father of Aias, in the background of *Aias*, Teiresias is accustomed to being obeyed and does not easily brook opposition. Teiresias' early statement here of his authority prepares us for the outcome of his conflict with Kreon.

1056 / 994 *captained this ship of a city rightly* Teiresias echoes the nautical imagery with which Kreon described his rule in his first speech (**182–83 / 162–63, 212–13 / 189–90**), but in a very different tone that suggests the limits of Kreon's initial confidence and egotism.

1057 / 995 Literally, "By my own experience [or, suffering] I have cause [am able] to bear witness to (your) useful (things)." The Greek grammar suggests that Kreon means he himself has experienced Teiresias' "useful things/ benefits" and can testify to them. If there is an allusion here to Teiresias' having prophesied the need for Kreon's other son to die for Thebes (as in Euripides' *Phoinikian Women*), the phrase "by my own experience," *peponthôs*, perfect participle of the Greek verb *paschein*, could have its other meaning of "suffer" and not just the neutral "experience." Sophokles, however, may be alluding to a somewhat different version of the myth. See notes on 1127 / 1058 and 1387–92 / 1301–5.

1058 / 996 *fortunes stand once more on the razor's edge* A common expression in Greek literature for being at the edge of extreme danger. The word "fortunes" here translates the Greek *tukhê*, "chance," often an important term in Greek tragedy, indicating the uncertainties of mortal life. Teiresias' prophecy is fulfilled in the Messenger's heavy emphasis on just these vicissitudes of "fortune" when he begins his account of the catastrophe, 1229–30 / 1158–59. Compare also Eurydike's "chance" exit from the house at 1256 / 1182 (see note on 1255–61 / 1182–86).

1060–62 / 998–1000 *signs of my craft . . . bird-divining* The ancient Greeks, like the ancient Romans, practiced divination through the movements and cries of birds in the sky.

1063–64 / 1001–2 Literally, something along the lines of "noise as they screamed a barbarous cry, stung by some awful madness." Teiresias, as befits a prophet, speaks in grandiose language. His expression, *barbaric maddened gibber-jabber*, refers to the unintelligible speech of non-Greeks, whom the Greeks called *barbaroi*. The word suggests that in the present crisis the communication between gods and mortals through the language of bird signs has become ominous and dangerous. The whole phrase conveys the utter strangeness and horror in the cries of these birds that Teiresias has been listening to all his life

1071–75 / 1006–11 *instead, the fatty thighbones . . . lay exposed . . . covered them* Teiresias' description shows the disorder in the natural world through the motif, common in tragedy, of corrupted sacrifice. The thighbones of the sacrificial animal (in this case, presumably an ox) were wrapped in fat and placed on the altar and burnt with incense. Teiresias' language also echoes a word used to describe the rotting corpse of Polyneikes in 454 / 410 and so suggests a causal connection between the body that should have been put beneath the earth in reverence for the gods below and these offerings whose fragrant smoke should have mounted to the heavens in prayer to the gods above. Instead, the fire smolders, the fat fails to burn and runs downward, and what reaches the heavens is the bitter gall as it explodes upward. The Greek syntax in the description of the dripping thighbones might evoke a macabre image of the fat of the bones turning into a wet slime.

1078–79 / 1015 *from your thinking . . . the city is sick* Kreon's legalistic attempt to avoid pollution in the bloodless killing of Antigone rebounds on the city in a much larger and more dangerous form. Such a pollution (*miasma*) is felt to be a kind of infectious disease that can bring plague, sterility, and death to the city and its environment. See notes on 467 / 421, 944–50 / 885–90, and 1371 / 1284.

1080–81 / 1016–18 *food brought by the birds and dogs . . . son of Oidipous* Teiresias recalls the descriptions of the exposed corpse of Polyneikes in both Antigone's and Kreon's early speeches in the play (31–38 / 26–30, 233–35 / 204–6). Now, however, the fearful results of that exposure are becoming visible on the plane of divine action. By referring to Polyneikes by his patronymic, he also evokes the curse on the house of Oidipous.

1085–86 / 1022 *eaten the blood-streaked fat* The language recalls the chorus's description of the bloodthirsty attack on Thebes by Polyneikes and his army in 139 / 121–22 and Kreon's description in 227–28 / 201–2. Now, however, the tasting of Theban blood has taken on a different meaning as the threat to the city has shifted from outside to within, from the attackers to the ostensible defender.

1086–89 / 1023–26 *Know this . . . ill-advised . . .* Teiresias takes up the "good sense" or "wise counsel" that Kreon has claimed for himself against the folly of Antigone.

1092–93 / 1027–28 *He will not move. Stubbornness . . . botching things* Teiresias' advice about the dangers of inflexibility recalls the warnings of Haimon in 768–77 / 710–17. *Stubbornness* implies a self-will that resembles that of Antigone. The accusation of ineptitude or stupidity must be particularly infuriating to Kreon, who prides himself on his logic and intelligence.

1098 / 1032 *your profit* Teiresias reiterates this dominating preoccupation of Kreon, but takes it in a direction that will soon enrage the ruler; see note on 1102–5 / 1035–39.

1099 / 1033 *you all, like archers* Kreon may be thinking of the previous mutterings against him. See 747–55 / 693–700 and note on 333–38 / 289–92.

1102–5 / 1035–39 Kreon's language of profit, trade, and mercantilism repeats his suspicions of bribery and conspiracy; see 252–53 / 221–22, 354–59 / 310–14,

508–10 / 461–62, 1098 / 1032, 1130 / 1061, 1132 / 1063, and notes on 1116 / 1047 and 1409 / 1326. However, Kreon will soon be put on the defensive.

1104–5 / 1038–39 *gold from India* Stephanie West (see note on 967–79 / 905–15), 113–14, has plausibly suggested that this reference to Indic gold is indebted to Herodotos' *Histories* (3.94.2), as India is not generally mentioned as a source of gold.

1107–12 / 1040–44 *eagles of Zeus . . . fear of pollution . . . power to stain the gods* Kreon's hyperbole puts him on dangerous ground, particularly as he touches so scornfully on the serious matter of pollution. With characteristic confidence, he presupposes a clear separation between human and divine realms and identifies the gods with his own policies. In what follows, however, his confidence about limiting and controlling pollution—like his confidence about controlling Hades and Eros—proves ill-founded; see Introduction, 31–32. For his cavalier way of dismissing Zeus, see notes on 348 / 304 and 535–38 / 486–87.

1116 / 1047 Kreon ends his tirade by repeating his accusations of profit from 1103 / 1037 and his recurrent suspicions of monetary gain and bribery. See note on 1102–5 / 1035–39. Oidipous' accusations in *Oidipous Turannos*, 532–42, mine this theme for similar effects.

1125 / 1056 Teiresias takes up the criticism of Kreon's autocratic behavior raised by Antigone and Haimon earlier and turns the charge of greed back on the king.

1126 / 1057 *your sovereign* In Greek, this is the rare and archaic-sounding *tagos* (found only here in Sophokles' extant plays). Kreon perhaps uses it to emphasize his power and perhaps also to neutralize the pejorative associations of Teiresias' "tyrants" just before (both words are generalized by being in the plural).

1127 / 1058 *It was through me that you have saved this city* This assertion may allude to Teiresias' prophecy that only the blood of one descended from the original Theban Planted Men could save Thebes; see notes on 1057 / 995 and 1387–92 / 1301–5.

1133–34 / 1064–65 *complete many swift courses of the racing sun* The prophecy of tragic doom coming in terms of days, or a single day, is a recurrent motif in Sophokles (e.g., *Aias*, *Trakhinian Women*, *Oidipous Turannos*);

see note on 1189–90 / 1113–14. Kreon's doom will come within a few hours.

1135 / 1066 *your own gut* The Greek word is used more commonly of the mother's "womb" rather than the father's "loins." Antigone uses a form of it to describe her brother as born *from the same womb*, in 562 / 511. Kreon has hitherto treated the realm of marriage and generation with scorn. Now, rather than producing a living child, Kreon's male "womb"—his male way of being—will figuratively produce the death of his living child.

1138–39 / 1069 *dishonorably compelling her, a human spirit* The Greek for *human spirit* is *psukhe*, which may also suggest "shade" and so points to the ambiguity of Antigone's present position between living and dead at this point, as she lamented in her last lyrics. It is part of Kreon's violation of the order of things that he has made her a "shade" when she is still alive and in the upper world. The word "dishonorably," Greek *atimôs*, has a wide range of associations. It implies Kreon's harshness to a member of the royal family (and his own family), his "dishonoring" of the gods, and probably also, as Griffith suggests, his "disenfranchisement" of Antigone, that is, her loss of civic rights. But it can also include her loss of the rites and honor of a proper burial.

1141 / 1070 *body with no share of the gods* The text is uncertain here and has often been emended to something like "no share of offerings" or "of rites." Alternatively, *of the gods* may be construed with "those below" in the previous line ("one of those who belongs to the gods below"), though this disturbs the parallelism with "someone from here above" just before. In that case, "rites" or some such word would be understood with the phrase "with no share."

1142–44 / 1072–73 Another difficult and much discussed passage: the meaning seems to be that the burial of the dead belongs neither to Kreon nor to the gods of the upper world, but that the latter have nevertheless suffered "violence" or outrage from the pollutions of the human carrion that the birds and dogs have carried to their altars (1079–86 / 1016–22). Hence the Furies mentioned in the subsequent lines (1145–47 / 1075–76) avenge the gods of both the lower and upper worlds.

1145–46 / 1074 *late-destroying* Teiresias uses a grandiose compound of which the first part evokes the old, archaic (and tragic) idea that the gods may be slow to punish but are inexorable. The suggestion that Hades has its "avengers" (here identified with the Furies) gives a darker meaning to Kreon's scornful references to Hades earlier (see note on **495–518** / 450–70 and **838–42** / 777–80; compare also **352** / 308) and points toward the peripeteia, or reversal, in his circumstances. The Furies are dread goddesses of the underworld and always evoke horror, particularly here, where their epithet suggests their inexorable pursuit and punishment of their victims.

1146–47 / 1075 *who avenge Hades* Hades stands here collectively for the gods of the lower world, whose Justice Antigone had invoked in her defiant speech of **495–518** / 450–70. Teiresias, however, says nothing specific of Antigone, though she seems to be clearly implied in **1136–38** / 1068–69. The silence about her name has the effect of making Kreon's punishment appear as part of a broad reaction of Sophokles' characteristically remote gods to a disturbance in the balance of nature rather than as revenge for a human crime against a particular individual.

1150–51 / 1078 *Time will test my mettle* We try to keep a word play in the Greek, as the word for "time" here can mean "delay" and but also "rubbing" to test true metal and distinguish it from false. Thus it continues the motif of *given silver* in the previous line, which literally means "covered over with silver," as if the bribery of Teiresias were analogous to making false coinage, that is, false prophecy. With slightly different punctuation and consequently different syntax, the lines can also mean, "much wailing of men and women—and there will be no long delay of time—will reveal (these things) to your household."

1153–58 / 1080–83 Some editors place these lines after Teiresias' earlier description of the pollutions of the cities ending at **1086** / 1022, and others delete them as spurious or suggest that a line or two has dropped out before them. The lines, however, are in keeping with the widening scope and mounting authority of Teiresias' prophecy. Sophokles here seems to be alluding to a version of the story told in Euripides' *Suppliants*, in which Kreon refuses to bury the fallen Argive attackers and is then forced to do so by the armed intervention of the Athenian king, Theseus. As part of Athenian patriotic lore, the allusion would be easily recognized by Sophokles' audience. This "burial" by *dogs, beasts, and wingèd birds of prey* is to be understood ironically: the only "burial" of the corpses has been in the bellies of these scavengers. Gorgias of Leontini, a contemporary sophist and rhetorician, called vultures "living tombs." The Greek has a single verb for *have purified in burial* in **1155** / 1081, for which the manuscripts offer two variants, *kathêgnisan* or *kathêgisan*.

The former contains the root of the word for "pure," *hagnos*, in the sense of "make pure by (proper) burial" or "sanctify," and so would continue the motif of "purity" and pollution in the play. This reading is supported by the fact that Sophokles uses other forms of this verb in 220 / 196 and 596 / 545. With the majority of editors, therefore, we read *kathêgnisan*. The verb *kathêgisan* means "consecrate by offerings" or "dedicate," and is explicitly associated with burial only in later writers. On the other hand, this latter reading finds some support in the fact that the same root occurs in 282 / 247, *kathagisteuein*, literally "avoiding pollution," in the context of burial.

1159 / 1084 *like an archer* Teiresias throws back at Kreon his own metaphor accusing prophets at 1099–1100 / 1033–34.

1170ff. / 1095ff. For the issue of "giving way" or "yielding" in Kreon's character see 521ff. / 473ff., 729–34 / 677–80, 771–77 / 712–17, 1093–94 / 1029–30, 1177 / 1102. Teiresias describes Kreon's "unyielding" temperament as *stubbornness* in his warning at 1092 / 1028. "Giving way" in general is a major test of the Sophoklean hero, and the true hero, like Aias or Elektra or Antigone here, does not give way. See in general Knox, *Heroic Temper*, chapters 1 and 2.

1174 / 1099 *I will obey* Kreon's assent recalls Teiresias' insistence that he obey, at the beginning of the scene (1054ff. / 992ff.), but now Kreon is in a very different mood. This is the first time that he eagerly asks for advice, and also the first time that the chorus takes a forceful initiative in suggesting it in the following lines.

1175 / 1100–1101 *Go send the girl up* The word *anes* here may recall the Eleusinian myth of Persephone and her *an-hodos*, or road upward, when her mother, Demeter, secures her temporary liberation from Hades. The hope of restoring Antigone to the upper world, however, is to prove futile. See note below on 1195 / 1120 and Introduction, 28–29. The chorus's description of Antigone's underground tomb echoes earlier language, of Kreon himself at 834–35 / 774 and of Antigone at 907–09 / 848–49.

1179 / 1103–4 *Bringers-of-Harm.* This is another allusion to the Furies. See notes on 647–50 / 598–603 and 1145–46 / 1074.

1183–90 / 1108–14 Kreon's instructions imply that he will send his attendants to bury Polyneikes while he simultaneously will go to set Antigone free. In the

Messenger's subsequent narrative, however, it appears that Kreon first accompanied his attendants to Polyneikes and only afterwards went to liberate Antigone (1271–83 / 1196–1205)—a delay that may have been fatal for all concerned. His emphatic *I . . . myself* in 1186–89 / 1111 implies his acceptance of responsibility for his punishment of Antigone, but at the end of the play he will also have to accept the more agonizing responsibility for his *foolish heedlessness* and *foolishness* (1347–56 / 1261–69) when his intended rescue of Antigone fails and recoils back on himself.

1189–90 / 1113–14 *I am afraid it's best to observe the established laws through all one's life, to the end* At this point of reversal, Kreon seems to recognize, too late, an area of "law" apart from his authority in the city. The phrase could suggest those "unwritten laws" that Antigone invoked at 495–518 / 450–70 and that Kreon dismissed. *Through all one's life, to the end* carries an ominous ring in tragedy, which often emphasizes how uncertain is the final end of a human life. Kreon here looks to the completion of a more or less normal life, whereas Teiresias framed his prophetic warning in terms of a cycle of days (1133–34 / 1064–65), and this is in fact fulfilled at the end as Kreon experiences the tragic reversal of his life in a single day (1412–15 / 1329–32), as often happens in Sophoklean and other tragedy (e.g., *Aias*, 753–57, *Oidipous Turannos*, 438, 1283). We may recall also the "one day" of the fratricidal deaths of Polyneikes and Eteokles (19 / 14, 69–71 / 55–57, 190–91 / 170–71). The contrast between the respective exits of Kreon and Antigone is striking: he leaves the stage yielding, as she does not, and his final words are about his fear, whereas hers were about her *reverence*.

1191–1224 / 1115–54 Fifth stasimon (sixth ode) This ode of supplication, the last ode of the play, summons Dionysos, patron god of Thebes, to come to his birthplace and save his city by warding off the *disease* of pollution about which Teiresias has just warned (compare 1215–16 / 1140–41). The ode is an important part of the structural design of the play, for it answers the parodos, the first ode, which ends with Dionysos and nocturnal ritual (171–74 / 152–54). Now, however, joyous thanksgiving gives way to anxious prayer, civic choruses in the temples within the city change to a figurative chorus of fiery stars in the heavens, and citizens are replaced by the frenzied female worshipers of Dionysos (1218–24 / 1146–52).

1191 / 1115 *God of many names* Greek gods typically have many epithets to denote their different functions or different local cults, and it is important to address the deity by the appropriate name. So here the chorus invokes Dionysos, in hymnic fashion, by referring to several of his places of worship.

1191 / 1116 *Glory of the young wife* Semele, daughter of Kadmos, is the mother of Dionysos by Zeus and gives birth to him prematurely when Hera, Zeus's Olympian wife, tricks her into asking Zeus to show himself to her in his full divine glory. She is killed by his lightning, but Zeus saves the infant. The myth, told at length in Euripides' *Bakkhai*, is the basis of Thebes' special claim on Dionysos.

1192 / 1115 *Kadmos* The founder of Thebes, Kadmos is the father of Semele, Dionysos' mother. See note on 144 / 126.

1193 / 1119 *Italy* The worship of Dionysos was especially popular in the Greek colonies of Sicily and southern Italy (Magna Graecia, or Great Greece, as it came to be called), which was also noted for its wine production. Some have seen here a possible indication of particular Athenian interest in the area with the founding of its colony, Thurioi, in 443/442. The suggested emendation to "Ikaria," a village northeast of Athens famous for its worship of Dionysos, is unnecessary.

1195 / 1120 *Eleusinian Demeter, shared by all* Dionysos, in the cult form of Iakkhos (the last word of the ode in Greek at 1224 / 1152), has an important place in the rites of Demeter at the panhellenic sanctuary of Eleusis, on the southern outskirts of Athens. The rites are open to all who undertake initiation (hence *shared by all*) and promise to the initiates a blessed life in the hereafter. Demeter is here paired with her daughter, Persephone, and in fact the rites (which were kept secret) gave a prominent place to the myth of the latter's rescue from Hades by her mother. Both the promise of return from Hades and of some kind of personal salvation that mitigates the pain of death stand in ironic counterpoint to the events of the play. See note on 954 / 894 and 1175 / 1100–1101, and also Introduction, 28–29.

1196 / 1121 *Bakkhos* This epithet of Dionysos is used especially in connection with his role as wine god and with his ecstatic cult of frenzied processions and dances.

1197 / 1122 *Thebes, mother-city of the Bakkhai* Thebes is the birthplace of Dionysos (see note on 1191–1224 / 1115–54) and therefore is a place where the

Bakkhai, the female worshipers of the god in his dances and processions, have special prominence.

1198 / 1124 *Ismenos* This river flows through Thebes.

1200 / 1124–25 *Savage serpent's teeth were planted* See note on **144 / 126**.

1201–5 / 1126–30 *pine torches . . . double peak of rock . . . Korykian nymphs. . . . Kastalia flows down* Sophokles here refers to an important aspect of the Theban cult of Dionysos. His *Bakkhai,* or female worshipers, honor the god in a nocturnal procession every other year on the heights of Mt. Parnassos, above Delphi, accompanied by torches, ecstatic dances, and the tearing apart of wild animals. The *double peak* refers to the twin crags prominent above Delphi, known as the Phaidriades, which these processions pass. In these upland plateaus of Parnassos is also the cave sacred to the Korykian Nymphs, who are closely associated with the god and are here imagined as accompanying these nocturnal processions. The spring of Kastalia flows down from these heights to Delphi below. Its water is sacred and was thought to bring poetic inspiration.

1205–8 / 1131–33 *ivy slopes of Nysaian hills send forth . . . coast rich with grapes* More cultic details of Dionysos: Nysaian hills refer to Nysa, a mountain sacred to Dionysos located variously in Egypt, Italy, Asia Minor, and Thrace. The ivy, because of its deep green, curling vine, is associated with the god's vital energies and vegetative power, and the grape (with its vines) belongs to Dionysos as god of wine. The Greek verb for *send forth* (*pempei*) connotes an escort or ritual procession (*pompê*), and Dionysos is often depicted on contemporary vases as arriving in such processions, escorted by nymphs and satyrs. The figurative use here makes it seem as if the god leads his own Dionysiac landscape in such a procession.

1208–9 / 1134–36 *immortal followers cry out the Bakkhic chant* Sophokles is using a verb that means to "utter *euoi*," the cry of the Bakkhants in their excited worship of Dionysos. Dionysos is himself sometimes referred to as "the Euian one," the god worshiped by the shouts of *euoi!* The word *followers* is a widely accepted emendation for a Greek word meaning "songs," "verses," "chants" in the manuscripts, which some editors accept. To have "songs cry out the Bakkhic chant," however, seems redundant; and *followers* suits the idea of a Bakkhic procession here; see the previous note.

1211–13 / 1139 *Your mother, she who was struck by lightning* Semele gives birth to Dionysos amid the lightning flashes of Zeus's majesty; see note on **1191 / 1116**.

1215–16 / 1140–41 *Disease . . . the city . . . and all its people, come cleanse us* The chorus calls on Dionysos to bring an end to the pollution caused by the unburied corpse of Polyneikes, which both is a "disease" and also may be the fearful cause of diseases; see notes on **467 / 421** and **1078–79 / 1015**. The pollution, or *miasma*, is feared as a kind of infectious stain or filth that needs "cleansing." The present anxiety undercuts Kreon's earlier confidence about avoiding pollution; see note on **944–50 / 885–90**. Note too the contrast with the confidence in the human power to overcome disease in the Ode on Man (**405–6 / 363–64**). Scattered references to Dionysos as healer occur in the ancient sources; this is the earliest. In the Greek, our wording *come cleanse us! Stride . . .* is literally "come with cleansing foot," which may be a reference to the cathartic effect of ecstatic Dionysiac dance, given the emphasis on ecstatic dancing throughout the ode; see Scott Scullion, "Dionysos and Katharsis in *Antigone*," *Classical Antiquity* 17 (1998), 96–122. As Griffith notes re: Greek lines 1140–45, "*katharsis* can be painful." Kreon discovers this for himself: see note on **1371 / 1284**.

1217 / 1144–45 *slopes of Parnassos . . . moaning narrows* Dionysos would come to Thebes either from the west via Parnassos and Delphi, where he is worshiped, or from the northeast across the narrow channel of the Euripos, which lies between the mainland of Boeotia and the island of Euboea.

1218–20 / 1146–48 *Lead the dance of the stars . . . the voices sounding in the night* This beautiful and remarkable image projects into the night sky the dances of Dionysos and his worshipers in their nocturnal processions on earth. The Dionysos who watches *over the Sacred Ways of Thebes* at the end of the previous antistrophe (**1210 / 1135–36**) now extends his presence to vast cosmic distances. This shift from the city to the heavens parallels the shift from the nocturnal processions of joy in the parodos to these more remote, figurative choruses of fiery stars at a time of anxiety; see note on **1191–1224 / 1115–54**.

1221–24 / 1149–52 *show us Your Presence . . . Bakkhantic Nymphs . . . frenzied dance* Dionysos often makes his appearance in sudden, unexpected, spectacular ways, and the Greek verb here, *pro-phanêthi*, implies a request for such a Dionysiac "epiphany." These female worshipers and attendants of Dionysos accompany the god in his processions and share the madness or "frenzy" of his ecstatic dances; see notes on 1196 / 1121 and 1201–5 / 1126–30 The word translated as "Bakkhantic Nymphs" is the Greek *Thyiades*, women or nymphs caught up in the ecstatic worship of Dionysos, from a verb meaning to "rush or leap furiously." Sophokles offers his own implicit gloss in the following phrase, "frenzied dance," where "frenzied," or "maddened," *mainomenai*, evokes the more familiar term, *mainades*, maenads, literally "maddened women," although the Thyiades here are probably to be thought of as nymphs rather than mortal women. Though Dionysos is here invoked as a savior god of the city, the reference to the Dionysiac madness continues the mood of mounting emotional violence that begins with the second stasimon and continues in the erotic subject of the third. It also resumes the theme of Dionysiac madness in the story of Lykourgos, who attacked the god's female followers in the fourth stasimon (1022–31 / 955–65).

1225–1342 / 1155–1256 The sixth episode constitutes the reversal or peripeteia of the play. The chorus's hopeful prayer for help and release from pollution in the preceding ode is immediately answered by the wrenching events of the Messenger's speech and by the accumulating pollutions in the house of Kreon. Sophokles often exploits this sharp contrast, notably in *Aias*, *Oidipous Turannos*, and *Elektra*. The following scene has been carefully arranged so that the Messenger reports the events not merely to the elders of the chorus, whom he addresses in his opening line, but also to Eurydike, wife of Kreon and mother of Haimon, who enters at **1254 / 1180**. She has not previously been mentioned and may well be Sophokles' invention (see note on **1255–61 / 1182–86**). Her response then leads directly into the final catastrophe and the final blow to Kreon's life.

1225–26 / 1155 *live near . . . both Kadmos and Amphion* The Messenger addresses the citizens of Thebes (and particularly the Theban elders of the chorus) in terms of the founders of the city—Kadmos who slew the dragon that guarded Thebes' sacred spring (see note on **144 / 126**), and Amphion, who built the walls of Thebes by causing the stones to leap into place through the magical power of his lyre, thereby resembling Orpheus in the power of his music over the natural world.

1229–30 / 1158–59 *Fortune . . . the fortunate and unfortunate* Such generalizations on the precariousness of human fortunes are common in messenger speeches and indeed in tragedy generally. The fourfold repetition on the root of the word for "fortune" or "chance" here, *tukhê*, reinforces the point. See notes on 1058 / 996, 1255–61 / 1182–86, and 1292 / 1213.

1231 / 1160 *things that stand established* The sense seems to be that no one can foresee how long the present circumstances can last for mortals. The phrase harks back to Kreon's obedience, too late, to the *established laws* in 1190 / 1114.

1235–36 / 1163 *absolute command* The Messenger means this as a compliment, but it also recalls Kreon's too absolute view of his authority; compare 194 / 173 and 796–99 / 736–39.

1237 / 1164 *seeds of noble children* The phrase echoes Haimon's still gentle attempt to persuade his father in 760–61 / 703, and so reinforces the Messenger's contrast here between Kreon's previous prosperity and his present precarious situation.

1238–39 / 1165–66 *when a man's enjoyment betrays him* The text is somewhat uncertain, but the general sense is clear. A variant reading, with weaker manuscript authority, would give the sense, "When men betray (i.e., abandon or lose) their pleasures"; another would give "When pleasures betray (abandon) men." We follow the majority of the manuscripts in reading *a man's enjoyment* (literally, "pleasing"), with the singular *man's*, which is supported by the scholia and better fits the specific application to Kreon. This hedonistic statement is revealing for the degree to which the Greeks view human life in terms of enjoyment or pleasure, in contrast to mere biological existence. The Messenger's generalization (which should not necessarily be identified with Sophokles' own philosophy) doubtless reflects popular sentiment. Brown aptly cites a fragment of Simonides, "Without pleasure what life of mortals or what absolute rule is desirable?"

1242 / 1169 *live in the style of a king* The tyrant, who rules by his own authority and without being responsible to other authorities, is the model of the happy life. Yet "tyranny" may also carry ominous associations of absolute power.

1249 / 1175 *bloodied by a hand close to him* The second half of this line, *autokheir haimassetai*, literally, "self-handed he was bloodied," plays on the two Greek words of which it consists. *Autokheir* can refer either to killing by one's own hand (so later in 1401 / 1315, of Eurydike's suicide) or by a kindred hand. In the latter case, Haimon's death is assimilated to the fratricidal deaths in Antigone's house (e.g., **71** / 56), an association re-inforced by the "self-" language of the Messenger's reply in **1251** / 1177. The verb "spilled the blood," *haimassetai*, also plays on the name of Haimon, as if his destiny is foreshadowed in his name. Greek literature is fond of this kind of false etymology, e.g., Pentheus and penthos, "grief," in Euripides' *Bakkhai*.

1255–61 / 1182–86 *She comes... by chance... I chanced to loosen... the bolts* By calling attention to Eurydike's "chance" arrival, Sophokles perhaps in-dicates that her presence as the recipient of the Messenger's narrative is not part of the traditional tale but is his own invention. She does not occur in any earlier extant version of the myth. "Chanced" in **1260** / 1186 repeats the same root as the word "chance" in **1256** / 1182 (*tukhê ... tungkhanô*). See notes on **1058** / 996 and **1229–30** / 1158–59.

1259 / 1184 *Pallas* Pallas Athena, major Olympian goddess, daughter of Zeus, is an appropriate divinity for a woman to supplicate. Offering such prayers of supplication would be one of the reasons for women to leave the house. Compare Iokaste's emergence from the house in *Oidipous Turannos* (911–23) to pray to Apollo.

1266 / 1191 *as one who has lived through adversity* This may hint at the death of Kreon's elder son; see notes on **673** / 626–27 and **1387–92** / 1301–5.

1267–70 / 1192–95 The Messenger's promise of an accurate account assures the ve-racity of what follows but also proves to be fatal for Eurydike.

1271–1328 / 1196–1243 The Messenger relates the deaths of Haimon and Antigone. Greek tragedy rarely shows scenes of violence on stage but prefers to narrate them through a messenger's speech, as here. The ancient au-dience was accustomed to the oral performances of the Homeric poems and of choral song and so, one imagines, would enter fully into the story. This is one of the most powerful such speeches in Greek tragedy. It completes the motif of Antigone's "marriage in Hades" and marks the reversal in Kreon's fortunes, from power and prosperity to help-lessness and misery. Four narrative devices contribute to its effective-ness: (1) the tenses shift back and forth between past and present as the Messenger begins the account of the encounter between father and son at **1285ff.** / 1206ff.; (2) the quotations in direct discourse make this encounter very vivid; (3) the sequence of events is clear and rapid; (4) Sophokles keeps the emphasis on the interaction between father and son but does so in a way that reveals its fully tragic character. Though the Messenger reports Kreon's words to his son, all verbal communication fails. Haimon refuses to answer and instead replies only with silent, violent gestures, culminating in his bloody embrace of Antigone's corpse as he dies. (See also note on 1401 / 1315.)

1271–83 / 1196–1205 On Kreon's change from his earlier intention first to rescue Antigone and then to bury Polyneikes, see note on 1183–90 / 1108–14.

1275–81 / 1199–1204 This account of the formal burial of Polyneikes not only gives closure to the motif of the unburied corpse; it also gives him the full rites of burial that Antigone could perform only in part. The culminating detail is that the tomb is formed by a *mound for burial straight and true.* Compare the first account of the burial in 290–91 / 255–56, where the Guard specifically states that the body was *not covered with a mound.* See note on 472–76 / 427–31. At the same time both the completed ritual and the visible mound contrast with the perverted "funeral" ritual of Antigone, buried out of sight in an underground chamber. See note on 962–65 / 900–903.

1283 / 1205 *bridal crypt of Hades . . . floor of rock* In the fusion of marriage and funeral Antigone's bed is in a stony cave/tomb instead of bridal chamber.

1291 / 1212 *Am I a seer?* Kreon's reference to prophecy here fulfills his earlier unknowing foreshadowing of the tragic events in the play, notably his description of Antigone as a "cold embrace" for Haimon, 699–700 / 650.

1292 / 1213 A *path that's more unfortunate* This echo of the word for "fortune" or "chance" puts into Kreon's own words the Messenger's initial generalization about the reversal of his situation; see note on 1229–30 / 1158–1159.

1296 / 1216 *fitted stones* We keep the manuscript reading, *harmon* (lit. "joint," "fitting"). The passage is difficult. Lloyd-Jones and Wilson emend to *agmon,* with the sense, "the gap made by tearing away the stones." Dawe supposes that some lines have dropped out after this verse. The cave presumably has a mound of earth and stones at its entrance, perhaps blocking the passageway into a Mycenaean chamber tomb or *tholos,* as Griffith plausibly suggests, which has been reused for this purpose. In any case, the entrance, or mouth, would have been sealed with piled up earth and a loose "fitting" of stones, which (as we subsequently learn) Haimon has "torn away" to open his access.

1298–99 / 1217–18 *hearing . . . the gods are tricking me* Kreon's fear introduces the important motif of communication (see note on **1271–1328 / 1196–1243**) and also admits the possibility that the gods may not be entirely on his side and that he may not understand their actions.

1302–3 / 1222 *noose tied of fine-woven linen* Wedding and funeral again come together, as the description suggests a veil, used in both marriage and burial ceremonies.

1305–8 / 1224–25 *bed . . . marriage* Both of these words in the Greek mean both *bed* and by metonymy *marriage*. Some editors have therefore suspected that the second line is an interpolation. Although Haimon does not mention Antigone by name, the *bed* can also stand by further metonymy for the bride. The *spoiling* or "corruption" of the bed (and bride) is soon answered by the spoiling or ruin of Haimon himself (i.e., of his sanity, as Kreon fears in **1310–12 / 1228–30**), and then by Haimon's suicide.

1309–10 / 1226–27 *moaning . . . wailing cries* Lamentation engulfs this family, as it had Antigone's, and it will continue in Eurydike's lament later.

1310–11 / 1228–29 *You desperate boy . . . in your mind?* Kreon's exclamation here can indicate both disapproval (of Haimon's "reckless" or "desperate" behavior) and compassion. Though Kreon's cry might at first be understood as possibly addressed to the dead Antigone, the context makes it clear that he is thinking entirely of his son.

1314–15 / 1232 *spits in his face* Perhaps this is an ironic reversal of Kreon's paternalistic urging of Haimon to "spit out" Antigone as an enemy in **702 / 653**.

1316 / 1233 *two-edged* The adjective can also mean "double-hilted," which some interpreters prefer.

1318 / 1235 *furious at himself* Combined with the silence, the spitting, and the drawn sword, the phrase indicates the total breakdown of communication between father and son, as well as Haimon's wild passion.

1320–21 / 1237 *wraps the girl in the weak crook of his arm* See notes on **699–700** / 650 and **945** / 886. The figurative "embrace" of Antigone by her tomb has now become an actual embrace, but both acts fuse marriage and death.

1327–28 / 1242–43 Messengers in tragedy often end their narratives with similar generalizations on the human condition.

1330 / 1245 *without a word* Eurydike's silent exit, which resembles that of Iokaste in *Oidipous Turannos* and of Deianeira in *Trakhinian Women* at analogous crises, continues the motif of silence and failed communication in the Messenger's narrative. The Messenger and chorus immediately reflect on the meaning of this silence (**1337–42** / 1251–56).

1334–35 / 1247–49 *But in the shelter . . . among her servants* Literally, "will not utter forth/cry forth her cries (*goous*) into the city, but rather beneath (the shelter of) her house will bring forth her private (literally, belonging to the house, *oikeion*) grief to her servants." Women in fifth-century Athens were not expected to lament in public, and the mourning for warriors killed in battle was taken over by a public ceremony at which the chief magistrate pronounced a funeral oration. In the most famous extant example of such funeral orations, Perikles' speech in Thucydides' *History of the Peloponnesian War*, 2.34–46, Perikles says that a woman's reputation consists in being least talked about among men "either concerning excellence or blame" (2.45.2). Sophokles heavily overdetermines the contrast between house and city by the repetition "under her own roof / in private," as the latter word, *oikeion*, means, literally, "belonging to the house," *oikos*.

1343–1431 / 1257–1353 The final scene, or *exodos*, of the play begins with another *kommos* (see note on **866–941** / 806–82), an emotional exchange largely in lyric meters, between Kreon and the Chorus. Kreon enters in what is essentially a funeral procession, either carrying (or more probably supporting with attendants) the body of Haimon. If the body is represented by a dummy of some sort, it is possible to understand *in his arms* (**1344** / 1258) literally, but it is perhaps more likely that the corpse is carried or wheeled in on a bier by his attendants. This arrangement is perhaps suggested also by the chorus's words at **1365** / 1279 (literally, "These things you hold before your hands") and would make the actor's task easier. But there would obviously be a more graphic pathos if Kreon is actually carrying the body in his arms. Conceivably, he enters

carrying the body and is then relieved of it by attendants, as **1383–84 /
1297** implies. The carefully balanced antiphonal responsions between
single mourner and chorus throughout this scene evoke the ritual of
burial that often concludes Greek tragedies. The finales of Euripides'
Andromakhe and *Women of Troy* offer close parallels. Comparable too
are the funeral procession at the end of Sophokles' *Aias* and the entrance of Kadmos with the mutilated body of his grandson, Pentheus,
at the end of *Bakkhai*.

The shift to song and song meters here marks a strong shift of tone
after the long Messenger's speech. This last entrance of Kreon contrasts
with the energy he displays earlier when confronting Teiresias, at
1050ff. / 988ff. So forceful and confident before, Kreon is now a broken
man, and this radical change is indicated in part by his singing for the
first time in lyric meters, the emotional rhythms of dochmiacs (essentially syncopated iambics). His only previous utterances outside of the
dialogue meter of iambic trimeter were his short anapestic exchanges
with Antigone at **999–1000 / 931–32, 1003–4 / 935–36**. The lyrical *kommos* not only shows his changed relation to those around him but also
harks back to the lyrical laments of Antigone with the chorus just before
she is led off to the cave.

1344–45 / 1258–60 *conspicuous sign . . . a memorial, his own ruin* This now answers
the previously absent or "unclear" or "unintelligible" signs, e.g., the
marks of burial at **287 / 252**, the cries of the birds of omen at **1060–67
/ 998–1004**, and the shout from the cave in **1288–89 / 1209–10**. Haimon's
body, on the stage, is now both the visible "sign" of Kreon's "ruin" and
its concrete, physical embodiment.

The word translated as "ruin," *atê* (**1345 / 1260**), also means the "infatuation" or "madness" that leads up to the ruin. That is, it refers both
to the subjective mental disposition that caused the disaster and to the
objective result, the disaster itself; see note on **671–72 / 624–25**. In the
former sense, Haimon's body now makes tangible Kreon's inner disposition, which has led him to this terrible moment. So understood,
these lines can also be seen as a kind of metatheatrical discourse, calling attention to the drama's ability to reveal, in visual "signs" on stage,
the invisible causes of the tragic events in the emotional and moral
behavior of the characters.

Kreon's vocabulary here also seems to echo that of the Athenian
funeral speech or *epitaphios logos*, a public discourse pronounced over
fallen warriors at a state funeral in the fifth century (see note on **1334–
35 / 1247–49**). If so, there is a deep irony because Kreon is lamenting
a private, not a public loss, and his son did not die heroically for the

city, like his brother Megareus (see note on **1387–92** / 1301–5), but because of a wild, individual passion for a girl condemned by the city. This "illustrious memorial" would also suggest both a parallel and a contrast to the "glorious bier" of the dead Megareus (if that is the correct reading) in **1387–92** / 1301–5.

1345 / 1260 *His own ruin—no one else's* The chorus, which previously has mentioned "ruin," *atê*, in general terms (**661** / 614, **671–72** / 624–25), now attributes it specifically to Kreon. This does not mean that Antigone has not contributed to the disaster, but not through the kind of "infatuation" that *atê* here implies.

1357 / 1270 *recognize what justice is, too late* The chorus implicitly validates Antigone's claim to justice in her defiant speech to Kreon in **495ff.** / 450ff. and reverses its view of Antigone's "stumbling against the throne of Justice" in **914–15** / 854–55. The chorus also acknowledges the retributive justice for which Antigone prayed in what were almost her last words, **995–96** / 927–28.

1363 / 1276 *burden . . . exhausting burden* The Greek word *ponos* means "pain," "suffering," "effort," "toil," etc., and has earlier been used for Antigone's acceptance of the "burden" of burying Polyneikes (**52** / 41, **967** / 907) and for the guards' "task" of enduring the stench of Polyneikes' rotting corpse (**458** / 414). The phrasing here, with its bleak repetition of "burdens," expresses Kreon's utter despair. His language uses the same lyricism of the dirge that had characterized Antigone's final laments.

1364ff. / 1277ff. The final blow to Kreon comes from the news of Eurydike's death, brought by the Messenger. The staging probably made use of the *ekkyklêma*, a low platform wheeled out from the central door of the scene building, which represents the royal house of Kreon. Thus we are reminded both of the play's opening scene, when Antigone and Ismene stand before that door, and of the increasingly domestic and personal nature of a catastrophe for one who had placed city over house.

1368 / 1282 *mother absolute* For *pammêtor*, literally, "the all-mother" (a single word in the Greek), there is no easy English equivalent. It conveys the sense of the wholly devoted mother, the mother in the very fullest sense of the word, the one who defined herself as totally mother and so feels most keenly the loss of a son, whose death she does not survive. The juxtaposition with *nekrou*, corpse, adds pathos. She is now mother only of a dead son and so has gone from all-mother to no-mother. This highly poetical word recurs elsewhere as an epithet of Earth or of the venerable Rhea (mother of Zeus and Hera) as the "mother of all." In its evocations of a universal maternity, both divine and human, the epithet may also recall the female goddesses of death and rebirth, Persephone and Demeter, in the background, or the ever-grieving Niobe of Antigone's lament after the second stasimon, or the mourning mothers of the fourth stasimon. See Introduction, 29–30.

1371 / 1284 *Harbor of Hades, never to be purified* In contrast to his earlier confidence about avoiding pollution for the city (944ff. / 885ff.), Kreon finds a pollution in his own case that he cannot "cleanse" or "purify." See notes on 1078–79 / 1015 and 1215–16 / 1140–41. The metaphor of his own house as a "harbor of Hades" also contrasts with his previous nautical imagery (182–83 / 162–63, 212–13 / 189–90) and with his use of Hades (death) as an instrument of his own power (e.g., 352 / 308, 838–42 / 777–80). See notes on 495–518 / 450–70 and 559–74 / 508–23. Antigone, meanwhile, has invoked Hades as the divine authority for her insistence on burying Polyneikes (e.g., 570 / 519).

1376–79 / 1289–92 *Of what new killing . . . piled on top of death* The Greek is very dense here. The last element of the total collapse of Kreon's ordered world is that this death at an altar (*bômia*, 1387 / 1301) is a kind of perverted ritual of sacrifice, as *sphagion* literally means "sacrificial victim." The altar here, moreover, is presumably that of *Zeus Herkeios* — the household shrine of Zeus who protects the family — which Kreon had so confidently scorned in his condemnation of Antigone; see note on 535–38 / 486–87. That a woman should kill herself in so agonizing a way adds to the horror (see note on 1401 / 1315).

1380 / 1293 *See her* For the probable use of the *ekkyklêma* here to display Eurydike's body, see note on 1364ff. / 1277ff.

1383–84 / 1297 *Only now I held my son in my arms* If Kreon did enter actually carrying the body, he has now put it down or it has been taken by his attendants. See note on 1343–1431 / 1257–1353.

1387–92 / 1301–5 These lines present a number of textual and interpretative problems. The manuscripts are divided between assigning the speech to the chorus or the Messenger, but the latter is far more likely. At least one line has dropped out after 1387 / 1301, which does not make a complete sentence and in any case is corrupt. We have adopted a plausible emendation for 1387 / 1301 and have added a possible version of one missing line. The lost verse or verses presumably described Eurydike's approach to the altar and gestures preliminary to stabbing herself. In 1390 / 1303 the manuscripts read "dead Megareus' glorious bed," or perhaps "glorious bier," which most editors emend either to "glorious lot" or to "empty bed," both readings involving the change of a single letter of the Greek. Sophokles seems to be referring to a version of a story found in Euripides' *Phoinikian Women*, in which Teiresias tells Kreon that only the willing sacrifice of a descendant of the original Theban Planted Men can save Thebes from the Argive attack (see note on 1057 / 995). In that play, Kreon's son, there called Menoikeus (after Kreon's father), hurls himself off the wall into the Serpent's den and so saves Thebes. In the version that Sophokles seems to be following, Eurydike (rightly or not) seems to blame Kreon for Megareus' suicide, so that he is the killer of both his sons—Haimon in the immediate present ("this son") and Megareus. (In Euripides' version, Kreon, a much more sympathetic character, puts family ahead of city and tries to forestall his son's possible death.) But if Sophokles is following this version of the Theban legend, Megareus' death presumably must have been fresh, i.e., during the Argive attack, and so Sophokles has carefully kept it in the background. There are a few passing hints earlier; see notes on 673 / 626–27, 1127 / 1058, 1266 / 1191. If we keep the manuscript reading, "glorious bier" could refer to the honor of Megareus' patriotic self-sacrifice. We have, however, accepted the emendation "empty bed" for a number of reasons. Syntactically, it suits the following reference to Haimon's equally "empty bed" (although the possessive genitive of the manuscripts is also sometimes emended to the accusative, "looks to the bed and to this [other] one, Haimon"). "Empty bed" would also reflect Eurydike's grief at the loss of both of her sons' future marriages and so reinforce the parallel with Antigone. This interpretation is supported by the way it echoes Antigone's lament over Polyneikes like a mother bird *when she finds that her nest and bed are empty* (*orphanon lekhos,* 469–70 / 425) and by the fact that Antigone, like Eurydike, "curses" the perpetrator (473 / 427). We are reminded too of "the unfortunate bed" of Antigone over which Haimon groans and wails in 1305–8 / 1224–25. Yet both the reading and the exact sense of 1390–92 / 1303–5 remain obscure.

1395–96 / 1309 *two-edged sword* Literally, a "double-whetted sword," this is sharp on both edges. Kreon now takes up and applies to himself the Messenger's description of Eurydike's *sharp-edged blade* at 1387 / 1301.

1398 / 1312 *charged by the dead woman* The language is that of Athenian legal ter-
minology and may be an ironical reflection on Kreon's legalistic frame
of mind earlier in the play.

1400 / 1314 *torn away from us* Kreon repeats the verb he used for the death of Haimon at 1355 / 1268, thereby linking the two deaths.

1401 / 1315 *With her own hand . . . below her liver* The liver may be used here in a
general sense for the abdominal region, but it may also be intended as
the specific organ, as the liver is considered the seat of the passionate
emotions. This particularly bloody and painful death bears out the Messenger's language of a murderous sacrificial slaughter at 1387ff. / 1301ff.
and 1368–69 / 1282–83. Like Antigone herself, women in Greek tragedy
usually commit suicide by hanging (e.g., Iokaste in *Oidipous Turannos*). Deianeira's suicide in Sophokles' *Trakhinian Women*, who stabs
herself through her side "downward toward her liver and chest," is
another exception. Seneca's Jocasta, in his *Oedipus*, stabs herself in the
womb, a gruesome variant characteristic of that author. *With her own
hand*, in Greek *autokheir*, is the last occurrence of these "self-" compounds in the play, and it marks the climax of the destruction and
passion turned against oneself or one's family. The word was last used
of Haimon in 1249 / 1175. The whole passage has echoes of Haimon's
lament and suicide in 1305–8 / 1224–25 as well as of Antigone's lament
and curses over Polyneikes' body at 467–73 / 422–28. In the destruction
of Kreon's house, father and son and husband and wife communicate
in terms of murderous gestures rather than intimate communication.
Haimon does not answer his father's words (1313–15 / 1231–32), and
Eurydike exits from the stage in silence. Haimon spits in his father's
face before killing himself, and Eurydike calls down curses on her
husband at her death (1391–92 / 1305). Sophokles thus links the death
of Eurydike with the deaths of Antigone and Haimon as the steps that,
in retrospect, form the sequence leading to Kreon's destruction.

1402 / 1316 *sharp wailing* Literally, "when she learned this (present) sharp-bewailed
suffering of her son." The *sharp wailing* leads to the *sharp-edged* knife
of her suicide (1387 / 1301). There is a lot of "sharpness" here at the
end (also 1395–96 / 1309), which adds to the atmosphere of violence
and suffering. Is there tragic irony in the contrast between this sharpness and the chorus's exultation in the metaphorical *sharp bit* that
saved Thebes in the parodos (127 / 108–9)?

1408 / 1325 *no more than nothing* These words represent the climax of Kreon's utter spiritual and literal annihilation. The phrase takes up and fulfills, on stage, the Messenger's introduction to Kreon's disaster in 1240–45 / 1167–71: *a dead man who can still draw breath . . . the shadow of thin smoke.* Sophokles is fond of this figure of the tragic life as reduced to "nothing": e.g., *Oidipous Turannos,* 1186–88, *Elektra,* 1165–67, *Philoktetes,* 1018, 1217.

1409 / 1326 *profit* This is the last and most devastating iteration of what had been Kreon's obsessive preoccupation. See note on 1102–5 / 1035–39.

1420 / 1337–38 *destined for mortals . . . no deliverance* Greek tragedies often end with such moralizing generalizations by the chorus (as also in its final lines below on "teaching good sense"), but they constitute only one attempt to grasp the meaning of these devastating events, and not necessarily the most profound. See note on 1427–31 / 1349–53.

1421 / 1339 *Lead me away* This small touch subtly marks once more the total inversion of power and weakness at the end of the play, for such was Kreon's command regarding Antigone in 833 / 773 and 944 / 885.

1424 / 1342–43 *I do not know which one to look at* Like Eurydike in 1389–91 / 1303–4, he is divided between two sources of agony.

1425 / 1344–45 *everything is twisted* This completely overturns Kreon's earlier confidence in his ability to "direct" and keep his city "upright" or "right" (*orthos,* literally "straight") in his first speech (e.g., 182ff. / 162ff., 686ff. / 639ff.).

1427–31 / 1348–53 As the chorus chants its final moralizing song, Kreon leaves the stage, led away by his attendants, as he has twice requested (1406–8 / 1321–25, 1421 / 1339). In the Greek performance, we do not know what was done with the bodies of Haimon and Eurydike. They might have been left on the stage as the visible evidence of the tragic waste and loss, or they might have been carried back into the palace, or carried with the chorus as they exit after their final song, or possibly carried off with Kreon as he exits, as members of the house that he has destroyed. The final lines mention a number of important themes in the play: *good sense,* disrespectful actions toward the gods, excessive or boastful speech, and the contrast between the old and the young. As often in Greek tragedy, such gnomic closure offers a measure of continuity and communal solidarity after disorienting, chaotic violence. At the same time, the tendentious moral only points up the discrepancy between the tragic events and the construction of a rational, coherent world-order. *Happiness*, in 1428 / 1348 here, seems very far away; none of the major characters has shown *good sense*; Antigone has died for her *reverence*; and the young victims will have no chance to learn *in old age*. Whatever Kreon may yet learn as he grows old seems beside the point amidst the completeness of his destruction now.

APPENDIX 1. THE DATE OF *ANTIGONE*

The only external evidence for the dating of *Antigone* is a statement in the ancient Argument attributed to the Hellenistic scholar Aristophanes of Byzantium and prefixed to the play in the manuscripts. Thanks to the success of *Antigone*, the Argument reports, Sophokles was elected one of the ten generals to serve in the Athenian war against the revolt of the island of Samos, an important member of the Athenian naval empire. The Samian revolt took place in 441–439 BCE, and the connection of the play with it, even allowing for exaggeration, would suggest a date in 442 or 441. As the elections took place in late spring, *Antigone* would have been first performed at the great festival of Dionysos in March 442 or 441. The connection between the generalship and the play, however, may be the invention of the often unreliable biographical tradition and may mean only that the play was performed sometime around 440, plus or minus a few years. Some scholars, therefore, for various reasons, have preferred a slightly later date. There is no absolute certainty, but a date in this period would suit the play's style and dramaturgy, and it is widely accepted. In any case, the play seems to belong to Sophokles' full maturity. Born in 496/97, he would have written it in his mid-fifties, after he had been presenting plays at the dramatic festivals for some thirty years, since his first victory in the dramatic competitions in 468. The play would be about a decade earlier than the *Oidipous Turannos* (429–425), with which it shares certain features (e.g., an angry encounter between a king and a prophet and the silent exit of a queen to commit suicide).

APPENDIX 2. THE MYTH OF ANTIGONE, TO THE END OF THE FIFTH CENTURY BCE

The story of Oidipous and his children is referred to in Homer and was told in a number of epic and probably lyric poems of the seventh and sixth centuries BCE, of which only sparse fragments survive. We know very little of the story of Antigone herself prior to Sophokles. The ancient sources report various versions, many of uncertain date, no one of which exactly tallies with Sophokles' version.* It is uncertain whether Sophokles is the first to have Antigone sacrifice her life to bury her brother. It is probable (but by no means certain) that the framing of the conflict between Kreon and Antigone, her and Haimon's deaths in the cave, and the figure of Eurydike are Sophokles' inventions. The dramatists always felt free to add new details and to interpret the story in their own way. Euripides' lost *Antigone* of 431, for example, probably ended with Dionysos as deus ex machina rescuing the heroine from death.

Sophokles' most important predecessor is Aiskhylos, whose *Seven against Thebes* was performed in 467, and is the only surviving play of a trilogy that included *Laios* and *Oidipous*. Echoes of Aiskhylos' language suggest that Sophokles has *Seven against Thebes* in mind at several points.

Seven against Thebes dramatizes the events that immediately precede the action of *Antigone*—that is, the conflict between the two sons of Oidipous, Eteokles and Polyneikes, for the throne of Thebes. Eteokles, the defender of the city against his brother's army from Argos, puts a Theban warrior in command at six of the seven gates to defend them

---

*For a brief survey of the ancient evidence see J. C. Kamerbeek's "Introduction" to his commentary, 1–5; Griffith's introduction, 7–12 (full bibliographic citations at the beginning of the Notes, 117); also my *Tragedy and Civilization*, 190, with notes 111–14 on 449 (see Suggestions for Further Reading).

against seven captains of the Argive attackers, and he places himself at the seventh gate, where the two brothers kill each other in battle. *Seven against Thebes* ends with a lament over the two fallen brothers, which editors variously attribute to the chorus, divided into two halves, or to Antigone and Ismene. At this point a herald enters and announces the decree to the leaders of the city not to permit the burial of Polyneikes. Antigone states her determination to bury him, and the manuscript ends with the two half choruses divided in allegiance between Antigone and the city's leader's, respectively. In contrast to Sophokles' play, *Seven against Thebes* does not mention Kreon, nor does it isolate Antigone.

Unfortunately, there is considerable controversy about how much of this ending is due to Aiskhylos and how much may have been a later addition under the influence of Sophokles' own play. The issue remains unresolved. If the ending of *Seven against Thebes* is in fact by Aiskhylos, Sophokles has shifted the emphasis from Aiskhylos' central themes of inherited guilt and the family curse to the conflict between Antigone and Kreon and her heroic defiance of the latter's authority.

Some fifteen or twenty years after *Antigone*, Euripides' *Suppliants*, dated to the late 420s, uses a doubtless early version of the story, in which Kreon refuses burial to all of the Argive dead and not just to Polyneikes. This Athens-centered version has no place in it for Antigone. Here the Athenian king, Theseus, heeding the supplications of the mothers of the fallen warriors, finally compels Kreon to bury them. Sophokles seems to be alluding to this version in lines 1153–56 / 1080–83 of *Antigone*.

By the end of the fifth century BCE, Sophokles' version of the myth, with Antigone at its center, is familiar. In the *Phoinikian Women* of 409, Euripides tells the story of the two brothers' death at Thebes differently, but he ends with Antigone, who leads the old Oidipous into exile. The last scene includes her dialogue with Kreon, in which she defies his decree of exposing Polyneikes' corpse in a stichomythia that obviously echoes Sophokles' (1646–68); and she tells Oidipous of her determination to bury her brother even if it means her death (1745–46).

Sophokles himself returns to Antigone at the very end of his life in his *Oidipous at Kolonos*, composed some thirty-five years after *Antigone* and produced posthumously. This play, set at Athens in the last days of the aged Oidipous' life, is a "prequel" to *Antigone*. The father curses both his sons, predicting their death. After failing to dissuade Polyneikes from what will prove to be his fatal expedition against Thebes, Antigone at the end decides to go back to the doomed city and try to prevent the two brothers from killing one another. Although the ending says nothing about the burial of Polyneikes or Antigone's death, Sophokles clearly has his earlier play in mind.

APPENDIX 3. THE TRANSMISSION OF THE TEXT

Antigone, along with the six other extant plays of Sophokles (out of over a hundred that he wrote), survives primarily in numerous Byzantine manuscripts, ranging in date from the tenth to the fifteenth centuries CE. There is, therefore, a period of some 1,500 years between Sophokles' original text and our earliest manuscripts. In some cases the manuscripts can be supplemented by quotations or comments in other classical authors (themselves transmitted in medieval manuscripts) or occasionally by papyrus fragments preserved from Hellenistic and Greco-Roman Egypt, generally dating from the third century BCE to the fifth century CE. In the case of Sophokles, however, we are dependent mostly on the Byzantine manuscripts. The first printed edition appeared from the celebrated Venetian printing house of Aldo Manuzio (Aldus Manutius) in 1502.

Before reaching the medieval manuscripts, these texts (like those of most classical Greek authors) were copied, edited, and recopied numerous times. This process resulted in numerous errors or corruptions. Later scribes often made mechanical errors or misunderstood and hence miscopied the text because an earlier script was unfamiliar or because they did not fully grasp Sophokles' dense poetic vocabulary and syntax, especially in the choral odes. It used to be assumed that the earliest manuscripts were the most reliable (especial the tenth-century manuscript designated as L and now in the Laurentian library in Florence), but even these have many errors, and recent research has shown that good readings are to be found in a much wider range of manuscripts.

Since the Renaissance, classical scholars have worked intensively to restore the text to something like its original form through comparative study of the manuscripts and through close critical examination of Sophokles' language and meaning. The process still continues. In numerous passages, and not only in the odes, editors and translators have to choose among variant readings in the manuscripts or among the conjectures and emendations of modern scholars for passages that are clearly wrong in the manuscripts. Although no two modern editors agree on all parts of the text, there is a wide consensus on much of it, embodied in the editions of Jebb, Dawe, Lloyd-Jones and Wilson, and (most recently) Griffith (see beginning of Notes, 117). We have not followed any single edition and have indicated our choices for some of the most controversial passages in the Notes.

GLOSSARY

AKHERON: River in Epirus in northwestern Greece, supposed to lead to the Underworld. Popular etymology connected it with the Greek word *akhos* ("woe") as the "river of sorrow."

AMPHION: Early mythical king of Thebes, who helps build the city by the power of his magical lyre that causes the stones to leap spontaneously into their places in the walls. He is the husband of Niobe (q.v.).

ANTIGONE: Incestuously born daughter of the former king of Thebes, Oidipous, and his wife (and mother) Iokaste, and sister of Ismene, Eteokles, and Polyneikes (qq.v.). She is betrothed to Kreon's son, Haimon (q.v.).

APHRODITE: Olympian goddess of love. Often regarded as the mother of the god Eros, the personified force of erotic desire.

ARES: Olympian god, son of Zeus and Hera. The god of war, he is often imagined as violent and destructive and so is associated by the early Greeks with Thrace and the warlike Thracians.

ARGOS (ADJ., ARGIVE): Major city of northern Peloponnesos and the ally of Polyneikes (q.v.) in his attempt to overthrow his brother, Eteokles (q.v.), and win back the throne of Thebes.

ATHENA: See PALLAS.

BAKKHAI: Female worshipers of Dionysos (q.v.), particularly in the excited, ecstatic dances and processions that form a part of his cult.

BOREAS: God of the north wind, whose abode is in Thrace (q.v.). He carries off the Athenian princess Oreithyia to be his wife, by whom he has a daughter, Kleopatra, who marries the Thracian king Phineus (q.v.).

BOSPOROS: A narrow channel in Thrace separating what is now European from Asian Turkey and connecting the Sea of Marmara (ancient Propontis) with the Black Sea.

DANAE: Daughter of King Akrisios of Argos, who, learning of a prophecy that her child will kill him, imprisons her in a tower of bronze. Zeus, however, visits her in a shower of gold and fathers Perseus, who eventually fulfills the prophecy.

DEMETER: Olympian goddess of the fertile earth, of the harvest, of crops, particularly grain, and of fertility. She is the mother of Persephone (q.v.) by Zeus. When her daughter is carried away by Hades to be his queen in the Underworld, Demeter brings her back to the upper world for part of the year by withholding crops until Zeus accedes to her demand. This story forms part of the background to her cult at Eleusis (q.v.), her major place of worship in Athens.

DIRKE: A famous spring at Thebes where Kadmos, first king of Thebes, killed a huge serpent guarding the water, and thereby founded the city. See also KADMOS.

DIONYSOS: Divine son of Zeus and the Theban princess, Semele, he is a complex and multifaceted god, associated with wine, fertility, festive dance and song, the mask, and drama, but also with madness and ecstasy. He is often dangerous and vengeful in establishing his cult among those who resist him. He is frequently represented in processions of wildly dancing, ecstatic nymphs or women, his maenads (*mainades*, literally, "mad women"), sometimes escorted also by satyrs and wild animals. His rites at Thebes included nocturnal torchlight processions of women on nearby Mount Parnassos (q.v.). In another cultic form, as Iakkhos (q.v.), he is sometimes associated with the Eleusinian goddesses of fertility, rebirth, and the afterlife, Demeter and Persephone (qq.v.).

DRYAS: Son of King Lykourgos of Thrace. Lykourgos refuses to accept the cult of Dionysos (q.v.) and, in revenge, the god drives him mad so that he thinks his son is Dionysos' vine and chops him into pieces with an axe. In some versions, this act of bloodshed causes a plague, and Lykourgos is then imprisoned in a cave.

EDONIANS: Warlike Thracian people northeast of Greece, in the area of modern Bulgaria.

ELEUSIS: Town south of Athens, the site of the Eleusinian Mysteries, an important cult in honor of Demeter and Persephone (qq.v.) offering hope of a happy afterlife to those who were initiated into the rites at special ceremonies that were kept secret. The cult, though localized at Eleusis, was open to all and attracted initiates from all over Greece.

EREKHTHEIDS: Royal family of Athens, descended from the early king; Erekhtheus.

ERINYES: See FURIES.

EROS: Personification of the power of erotic desire. Sometimes regarded as the son of Aphrodite (q.v.).

ETEOKLES: Incestuously born son of the former king of Thebes, Oidipous, and his wife (and mother) Iokaste, and brother of Antigone, Ismene, and Polyneikes (qq.v.). He holds the throne of Thebes after the death of Oidipous and dies in a mutually fratricidal battle with Polyneikes at one of the seven gates of Thebes.

EURYDIKE: Wife of Kreon and mother of Haimon and his brother Megareus (qq.v.).

FURIES: Dreaded vengeful deities of the Underworld. They particularly punish crimes of bloodshed within the family, and they often drive their victims mad.

HADES: God of the Underworld and husband of Persephone (q.v.), who shares his subterranean throne and his realm. He is often used as a synonym for death and for the Underworld, which the early Greeks imagined as a grim shadowy place for the lifeless shades of men and women after death. Hades the god shares the world with his brothers Zeus, the god of the sky, and Poseidon, the god of the sea.

HAIMON: Surviving son of Kreon and Eurydike and betrothed to Antigone (qq.v.).

IAKKHOS: A youthful divinity, closely associated with Demeter (q.v.) as the divine child; he has an important place in her mystery cult at Eleusis (q.v.). Though originally distinct from Dionysos (q.v.), he gradually becomes identified with him. His name may originally have meant "Lord of the shouting," derived from the "shouting" (in Greek *iakkhein*) that attended the processions and rites at Eleusis.

IOKASTE: Wife of King Laios (q.v.) of Thebes and mother of Oidipous (q.v.), whom she allows her husband to order killed by exposure, after learning of a prophecy that the infant son will grow up to kill the father. Years later, after the death of Laios, Iokaste marries Oidipous, ignorant of who he really is. This incestuous union produces two sons, Oidipous' successors to the throne of Thebes, Eteokles and Polyneikes (qq.v.) and two daughters, Antigone and Ismene (qq.v.). When Iokaste discovers the truth of Oidipous' birth, she hangs herself.

ISMENE: Incestuously born daughter of the former king of Thebes, Oidipous, and his wife (and mother) Iokaste, and sister of Antigone, Eteokles, and Polyneikes (qq.v.).

KADMOS: Mythical founder of Thebes. Arriving from Phoinike (Phoenicia) in search of his sister, Europa, he encounters a huge serpent at the spring of Dirke (q.v.) at Thebes, which he kills in a heroic battle. He plants the teeth of the serpent in the ground, and from this spring the ancestors of the future Thebans, known as the Sown Men or Planted Men. See also DIRKE.

KASTALIA: A spring sacred to Apollo at Delphi on Mt. Parnassos. Its water was traditionally considered a source of poetic inspiration.

KORYKIAN NYMPHS: Minor female divinities, worshiped in a cave high on Mt. Parnassos in central Greece, and closely associated with Dionysos (q.v.).

KREON: Successor of Oidipous (q.v.) as king of Thebes, and brother of Iokaste and so the maternal uncle of Antigone, Ismene, Eteokles, and Polyneikes (qq.v.). Kreon's son Haimon is betrothed to Antigone (qq.v.).

LABDAKOS: Father of King Laios (q.v.) of Thebes and so ancestor of the line Theban royal line known as the Labdakids.

LAIOS: King of Thebes and father of Oidipous by Iokaste. Receiving a prophecy that he will be killed by his own son, he orders the infant Oidipous exposed to the elements on Mt. Kithairon near Thebes, so that he will die. But Oidipous is rescued by a shepherd and, when grown to adulthood, ignorant of his true identity, kills his father at a chance meeting on a highway, fulfilling the prophecy. See OIDIPOUS, IOKASTE.

LYKOURGOS: See DRYAS.

MEGAREUS: Deceased son of Kreon and Eurydike and (probably elder) brother of Haimon (qq.v.). If he is to be identified with the Menoikeus elsewhere in the literary tradition, he has sacrificed himself to save Thebes, and somehow (in Eurydike's view) Kreon can be blamed for his death.

MUSES: Nine goddesses of song, dance, and poetry, daughters of Zeus and Mnemosyne (Memory), often closely associated with Dionysos (q.v.) in his festive aspect.

NIOBE: Daughter of the Phrygian king Tantalos (q.v.) and later the wife of Amphion (q.v.), an early king of Thebes. She boastfully compares her seven sons and seven daughters to the two children of the goddess Leto. She is then punished by Leto's children, Apollo and Artemis, who kill all of hers, whereupon in her grief she is transformed into the rocky face of Mt. Sipylos in Phrygia (qq.v.), which was thought to resemble the face of a weeping woman.

OIDIPOUS: Son of Laios by Iokaste (qq.v.). Left exposed to the elements by his father's orders at birth, because of a prophecy that this son would kill his father, Oidipous is rescued and raised at Corinth by the childless royal couple. When he reaches manhood, he goes to Delphi to discover his identity, then kills Laios in a chance quarrel on the road between Delphi and Thebes. He arrives at Thebes, solves the riddle of the Sphinx, a monster that is ravaging the city, and marries the queen, the now widowed Iokaste, not knowing that she is his mother. Oidipous has four children by Iokaste—his sons (and half-brothers) Eteokles and Polyneikes, and his daughters (and half-sisters) Ismene and Antigone. When Oidipous discovers the truth of his birth, Iokaste commits suicide and Oidipous blinds himself. The story was the subject of a lost tragedy by Aiskhylos performed about fifteen years before *Antigone,* and of Sophokles' *Oidipous Turannos,* ten to fifteen years after.

OLYMPOS: Mountain in northeastern Greece, the peak of which is traditionally considered the abode of the gods, who are therefore called Olympians.

PALLAS: An epithet of Athena, daughter of Zeus and one of the major Olympian divinities. She is sometimes invoked by women as a protective divinity.

PARNASSOS: Mountain to the west of Thebes, the site of Apollo's sanctuary at Delphi, and also associated with the cult of Dionysos (q.v.).

PERSEPHONE: Daughter of Zeus and Demeter (q.v.), who is carried off to the Underworld by its god, Hades (q.v.), as his queen. Her annual return to her mother and the upper world for part of the year formed part of the mythic background to the Eleusinian Mysteries, which offered to initiates hope for a happier afterlife. Along with her mother, Persephone is also worshiped as a goddess of fertility. See also DEMETER, ELEUSIS, IAKKHOS.

PHINEUS: King of the Thracian city of Salmydessos, husband of Kleopatra, daughter of Boreas (qq.v.). He divorces Kleopatra to marry a second wife, named Eidothea or Idaia, and imprisons or otherwise maltreats Kleopatra. His second wife blinds Kleopatra's two children.

PHRYGIA: An area in what is now western Turkey, the location of Mt. Sipylos, where Niobe (q.v.) is transformed into stone.

PLUTO: Another name for Hades, god of the Underworld (q.v.).

POLYNEIKES: Incestuously born son of the former king of Thebes, Oidipous, and his wife (and mother) Iokaste, and brother of Antigone, Ismene and Eteokles (qq.v.), his rival for the throne. After he and Eteokles kill one another in the battle at the gates of Thebes, Kreon forbids the burial of Polyneikes' body, thereby impelling Antigone to the act of defiance that sets the tragedy into motion.

SALMYDESSOS: A Thracian city on the southwestern shore of the Black Sea.

SERPENT: See KADMOS.

SIPYLOS: Mountain in Phrygia (q.v.) whose shape suggested to the ancients the face of a weeping woman. Hence the myth of Niobe (q.v.), who in her grief for her dead children is turned into the stony shape of this mountain.

TANTALOS: Mythical king of Phrygia in Asia Minor, father of Niobe (q.v.). Elsewhere in Greek myth he is one of the sinners punished in Hades (q.v.) for sharing the gods' divine food, ambrosia, with mortals after he has been invited to a feast on Olympos.

TEIRESIAS: An aged, blind seer of Thebes, who plays an important role in other Theban myths and in other Greek tragedies set in Thebes, such as Sophokles' *Oidipous Turannos* and Euripides' *Bakkhai*.

THEBES: Ancient city in central Greece, the site of the action of *Antigone* and of Sophokles' other Theban plays, *Oidipous*

Turannos and *Oidipous at Kolonos*. It was founded by Kadmos (q.v.) from Phoinike (Phoenicia, in the more familiar Latin form), and came to be ruled by the Labdakids (see LABDAKOS), the family of Oidipous (q.v.). It was guarded by a massive wall with seven gates, at one of which Oidipous' two sons, Polyneikes and Eteokles (qq.v.), rivals for the throne of Thebes, kill one another.

THRACE: Area to the northeast of Greece, extending north into what is roughly modern Bulgaria and along the eastern shores of the Black Sea. It was regarded by the early Greeks as a remote and savage place, inhabited by warlike tribes.

THYIADS: Female worshipers of Dionysos who accompany the god in processions marked by ecstatic dances and singing.

ZEUS: King of the Olympian gods and divine ruler of the world. Initially a sky god associated with celestial phenomena like lightning and thunder, he later comes to be considered the administrator of cosmic order and the guardian of law and justice. In one of his many cults, he is also worshiped as guardian of the family, Zeus Herkeios, an image of which stood in the courtyard or enclosure (*herkos*) in front of the house.

SUGGESTIONS FOR FURTHER READING

Kitto, H. D. F. *Form and Meaning in Drama*. London, 1956.

Letters, F. J. H. *The Life and Work of Sophocles*. London, 1953.

Reinhardt, Karl. *Sophocles* (1947), trans. H. and D. Harvey. Oxford, 1979.

Seaford, Richard. "The Tragic Wedding," *Journal of Hellenic Studies* 107 (1987), 106–30.

Seale, David. *Vision and Stagecraft in Sophocles*. Chicago, 1982.

Segal, Charles. *Interpreting Greek Tragedy*. Ithaca, 1986. Essays using a variety of contemporary critical approaches to Greek drama.

———. *Sophocles' Oedipus Tyrannus: Tragic Heroism and the Limits of Knowledge*. Second ed. New York and Oxford, 2001.

———. *Sophocles' Tragic World*. Cambridge, Mass., 1995.

———. *Tragedy and Civilization: An Interpretation of Sophocles*. Cambridge, Mass., 1981; reprint Norman, Okla., 1999.

Vernant, Jean-Pierre, and Pierre Vidal-Naquet. *Myth and Tragedy in Ancient Greece*, trans. J. Lloyd. New York, 1990.

Winnington-Ingram, R. P. *Sophocles: An Interpretation*. Cambridge, Eng., 1980.

Zeitlin, F. I. "Thebes: Theater of Self and Society in Athenian Drama." In *Nothing to Do with Dionysus?* ed. J. J. Winkler and F. I. Zeitlin, 135–36, 148–50. Princeton, 1990.